The 7 Levels of Change

The 7 Levels of Change

Diffferent Thinking for Diffferent Results

Third Edition

by

Rolf Smith

Tapestry Press
Reading, Pennsylvania

Tapestry Press
1401 Parkside Dr. North
Reading, PA 19610
610-375-1422   www.tapestrypressinc.com

Printed in the U.S.A.

11 10 09 08 07   2 3 4 5

Library of Congress Cataloging-in-Publication Data
Smith, Rolf, 1940-
   The 7 levels of change : diffferent thinking for diffferent results / by Rolf Smith. -- 3rd ed.
      p. cm.
   Includes index.
   ISBN 1-930819-50-1 (trade paper : alk. paper)
   1. Organizational change. I. Title.

HD58.8.S638 2007
658.4'06--dc22

                                             2006031888

Cover and book design and layout by
D. & F. Scott Publishing, Inc.
N. Richland Hills, Texas

☑ TIP!

If we keep going where we are going,
we are going to get where we were going . . .
not where we weren't going,
unless we go where we weren't going.
Then we will get where we are going.

—Leonard Pray, philosopher

☑ TIP!

Let us admit the case of the conservative:
if we once start thinking, no one can guarantee where we shall come out;
except that many ends, objects, and institutions are doomed.
Every thinker puts some portion of an apparently stable world in peril,
and no one can wholly predict what will emerge in its place.

—John Dewey

☑ TIP!

*Man's mind stretched to a new idea
never goes back to its original dimensions.*

—Oliver Wendell Holmes

Dedicated

To the unconventional thinkers,
to those who dare to think diff*f*erent.

LEVEL 7
Impossible—Doing things that can't be done
to my wife, Juliane, who kept pointing out, "You're never
going to rewrite your book if you don't rewrite it."
And then once I'd started . . .
"Keep trying, one of these times you'll have a good idea."

LEVEL 7
Impossible—Doing things that can't be done
to Durwin Sharp, without whom I could not have,
and would not have, rethought and rewritten this book.

LEVEL 7
Impossible—Doing things that can't be done
to my sister, Bozier Demaree, who said,
"I can't believe it—I saw your book in a bookstore!"

LEVEL 8
Beyond Impossible
to my son Rolf, who pointed out
"Hmmm, 'Never again' came around pretty fast, didn't it?"

Contents

The Rewrite Expedition of 2002

Putting this book together was a Level 7 experience and a very big expedition. It brought home to me some ideas I've been talking about for a long time: It's not the summit, it's the climb that makes the expedition. That, and getting back alive. Feel the fear and do it anyway.

And don't climb without a team. The team on this rewrite expedition of 2002 were: My wife Juliane, my partner Durwin Sharp, my other partner and daughter Thea Goldin Smith, and myself.

Durwin was our "base camp manager," and I could not and would not have been able to pull this off without him. He initially ran interference in the office on the front end so I could get started and stay focused on rethinking and rewriting. But then he clipped in too, and took care of all the Microsoft challenges, and the graphics and inserts throughout the text, plus he wrote a chunk of Level 5 about trends. And he constantly challenged my ideas and pushed back on my thinking.

Thanks again to my family for putting up with me this second time around. It was a much more demanding expedition than the first one! Like the first time, they clipped in and belayed me a lot. My wife, Juliane, even listened to most of my ideas again. And again. And again. And over and over. "Keep trying—one of these times you'll have a good idea," was her mantra. She's a terrific copy editor and dropped whatever she was doing each time I'd finish a major section in order to read it.

The idea of writing a book started with my Mom, Sue Felder Smith. She loved books and she loved to write. She and Father John Bremner, my mentor at University of San Diego, ganged up on me and made sure I had an English and journalism major hidden behind my B.A. in mathematics.

☑ TIP!

Always read stuff that will make you look good
if you die in the middle of it.
—P. J. O'Rourke

The History of the 7 Levels of Change

HOW EXPEDITIONS HAPPEN

"Where did this start?" was a question I found myself often thinking about. Back in 1989, while I was working with Exxon in the Innovations Group in Marketing, Don Taylor, the group coordinator said: "We need to figure out a way to connect continuous improvement and innovation." To the best of my recollection, that's when I started playing around with the idea of levels—first as levels of innovation—and I started feeling out the concept with the Innovation and Continuous Improvement workshops we were running all over Exxon. Don had pushed me into coming up with something that looked interesting.

EXPEDITIONS WITH THE SCHOOL FOR INNOVATORS

Every School for Innovators has been an operational research and development cauldron for the 7 levels of change. School XVIII was probably the first one in which the 7 levels had an integral part and from then on the model was a mainstay in one form or another. I owe many, many thanks to all the graduates—they served as an operational testbed for the 7 levels of change concepts.

Hoechst Celanese Corporation sent Randy McSwain to the first School for Innovators (1991) in which we connected rock-climbing and expeditionary thinking with the 7 levels of change. And Randy, in turn, came up with the basics for the mindshift model—thinking about thinking—which underlies all the thinking connected with each level of change.

Eight Schools for Innovators have been run in full expedition mode, sponsored primarily by single corporations. These schools allowed us to explore a variety of ways to apply the concept of the 7 levels as a creative problem-solving tool and to develop supporting processes and techniques for the model in large organizations. The sponsoring companies were: IBM, Hoechst Celanese, KFC Australia & New Zealand, Johnson & Johnson and most recently, Halliburton Company. These expeditions played heavily into the development of my ideas for the 7 levels.

Since 1997, when *The 7 Levels of Change* was first published, we have run nineteen more School for Innovators. As soon as the book was published, I began using it as both a textbook in the schools and as a field guide for Thinking Expeditions and Thinking Adventures. This new book is based on five years of R&D in the Schools for Innovators and on solid applications in major corporations.

Gwen Keith, principal of Campbell Junior High School in Houston's Cypress

xviii

The Expedition School

Fairbanks Independent School District (CyFair ISD), has taken everything she learned in the School for Innovators (Expedition XIV, 1995) and has turned Campbell JHS into an "expedition school" over the last six years. She has used the 7 levels and the mindshift model continuously and keeps giving me new insights and ideas on how to refine it further as a field guide for principals and educators.

Building on Gwen Keith's work, from 1998–2001, we designed several "Educators Expeditions" for Sharon Koonce, director of professional development for Houston Independent School District's Department (HISD), and Joe Nuber, an HISD district superintendent. The objective has been to transform thinking at the leadership level, and then bring it down into classrooms in new and different teaching and learning. Both Sharon and Joe are School for Innovators graduates and drivers of change and positive reform in education.

THE SEARCH FOR IDEAS: WHERE ARE THEY?

Ideas are the lifeline of every Thinking Expedition. The "long trek" into the unknown, moving from the staging area to Thinking Base Camp and the mess, is a continuous search for ideas and discoveries. When I looked back down the trail of my own long trek into the unknown of writing and rewriting this book, I had some real insights.

I've been a member of the Association of Managers of Innovation (AMI) since 1986, and have used AMI as a source of ideas and sanity checks for a long time. AMI is a loosely-coupled group of Fortune 500 thinkers and leaders who are making innovation happen in their organizations. In the Spring of 1989, I tried out my original "Levels of Innovation" concept on them. I took away some great observations and suggestions that led me into looking at the ideas and the sizes of change behind innovations—and ultimately at scale.

TEAMS: CREATIVE THINKING STYLE AND TYPE

Before you can change others or the organization, you must first change yourself—and understand what that means and how it works. Change and innovation always start with individuals. Because of that, and discoveries I've made over the last five years on Thinking Expeditions, I've expanded significantly in this rewrite on the implications of type and style for teams and leaders dealing with change.

Michael Kirton's Adaption Innovation theory and his KAI Inventory have been invaluable to me right from the start, clarifying the idea of relative change and differing perspectives. Even more than I did before, I think that the KAI is the most powerful instrument there is for working with teams doing creative thinking. In the last five years, we've used the KAI more and more and gone deeper and deeper with it. I require everyone who joins our Virtual Thinking eXpedition Company (vTx) as a thinking guide to become certified first in the KAI and then qualified in the Meyers Briggs Type Indicator (MBTI); the depth of understanding that the two instruments give you into how people think and deal with change is nothing short of amazing.

To that end, my son-in-law, Grant Goldin, fell into one of his 101 goals and ended up on Mt. Everest with a NASA, Yale, and International Explorers Club research team in May 1999. In October 1999, two of my daughters, Thea and Kristin, went on an expedition to Mt. Everest as well. On both expeditions, we were able to collect some data on thinking type and style, and personality shifts under extreme conditions and changes—as well as stress. Thea did the analysis and wrote the findings, and that led to a major new section: "The Change Factor in Teams and Organizations."

OTHERS' THINKING BEHIND MY THINKING

Back in May 1991, Ray Slesenski and I teamed up and wrote the first article on the 7 levels of change for Stephen Covey's *Executive Excellence* magazine. Writing that article with Ray clarified my thinking on the distinctiveness of each of the levels. Then, sparked by DuPont and a major meeting at which I had been invited to speak, Ray, Al Lewis, Jim Brown, and I spent a late evening in the Innovation Center brainstorming "The 7 Levels of Change for Work & Home." More importantly, we developed the ideas into the yellow card with the 7 levels on each side of it that we still use today. It was designed to go on a refrigerator door—and I actually got a number of "thank you" letters about it from attendees at the DuPont meeting.

I had lots of different kinds of help from good friends and special people, and some of them often didn't even

xix

Psychometric Instruments

XX

Those who've helped me Think different

realize they had said something worth listening to. I've mentioned several of them multiple times in different ways, which is a strong indicator of just how much they contributed. I owe each one of them very special thanks:

Boaz Arch. Bill Olsen. Henry Osti. Scott Swanson. Bozier Demaree, my sister. My daughters, Amanda and Amy. My son, Rolf III. My dad. Al Wilson. Bill Keeter. Bruce Hogge. Cathy Mathai. Charlie Weaver. Chuck Grey. David Hardy. David Purkiss. David Tanner. Dennis Behrens. Duke Rohe. Durwin Sharp. Ed Varian. Bill Shepherd. Eileen Ong. Fred Faiks. Paul Krause. Paul Germeraad. Peter Hearl. Randy Randol. Rod Tozzi. Joe Nuber. Al Lewis. Frank Luton. Glen Fayolle. Dale Clauson. Tom Martinez. Mike Donahue. Nadir Muwwakkil. George Abide. Jean Chatigny. Dave Wisch. Greg Beckler. George Gammon. Gerry Eckstein. Irene Eckstein. Stan Cutherell. Topher Donahue. Michael Legan. J.B. Groves. Jim Baskerville. Juliane. Karen van Wagenen. Kent Malone. Lynn Lee. Mary Wallgren. Matt Hoffner. Mike Brezina. Ron Bowen. Sharon Koonce. Jerry Zahourek. Joe Miguez. Sherman Glass. Stan Gryskiewicz. Thea. Tom McMullen. Bobby Wadsworth. Rod Tozzi. Bob Vernon. Betty Zimmerman.

In the first edition, Robin Dalred and OPTIMA Image brought some amazing talent to bear in creating and evolving the 35mm slides and art work. His images really made the 7 levels of change come alive in workshops and on Thinking Expeditions—the test bed for the book.

The Houston Executive Club played into and tested a lot of ideas I came up with. When Bob Holloway, a long-time member, realized that I really did want to write a book, he made the initial connection for me with Summit Publishing Group, and flew up to Fort Worth with me to make the first edition happen.

A large number of companies have invited me to come in and talk specifically about the 7 levels of change at meetings and conferences: Exxon, of course, company-wide (1988-1992); IBM through John Barnshaw; the DuPont OZ Group twice, and once to a worldwide maintenance conference; R J Reynolds' BIG BANG; Hoechst Celanese; Procter & Gamble (five Thinking Expeditions); General Mills (five Thinking Expeditions); Fletcher Challenge in New Zealand; Cadillac Fairview in Canada; the U.S. Navy; the Excellence in Government conferences; several U.S. Army Program Management teams; Boeing, EDS, Bosch, and Ford Motor Company. Every one of these companies added breadth and depth to my own understanding of the 7 levels of change.

Each time I've worked with companies like these, three things have happened: (1) While I was preparing, I made lots of changes and updates to what I'd presented or done the previous time; (2) I made the sessions heavily interactive and as a result, I got lots of ideas and input on ways to make the 7 Levels connect with people even better; and (3) in each of these companies, there were some people who really gave me some deep insights into what I was doing.

The Creative Problem Solving Institute (CPSI—1994–2000), and my six years on the board of trustees of the Creative Education Foundation (CEF), offered me some wonderful forums and testbeds to develop the 7 levels.

We built the 7 levels, Me, Inc.®, and the mindshift model heavily into R. J. Reynolds' BIG BANG and Innovation Week. Major new connections came out of that operation for me. It was the forerunner of the Thinking Expeditions of today. The sponsors there were: Harold Crayton Threatt, Tom Perfetti, Alan Norman, and Mike Dube.

ON EXPEDITION!

But in the end, it's been on Thinking Expeditions that I've gained the most insights and learned the most. There is something about focusing on urgent Level 6 and 7 results while ootching through the other five levels brings clarity to the concept that nothing else does. Since the book was first published, we have designed and led more than sixty Thinking Expeditions and Adventures for major corporations and the U.S. military—and *The 7 Levels of Change* has been used as field guide on every one of them.

Some of the earlier Thinking Expeditions where I personally got real mindshifts and breakthroughs in my own thinking were: Exxon, ARCO & British Petroleum; BOC Gases; Battelle Northwest Laboratories; General Mills (5 expeditions); Procter & Gamble (5 expeditions); Honeywell; Cadillac Fairview; Fletcher Wood Panels (Auckland, New Zealand); U.S. Navy SMART SHIP; U.S. Army Purple Ammo and TOCR (Total Ownership Cost Reduction Expeditions; the

xxii

The process and flow of an Expedition ("The Map")

Texaco Knowledge Management; and the Kellogg Brown & Root Barracuda Expedition in Rio de Janeiro.

Breakout Thinking: In early 1994, while leading a Thinking Expedition for a group of Quality Improvement Team (QIT) leaders from WMX Technologies in Chicago, I discovered the need for an expedition "process map." John Biedry, Manager of Quality for WMX, pushed me into coming up with something to show how we ran a Thinking Expedition. I sketched out the expeditionary process on a piece of bond paper. Shortly after that, for a keynote talk I gave on Thinking Expedition at the 1994 Houston Association of Quality and Productivity (HAQP) conference, I created the Thinking Expedition Map—"How Expeditions Happen." The map, more than any single item, has crystallized the concept of the Thinking Expedition for us. And in September 1997, I was a awarded a patent for it—making me an "inventor."

In 1999, we designed our fifth operational Thinking Expedition for Procter & Gamble. We invited several "outside stretchers," and one of them, Anna Muoio, was a staff writer for *Fast Company* magazine. I have included the article she wrote as a separate chapter leading into Level 6. It is an accurate description of a full-blown Thinking Expedition and it reads almost like a novel. The article led us into an exciting working relationship with *Fast Company* over the next two years. I have participated as a mentor at their biannual RealTime Gatherings, and we ran a series of mini-Thinking Expeditions in Orlando, Phoenix, and Philadelphia.

In 2000, Halliburton Company asked us to design a Project Management Leadership Development Program (PMLD), built on the framework of the School for Innovators Thinking Expeditions. We created the Vanguard Expeditions and used the 7 levels of change as the backbone. Robby Carr, Jim Smalley, and Kent Malone were drivers and backers that made it really happen. A number of Vanguard graduates rapidly became active practitioners in the company. That group has also created a Vanguard Network that meets regularly in Houston to share insights and tips: Martin Humphreys, Kent Malone, Cherri McNulty, Jim Smalley, Steve Gallagher, Michael Glover, Kim Fernandez, and Bruce Hogge—and I've gotten some great insights and ideas from them.

An indirect result of the Vanguard Network was an emergency Thinking Expedition for Kellogg Brown & Root in January 2002 in Rio de Janeiro, Brazil. We produced a Strategic Go-Forward Plan overlaid on the framework of the 7 levels of change.

xxiii

LOOKING BACK DOWN THE EXPEDITION TRAIL

Jill Bertolet, my publisher and coach at Tapestry Press, did heavy-duty work behind the scenes all the way through. It was Jill in particular who motivated me to go "on expedition" with the book again, and then kept after me and the continually slipping due date.

I owe much of my thinking about expeditions to my long-time friend, Colonel Dennis Behrens. I met Dennis at an Air Force rifle match in San Antonio in 1965. After that, I went through twenty-three years and a lot of adventures with him in while we were in the Air Force and NATO. We went through all 7 levels of change together a couple of times back then without even knowing it. Many of my insights into the expeditionary process have come out of our time together in Germany and Austria, and on safaris with Dennis in Zimbabwe, Kenya, Tanzania, and Namibia.

This time around, my wife Juliane and my two partners, Durwin Sharp and Thea Goldin Smith (my eldest daughter), clipped into the Rewrite Expedition to belay me. And all three ended up doing some serious climbing too.

In the process of first writing and then rewriting this book, I have rediscovered the depth to which I am personally "on expedition" and how much I live and move the reference points of the 7 levels of change every day. Who I am, what I do, and how I do it, all continuously change with every School for Innovators and with every Thinking Expedition we organize and lead. When we clip back out of our Virtual Thinking eXpedition (vTx) company mode, link up physically with a corporate team at some offsite location, and go into actual execution, we're once again moving out into the unknown on a new adventure through the 7 levels of change.

And, just like last time, I'm still not sure I fully understand everything I know about this.

Rolf Smith
Cypress, Texas
May 10, 2002

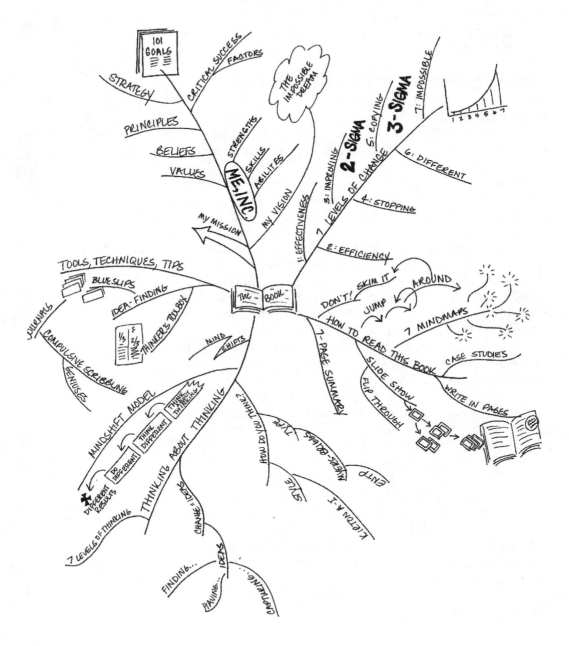

HOW TO USE THIS FIELD GUIDE
~~HOW TO USE THIS BOOK~~
~~HOW TO READ THIS BOOK~~

This book is diffferent.

It's a "Field guide for Innovators," a handbook for thinking diffferent, for doing diffferent, and for guiding others in thinking diffferent to get diffferent results.

It's based on five years of using the 7 levels of change as the backbone of operational Thinking Expeditions, in the School for Innovators, and internally by major corporations, schools and conferences. It's full of "how to" stuff that works.

Unlike many business books and works of fiction, you don't have to start at the beginning and read it straight through, although there are some advantages to doing it that way. Reading straight through from Level 1 to Level 7 helps to flatten out the rough spots between the mindshifts. The 7 levels evolved into their sequence because the sequence works, yet the concepts aren't increasingly difficult as they progress through the levels. They build on each other as they go (ootching). The changes they deal with, however, are typically more difficult to sell and to implement as they climb toward Level 7. Yet, you don't have to go through all of the lower levels of change to make a Level 6 or 7 change. That said, you may want to consider using the book in one of the following ways.

JUMP AROUND IN THE BOOK

The basic framework of the 7 levels is almost intuitively simple. After you understand the concept and the relationship among the 7 levels, it's easy to jump around. So, just read what is interesting to you. Flip through to each level, read the overview that begins the discussion of that level, and omit the sections that don't immediately connect with you. If you want to get a good feel for all 7 levels, go to the last couple of pages in the book. They're summarized back there very succinctly.

USE THE MINDMAPS

If you are a visual learner, there are eight "mindmaps" in this book to help you find your way through the 7 levels—one, on the opposite page, explains the overall design of the book—what's in it—and then one for each level of change. Mindmaps are a simple and fast method of capturing ideas in chunks in a way that makes them easy to see, understand, and remember. It also makes their relationships very clear in a big picture way. Your brain doesn't create ideas and thought in a linear fashion. It jumps around. Mindmapping allows you to use your whole brain—both the creative and analytical sides—by freeing you from the constraints of linear thinking. It also gives you an immediate

2

big picture of each chapter. The concept of mindmapping originated with Tony Buzan, author of *Use Both Sides of Your Brain,* who developed the technique based on research that indicates the brain fundamentally works with key concepts in an interrelated and integrated way.

A STRUCTURED LOOK

If the mindmaps don't quite work for you, try the structured conversion of them developed by Elivra Stesikova, a Conoco research scientist. In table format, she has listed for each level of change (see appendix D, pages 315–318):

1. Tools to use
2. Habits and characteristics
3. Thinking about thinking
4. Mindshift
5. Pros and cons
6. Levels of fear

TOOLS, TECHNIQUES, AND TIPS

Each chapter has a lot of tools and techniques for either mindshifting you into thinking different, or for doing things that will help you and other people think different and come up with ideas at that level of change. There is a handy index to more than seventy creative thinking tools and techniques in context in the book. They work.

MARGINALIA (MORE TIPS AND INSIGHTS)

I believe that when you write in a book you improve it. You are either adding something the author wished he or she had thought of, or you are building on something they wrote with an insight or idea of your own. In either case you've made it better, and, more importantly, you've made it yours. I've added a lot of stuff in the margins already, things that I forgot or thought of JTL. (Just Too Late) but that are just too important or useful not to include in the book.

FLIP THROUGH THE SLIDE SHOW

In the bottom left page margins throughout the book are copies of some of the 35 mm slides I've developed and used on Thinking Expeditions with some of the world's largest corporations to help them think different and be more creative and

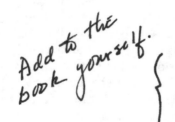
Add to the book yourself.

Change
is about
RESULTS

innovative. The slides themselves present a good sequential overview of the concepts in this book. By flipping the pages slowly with your thumb, you can visually move through the 7 levels of change at high speed. Try it!

WARNING!

These black and white slide copies are not intended to be illustrations for the book; they are meant to be a "flip-through slide show" —an overview of the 7 levels of change—and they are in a set sequence. As you read the book you'll quickly discover that *there is no direct correlation between the slides and the text on the page* on which they happen to be.

PROS AND CONS, FEAR, STRESS

I have expanded the summary of the "pros and cons" of each level of change and also included include the fears that we have seen creep in behind people's thinking when they move into a particular level of change (the 7 levels of fear, largely developed by Mike Donahue during School for Innovators Expeditions). In doing that, I realized that rewriting this book (not "updating" it) had turned into an expedition for me—and it was a pretty stressful one at that. My oldest daughter, Thea Goldin Smith, who is also one of my business partners, pointed that out to me. She also highlighted how often we explore stress in both the School for Innovators and on Thinking Expeditions and felt it would be valuable to include something about stress and its relationship to change. A School for Innovators graduate herself (Expedition XX, 1996), she went back and did the research on the stresses that seem to pop up most frequently with the mindshifts at each level of change, level of fear, and level of thinking.

TRANSITION FROM LEVEL 3 TO LEVEL 4
CPS (Creative Problem Solving)

This is a new chapter. Level 3 is the biggest chapter in the book and has the most tools and techniques in it as well; it builds heavily on the thinking and the tools from Levels 1

4

Fast company

GREAT STORY! Take your mind on Expedition...

and 2. So this transition chapter provides a framework to tie all those tools and techniques together. The Creative Problem Solving (CPS) model is the backbone of the School for Innovators and is a structure that can be used to lead (facilitate) a group in thinking different when working on a messy problem or when looking for innovative ideas.

TRANSITION FROM LEVEL 5 TO LEVEL 6
Thinking Expeditions

The transition out of Level 5 shifts into diff*erent*. This is a new chapter that describes a Thinking Expedition from end to end. A Thinking Expedition pulls together and focuses everything I do and focuses it all as a giant CPS model. This chapter is an extract of an article in the January 2000 issue of *Fast Company*, a magazine you should have subscribed to long ago. Anna Muoio, a senior writer at *Fast Company*, clipped into an operational Thinking Expedition as a "stretcher" and wrote the article. If the idea of an "expedition" grabs your mind, start here in the book.

THE BACK OF THE BOOK (MORE GOOD STUFF)
The appendices in the back of the book are all stand-alone pieces that I felt fit with the whole book as behind-the-scenes stuff.

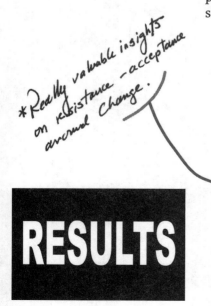

*Really valuable insights on resistance - acceptance around Change.

> *Updated and New Stuff.* There are several "case studies" of varying size that take you through how a number of different organizations and change agents have used the 7 levels of change as a framework to drive discovery, problem solving, and innovation. Several of them date back to 1994–96 and are still going strong, still changing, still innovating—only even more so.

> *Updated and New Stuff.* There is a major section that follows the 7 levels called "Getting Ready for Change" that goes into how different thinking styles and types deal with change, and some strategies and approaches for accelerating change. I believe it to be one of the most important sections of the book.

> *Diffferent Stuff.* You'll find the School for Innovators mentioned a lot in the examples in the book. There is a detailed "history" of Expedition XXXVII, Decem-

RESULTS

5

ber 2001, that was written day-by-day by the participants during the School.

> *New Stuff*. There is a copy of a corporate Innovation Strategy that I rolled out in 1986 when I was a Colonel in the U.S. Air Force. It worked then, and it has been copied and adapted by a number of major corporations to launch innovation and change initiatives. You might find it handy. Everywhere you see "U.S. Air Force" simply change it to your company's name.

> *Bibliography*: Go to our website (www.thinking-expedition.com) for an annotated list of books that I think should be on any innovator's bookshelf.

← website

HOW TO THINK ABOUT THINKING

Innovation and creativity start with ideas. We have to think before we can have an idea. To be creative, start by thinking about thinking. To be innovative, do something with your ideas.

> First, take time out to think. If you have to, actually put it on your calendar. Block out the time, hold your calls, unplug the phone. Or find a time outside of work conducive to thinking. Go outside. Don't just do something, sit there and think. Turn off your car phone. Take a quiet hour in the morning before the rest of the family is up. Give up worrying and start thinking about thinking. Don't think about anything in particular, just open your mind to your thoughts.

Tip! Set an alarm clock in your office to remind you to take a "think Break"

> Next, become aware of how you think. Take a look again at the 7 levels of thinking with this in mind. Remember, innovation involves doing things different, and to do something different, you must first think different. Before you can think different, you must think about the way you think—examine your basic thinking processes. Look at the thoughts that come into your mind as you think and reflect on them—deliberately and nonjudgmentally.

> Thinking comes before doing, and thinking about thinking comes before thinking. This triple mindshift is critical if you are going to get different results.

6

Me, Inc

Strategy
{ 1. My Vision
{ 2. My Mission
{ 3. My Strategy
Judgment 4. My Principles
Judgment 5. My Values
& 6. My Strengths
Strategy 7. My Major Goals

ME, INC.®

Many people never take the time to think about who they are, who they have been, and who they want to become. Me, Inc.® is the deeply reflective, deliberate process of mentally incorporating yourself, leading you to think about yourself as a personal business venture. By mentally incorporating, you move through a structured process to create a business plan for your life.

Me, Inc.® is a change process that moves you gradually through increasing levels of personal refection at the end of each of the 7 levels of change. The process of mentally incorporating helps you take inventory of your skills, abilities, traits, and unusual qualities. It helps you define your goals, wishes, and dreams, and focuses you on your basic beliefs, values, and operating principles. It examines your experiences and your personal vision and mission. Finally, Me, Inc.® helps you get to where you want to be.

The actual work of mentally incorporating is not a short or quick process. It's one that requires much introspection and is described in detail at each level of change throughout the book. And it's a process that works best when done in the order I've laid it out in the 7 levels.

ONE LAST POINT

Have fun with this book. I did while I was writing it. Both times, too.

Webster

re·sults (ri-zŭlts′)

noun. a measurable success

FAST-FORWARD OVERVIEW

Everyone wants to get *results*. Innovation is a new and different result. To be innovative you have to do things different. How do you do things different? Follow the Mindshift Model below, from left to right.

The MindShift Model

To get different results requires a first-order mindshift. You have to do things different. To do things different you have to make a second-order mindshift and think different. Thinking precedes doing. And before you can think different you have to think about your thinking. That's a third-order mindshift. Thinking about thinking is the biggest mindshift of them all because the vast majority of people have never thought about the way they think.

Focus on different. What's different around you? What's different as a result of what you just did? What's different about what you just noticed? How do you notice different? Start by noticing *same*. Mornings are often mired in sameness, in habits. Notice what you do when you wake up. Notice when you wake up. Is it the same time every day? Shake things up. Change your alarm clock by two or three minutes. Change something in your life that is the same every day. Do one thing different each day and notice it! Move one thing in your home or office each day to gradually change your perspective on what you're noticing. If you do that, you're on your way to innovation. Pick up the pace and do two things different each day and notice it. Move two things in your home. Three. Four . . .

There are two main sides to the 7 levels of change: at work and at home. They apply everywhere we find change, everywhere in life that we have to deal with change.

8

THE 7 LEVELS OF CHANGE AT WORK

Level 1: Effectiveness—Doing the Right Things
- ➤ Set priorities
- ➤ Focus!
- ➤ Do what's important first
- ➤ Become more effective

Level 2: Efficiency—Doing Things Right
- ➤ Follow procedures
- ➤ Clean up your mess
- ➤ Understand standards
- ➤ Become more efficient

Level 3: Improving—Doing Things Better
- ➤ Think about what you're doing
- ➤ Listen to suggestions
- ➤ Find ways to improve things
- ➤ Help, coach, and mentor others

Level 4: Cutting—Doing Away with Things
- ➤ Ask "Why?"
- ➤ Stop doing what doesn't count
- ➤ Use the 80:20 rule—simplify
- ➤ Refocus continuously

Level 5: Copying—Doing Things Other People Are Doing
- ➤ Notice and observe more
- ➤ Think before you think
- ➤ Read about best practices
- ➤ Copy!

Level 6: Diffferent—Doing Things No One Else Is Doing
- ➤ Think about thinking
- ➤ Ask "Why not?"
- ➤ Combine new technologies
- ➤ Focus on different, not similar

Level 7: Impossible—Do Things That Can't Be Done
- ➤ Question assumptions
- ➤ What's impossible today, but . . .?
- ➤ Defocus: Get a little crazy
- ➤ Wouldn't it be amazing if . . ."
- ➤ Break the rules!
- ➤ Where will it take pure magic?

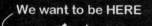

We want to be HERE

Diff/erent Results

THE 7 LEVELS OF CHANGE AT HOME

Level 1: Effectiveness—Doing the Right Things

- Talk and communicate
- Do your chores
- Keep your promises
- Start a savings program

Level 2: Efficiency—Doing Things Right

- Set family priorities for fun
- Praise and compliment
- Start an investment plan
- Actually listen

Level 3: Improving—Doing Things Better

- Be more loving and supporting
- Develop new habits—grow
- Become more cost conscious
- Increase amount of savings

Level 4: Cutting—Doing Away with Things

- Stop impulse buying
- Simplify your life
- Stop negative "self-talk"
- Detoxify your life
- Eliminate blaming and criticizing
- Turn off the lights

Level 5: Copying—Doing Things Other People Are Doing

- Copy what works
- Really take a vacation
- Stick ideas on the refrigerator
- Read, study, discuss

Level 6: Diffferent—Doing Things No One Else Is Doing

- Try something you've never tried
- Incorporate We, Inc.
- Get professional help
- Go on a family adventure!

Level 7: Impossible—Do Things That Can't Be Done

- Dream the impossible dream
- Enjoy each other
- "Wouldn't it be great if we . . ."
- Make a dream come true

10

THE 7 LEVELS OF THINKING

Each of the 7 levels of change requires a corresponding mindshift, a change in thinking. To do different, to make a change, you must first think different. Thinking always precedes doing.

Level 1: Focused Thinking
> ➤ Thinking that converges
> ➤ Concentrated thinking
> ➤ Awareness. Awareness. Awareness.

Level 2: Efficient Thinking
> ➤ Thinking with a minimum of waste, time, or effort
> ➤ Logical, analytical thinking
> ➤ Thinking with a high ratio of output to input
> ➤ Brainstorming

Level 3: Positive Thinking
> ➤ Thinking that adds to an idea to move it forward
> ➤ Thinking that suspends judgment
> ➤ Noncritical thinking
> ➤ Questioning
> ➤ Listening

Level 4: Refocused Thinking
> ➤ Concentration once more with greater intensity
> ➤ Undistorted thinking
> ➤ Clarifying

Level 5: Adaptive Thinking
> ➤ Visual thinking
> ➤ Seeing things
> ➤ Copying existing ideas
> ➤ Imitating someone else's thinking processes

Level 6: Lateral Thinking
> ➤ Shifting perspective
> ➤ Reversing basic assumptions
> ➤ Using intuition to reach a conclusion
> ➤ Nonnormal or abnormal thinking

Level 7: Imaginative Thinking
> ➤ Using the mind to form images of what does not exist
> ➤ Confronting and dealing with reality by using the creative power of the mind
> ➤ Breakout thinking

RESULTS

What Results do you want?

...BLUE SLIP

THE 7 LEVELS OF FEAR

Behind every level of change there is a hidden level of fear. The level of fear comes out when the mindshift is made into a new level of thinking. Fear is driven by reversed thinking, by thinking about what could go wrong as opposed to what could go right

11

Level 1: Paralysis

- Fear of doing the wrong things
- Doing nothing

Level 2: Inefficiency

- Fear of wasting time
- Fear of doing the right things wrong

Level 3: Catastrophizing

- Fear of things getting worse
- Seeing only the worst case

Level 4: Holding On

- Fear of letting go
- Focusing on the 80 percent that only brings 20 percent of the value
- Just-in-case fear: "Let's take everything just in case."

Level 5: Self-Doubt

- Fear of not being able
- Fear of not copying the right thing
- Fear of copying the right things wrong
- Fear of being laughed at
- Fear of criticism

Level 6: Normalcy

- Fear of being noticed
- Fear of rejection
- Fear of being different
- Fear of getting hurt

Level 7: Disbelief

- Fear of the unknown
- Fear of having no basis of comparison
- I *can t* do that.
- That won't work for me
- Fear of the point of no return
- Fear of death, of not coming back alive
- Fear of others dying
- The sum of all fears

12

THE MAGIC NUMBER 7 ±2

The 7 levels of change actually started out as three levels and evolved to seven levels. After many modifications, additions and subtractions, I arrived at the present version, which has remained stable for some time—primarily because it works.

In my work with large corporations and organizations, I have found several other lists that help people think about things differently. Guess what? Each is a list of 7 elements.

7 Differentiators in Unusual Thinkers
Rolf Smith

1. Noticing: An awareness of diff*e*rent
2. Openness: The ability to suspend judgment
3. Playfulness: The ability to play with ideas
4. Connecting: The ability to make idea connections
5. Tension: Continuous divergence-convergence
6. Quantity: Many different kinds of ideas
7. Compression: The ability to headline concepts

The 7 Major Changes in Life
Shad Helmstetter

1. Loss
2. Separation
3. Relocation
4. A Change in Relationship
5. A Change in Direction
6. A Change in Health
7. Personal Growth

After living with and using the 7 levels of change for more than 7 years now, I'm convinced that there is something mystical about the number "7." Among gamblers it's a lucky number, because it is the most likely combination to come up on a roll of the dice, and among authors and consultants, too, it would appear.

☑ TIP!

There is some scientific basis behind this. Knowing I had been a math major in college, a friend of mine, Chuck Brodnax, once sent me a scholarly paper entitled "The Magic Number 7

INSANITY

Doing what you've always done and expecting different results

Plus or Minus 2: Some Limits on Our Capacity for Processing Information." It was written in 1956 by George Miller, and was based on research that showed people max out at remembering seven digits or objects. After that, retention drops off quickly. Oddly enough (maybe not?) it's also used as a rule of thumb in brainstorming and Creative Problem Solving where we tell people to limit their ideas or problem statements to seven words. And it seems to have been applied to the thinking behind telephone numbers in the United States.

With that, here are some more lists of 7 to think about.

(handwritten: The Psychological Review 1956, vol. 63)

THE 7 CULTURAL FORCES THAT DEFINE AMERICANS
Josh Hammond & James Morrison

1. Insistence on choice
2. Pursuit of impossible dreams
3. Obsession with BIG and More
4. Impatience with time
5. Acceptance of mistakes
6. The urge to improvise
7. Fixation on what's new

THE 7 PRINCIPLES OF BREAKTHROUGH THINKING
Gerald Nadler & Shozo Hibino

1. Every problem is unique
2. Focus on purpose
3. Solution-after-next thinking
4. System-of-problems perspective
5. Limit information collection
6. People involvement in the design
7. Betterment timeline: Continual change

THE 7 HUMAN INTELLIGENCES
Howard Gardner

1. Linguistic
2. Logical-Mathematical
3. Spatial
4. Musical
5. Bodily-Kinesthetic
6. Interpersonal (Others)
7. Intrapersonal (Self)

14

THE 7 ELEMENTS OF ENGINEERING PRACTICE
John Gibson

1. Analytic, bottom-up approach
2. Absence of goal-definition
3. Absence of regard for human factors
4. Hierarchical, non-professional style
5. The fantasy of value-free design
→ 6. Separation of thinking from doing
7. Emphasis on reward for individual effort

THE 7 HABITS OF HIGHLY SUCCESSFUL PEOPLE
Stephen Covey

1. Be proactive
2. Begin with the end in mind
3. Put first things first
4. Think win/win
5. Seek first to understand
6. Synergize: creative cooperation
7. Sharpen the saw

THE 7 HUMAN NEEDS
Abraham Maslow

1. Physiological
2. Security and Safety
3. Love and feelings of belonging
4. Competence, prestige, and esteem
5. Autonomy and independence
6. Self-actualization and fulfillment
7. Curiosity and understanding

Hmm . . . George Miller closed out his thoughts back in 1956 with curiosity about his understanding:

> And finally, what about the magical number seven? What about the seven wonders of the world, the seven seas, the seven deadly sins, the seven daughters of Atlas in the Pleiades, the seven ages of man, the seven levels of hell, the seven primary colors, the seven notes of the musical scale, and the seven days of the week? What about the seven-point rating scale, the seven categories for absolute judgment, the seven objects in the span of attention, and the seven digits in the span of

Red
Blue
Yellow

Orange
Violet
Green

Results Are About Change

immediate memory? For the present I propose to with-hold judgment. Perhaps there is something deep and profound behind all these sevens, something just calling out for us to discover it. But I suspect that it is only a pernicious, Pythagorean coincidence.

☑ TIP!

When something works, and works well, use it—even if you aren't sure why it works.

INNOVATE OR DIE!

Today our thinking must shift. The world we live in is changing so rapidly that to survive, we must continually change *how we see it and we think about it*. Consider change and the rate of change in your own lifetime. Remember your home when you were growing up? When I was a kid, households only had one telephone, no dial and you had to talk to the operator to make a call. Only one television? Only a few channels on the TV set? Only one bathroom? Only one car? No computer? No E-mail? No internet?

Today we're constantly in touch with information. The infrastructure is a complex network of networks comprising satellites, fiber optics, wired and wireless local networks, and a host of others that most of us use but do not begin to understand. This supports an astounding array of interconnected devices in all shapes, sizes, capabilities and configurations. Taken together, this infrastructure and the connected devices provide an array of capabilities that encourage new and innovative uses daily. Fax machines thwart a revolution; world leaders communicate policy over CNN; online electronic transactions leverage traditional and virtual banking; information of all types is created, copied, sent, received, resent, and traded (to the delight of some and the chagrin of others); nations count (and recount, and recount) election results while the world watches; and E-mail travels worldwide with advertising and junk mail following. Of course, all of this communication and commerce precisely follows all existing rules, regulations, and geographic boundaries, even where these rules are in direct conflict.

And if we thought that the rate of change had accelerated over the past two decades, we suddenly had to think again.

16

Eleven September 2001 was a Level 7 change. We have been moved into high gear whether we want to be there or not.

> *The world we have created today has problems*
> *which cannot be solved by thinking the way*
> *we thought when we created them.*
> —Albert Einstein

Our thinking must shift. For our military, for our government, for businesses large and small, for schools, being proactive with change—being innovative and striving for continuous improvement—is going to be the key to survival and growth.

Still, many of today's corporations and organizations—built on yesterday's ideas—are continuing to live on those ideas today. Unless we innovate and continually change, we'll turn into tombstones and become memorials to our pasts.

Use what works. If something no longer works, stop using it. But it's not always easy to see immediately when something stops working. When theories or business models die, there is a similar effect. Newtonian physics was "proven true" repeatedly over a long period of time. But it didn't seem quite right to Einstein—there were some problems explaining absolute and relative speed when working with light. "Aha!" and one theory replaces another. Keynesian economics could not explain stagflation that would not respond to aggressive fiscal policies. Increasing numbers of leaders and thinkers began paying attention to monetary policy and economic indicators—the free market principles that had been presented and debated for years by Friedrich Hayek and others. Planned economies were slowly and grudgingly coming face-to-face with their failures. It just took a long time.

Many business models in use today are broken, but yesterday's managers haven't realized it yet. We have to "Innovate or Die!" It's that simple.

I consciously began focusing on innovation in 1984, while I was a colonel in the U.S. Air Force and director of long-range planning and strategy for Electronic Security Command (now called the Air Force Intelligence Agency—a big change!). Driven by change in technology and change in the world, Air Force senior leadership launched an initiative

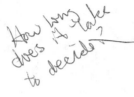

How long does it take to decide?

CHANGE

What is one thing you really want to Change?

...BLUE SLIP

deliberately focused on innovation. As the long-range planner, I was asked to develop a corporate strategy and action plan (see appendix C) to implement the initiative and translate innovation into a corporate value in our command. I launched the strategy by creating an Innovation Center to serve as a catalyst for ideas and as an extension of our long-range planning staff.

Within six months the Innovation Center and I were spun off from long-range planning, and I became director of the Office of Innovation, with the mission of sparking innovation throughout our worldwide command. We rapidly developed a network of innovation centers focused on operation innovation in our field units. By the time I retired, I was known as Colonel Innovation; even my Air Force name tag said "Innovation" instead of "Smith."

Surprisingly to me, this run at "Innovate or Die!" was a natural transition to civilian life and into some of the world's largest corporations. When I retired from active military duty in 1987, I walked into Exxon Corporation as a contract executive, and from 1987 through 1991 I had a mandate to stimulate creativity and innovative thinking throughout the organization—no different from my mission in the Air Force. Starting in Exxon marketing, where we created an Innovation Center along the lines of the Air Force model, the drive for innovation spread into virtually every area of the company.

In 1988, I created the School for Innovators to develop and train change agents and innovators in Exxon. Two years later it became an "open" school, drawing innovators primarily from Fortune 100 companies, working on real world issues and problems facing them. Today we have graduates not only at Exxon, but also at Texaco, IBM, DuPont, AT&T, Procter & Gamble, General Mills, Chase Manhattan Bank, Steelcase, R.J. Reynolds, Halliburton Company, EDS, Boeing, Timken Steel, Kellogg Corporation, Johnson & Johnson, Karastan Carpet, KFC, public schools, the U.S. Air Force, Navy, and Army. And my two oldest children are also graduates.

One of the most important ideas to come out of the School for Innovators is the 7 levels of change. The 7 levels evolved over several years as I was thinking about how to connect creativity, innovation and continuous improvement.

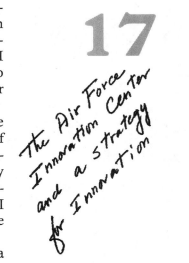

17

The Air Force Innovation Center and a Strategy for Innovation

18

Each of these goals—common to my clients in corporate America and to all of us as individuals striving to succeed in life—shares common themes. It struck me that that is all about ideas. Creativity is about having ideas and innovation and continuous improvement are about implementing ideas:

IDEA

+

CREATIVITY

+

ENHANCEMENT

+

EVALUATION

+

IMPLEMENTATION

INNOVATION!

Ideas are about change. When you implement a new idea, you cause a change. So all three of these—creativity, continuous improvement, and innovation—are about change. This led me to insights about the different sizes and levels of change. Not all change is the same. Adapting the work of quality gurus W. Edwards Deming and William Conway, and working with some of our country's greatest management minds—my clients—the 7 levels gradually evolved from three initial levels to five levels to six levels, and finally to seven and its present form. The number "7" was not a deliberate choice but rather one arrived at empirically over time. It works.

Change can be very difficult for companies of any size as well as for individuals. By breaking down change into different levels for my clients, I found them surprisingly successful at making significant changes that affected not only the company's bottom line but also its future path of success.

In the School for Innovators, I found our graduates making profound changes in their lives. When we integrated the structure of the 7 levels of change and the 7 levels of thinking into Me, Inc.® (the process we developed to help our graduates set new strategic directions and mentally incorporate themselves), they exploded with energy, commitment, and self confidence.

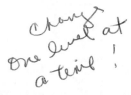

change one level at a time !

To Get Different Results ...

Mindshift

Different Results · Do Different

19

Continuously searching for ways to reduce fear of change in order to move groups and individuals more quickly through higher levels of perceived risk, I entered into a strategic relationship with Mike Donahue, director and owner of the Colorado Mountain School (CMS) in Estes Park, Colorado. In 1991 we integrated rock climbing into a School for Innovators we'd designed for IBM, and achieved some amazing results. We had discovered how to move people to Level 6, *different*, and to Level 7, *impossible*, first on the personal level and then on the business level, with correspondingly amazing effect.

In 1994, sparked by the insights we were gaining by using the 7 levels of change coupled with rock climbing and low-level mountaineering in the School for Innovators, I hit on the idea of "Thinking Expeditions" to operationalize the 7 levels and to leverage the ongoing stream of discoveries, learnings, tools, and techniques coming out of the School. The School for Innovators had become our research and development center. Working with Mike Donahue, we began to use the mountaineering metaphor as the baseline design for Thinking Expeditions built around a wide variety of real world challenges facing some of the world's largest corporations—Exxon, Arco, British Petroleum, Procter & Gamble, Hoechst, General Mills, Johnson & Johnson, and the U.S. Navy's Smart Ship—and led teams to achieve startling and exciting breakthrough results over the whole range of the 7 levels of change.

With every Thinking Expedition, we have developed new techniques, new tools, and new approaches to each level of change, both out of sheer necessity and also by building on the insights and experience of previous expeditions. Those discoveries and insights are what this book is about. This book explains those tools and techniques in details, in the context of how to use them, and when to use them at different levels of change. When you're finished with the book, you'll have your own tool kit for change loaded and ready to go on expedition.

By gaining insights into to the 7 levels of change, and by learning the tools to use at each level, and when to use them, I believe extraordinary summits, exciting discoveries, and exhilarating results can be yours.

On belay!

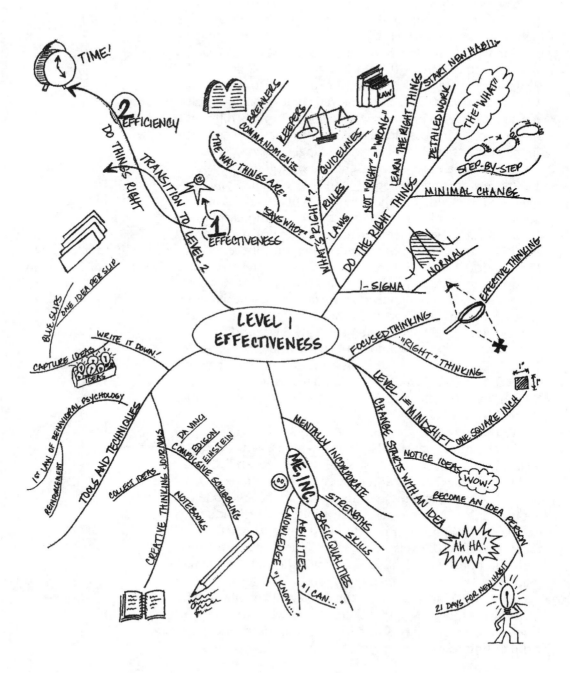

Level 1: Effectiveness
Doing the Right Things

UNDERSTANDING LEVEL I CHANGE

Imagine yourself on the first day of a new job or suddenly being in a brand-new situation. You have just moved into the unknown. And that is where Level 1 change starts. Typically, whether you are an executive or a worker on the line, you are highly focused on learning the basics of the job—the *"what"* that makes up the job. This is fundamental Level 1 change—doing the right things and becoming effective. Those first few days are full of Level 1 doing and learning—familiarizing yourself with the mission of your group, who's who, with whom you're going to work, what they do, what's in the office, the technology, the phones and other communications systems, the location of the coffee pot and the restrooms. The right things. The *what* to do.

LEVEL I CHANGES ARE ABOUT "WHAT"
Starting New Habits.

In most cases your new boss, or a supervisor, or an old hand who understands everything, walks you around and helps you understand what the right things are, what the roles are, and what to focus on. There are a lot of new ideas for you, and you either pay very close attention or you <u>write them down</u>—because you've got to turn them into changes in you, into new habits. Of course you weren't stupid when you took the new job. You know a lot of things, too, and have some pretty solid experience behind you. And you can draw on that. It turns out that the basics—the right things—are pretty much the right things everywhere. So these early changes you have to go through in a new job are predominantly incremental, relatively small, and involve low risk and low effort to get up to speed. Still, they are changes and there are usually a lot of them.

> *"There are two types of knowledge.*
> *One is knowing a thing.*
> *The other is knowing where to find it."*
> —Samuel Johnson

TOOL #1 (LEVEL 1):
Write It Down!

Writing down ideas is doing the right thing. For a lot of people who don't already make a habit of recording their ideas, that's a Level 1 change. The minute an idea or a new thought hits you, write it down. Whenever someone says something interesting, write it down. Win Wenger, in his book *The Einstein Factor*, highlights the first law of behavioral psychology: whatever you reinforce you will get more of. Every time you write down

22

Write an idea here in the margin NOW!

Write down your ideas!

an idea you reinforce the importance of having ideas, of being an idea person. And. . . whenever you don't write down an idea, you reinforce the behavior of not being an idea person. This is about habits. It takes 21 days to establish a new habit, or to replace an old habit with a new one—a change. Start now. Ideas are everywhere—in magazines, books, and newspapers. If you don't have anything to write with, tear out the ideas and collect them. Become aware of ideas.

"Awareness, Awareness, Awareness.
That's what awareness means.
It means awareness."
—Zen Master

UNDERSTANDING LEVEL I THINKING

Level 1 thinking is about awareness and focus—being aware of the right things and then focusing on doing them. When you begin thinking about your thinking at Level 1, you'll develop a new definition of what is right, internalize it, and shift back from thinking to doing with a new perspective about what is right.

The following diagram and definition illustrate Level 1 thinking and the mindshift you must make to achieve Level 1 changes—to get effective results. If you're going to do the right things, you have to make a mindshift, focus on what the right things are and not allow yourself to be distracted from doing them. You have to concentrate.

LEVEL I MINDSHIFT: EFFECTIVENESS

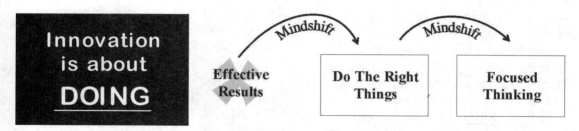

Innovation is about DOING

Effective Results → *Mindshift* → Do The Right Things → *Mindshift* → Focused Thinking

focused thinking (fō′kəs′d thĭng′kĭng) **n**.
1.   Thinking that converges on or toward a specific point. 2. Concentrated thinking; concentration.

23

Think about it: to get the right results you have to do the right things. To do the right things you have to really focus on what you are doing and the results you want to get. Your thinking at this level is about focus and awareness. What is the right thing to focus on—typically it's one thing at a time. Right thinking is fitting, proper, and appropriate. It's thinking that's in accordance with fact, reason, truth, or the commonly accepted way. It's thinking about the right things.

While Level 1 thinking is primarily focused on ideas—noticing them, capturing them—it is also often focused on facts as ideas—new "truths" that you didn't know that have been established previously. Because of that, learning at Level 1 will often tend towards rote and memorization, largely using routine or repetition, and acceptance of "the way things are" as givens—often without full comprehension.

THINKING ABOUT THINKING AT LEVEL I

Level 1 thinking—effective thinking—is focused on an intended or expected effect, thinking that produces the intended result. It's 1-sigma thinking, meaning that on the normal curve, it's inside the "normal" range. Take a look at the diagram below. Nearly 70 percent of the time, you will be thinking and doing in the "normal" or 1-sigma range. That's where Levels 1, 2 and 3 are. *These are the things you do everyday in your job.*

This is the vital heartbeat of any business— the things that keep it alive day-to-day.

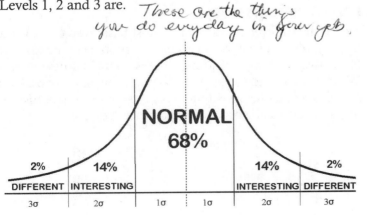

24

When you move past Level 3, you move over into 2-sigma or "interesting" thinking, where 28 percent of change is: Levels 4 and 5 change, cutting and copying. Finally, the smallest percentage of thinking, about 4 percent, lies at 3-sigma and beyond, out at the ends of the normal curve. That's where Level 6 and Level 7 change come from, the different and impossible, with corresponding quantum changes in performance.

Level 1 is the most normal of all the levels of thinking. When you are thinking about your thinking at Level 1, you constantly have to back up and ask yourself, "Is my thinking focused on doing something that will produce the right thing?" The ultimate check on your thinking is its effect on your doing and the results that you produce: "Am I getting the expected effect?" You look at the result and the effect. It means you have to have some clear definitions about what is right. Ask yourself what it is that you have defined as right for you and right for the job on which you are working.

Rock climbing is a good example of "right" or effective thinking. In rock climbing, to be safe, you have to focus on doing the right thing. You have to focus on your partner while your partner is climbing, anticipating what he or she is going to do—what move they're going to make. You focus on one thing at a time, so that you're thinking about the most important, most "right" thing to do at any one point. You focus only on where you're going to put your foot or your toe or where the next move is going to be—on the one square inch that is the "now." So Level 1 thinking tends to be very much in the moment, very much focused on getting results now—immediately.

LEVEL 1 RESULTS: IDEAS

At the micro level, ideas are the most basic result you get at Level 1. In any event, the first step is to become *aware* of ideas. How aware are you of ideas, of new thoughts, new things? Where do you find ideas? "Chic" Thompson, in his book *What a Great Idea!,* came up with a list of the ten most idea-friendly times. In increasing order of importance they are:

Idea
+
Creativity
+
Enhancement
+
Evaluation
+
Implementation

INNOVATION!

Source: U.S. Air Force Innovation Initiative, 1985

25

1. *While performing manual labor*
2. *While listening to a boring sermon*
3. *After waking up at night*
4. *While exercising*
5. *While reading*
6. *During a boring meeting*
7. *While falling asleep*
8. *While going to work*
9. *While showering or shaving*
10. *While sitting on the toilet*

What do all these times seem to have in common?

> *"The brain is a wonderful thing.*
> *It starts having ideas as soon as you*
> *get up in the morning and doesn't*
> *stop until you get to work."*
> —Robert Frost

You'll notice that most of these times are not while you are working or at work. They seem to be the times when you're *not* focusing! Not concentrating. Not really thinking about anything. Daydreaming? Maybe a Level "0" sort of thinking? And then BAM! Suddenly there's the idea.

When or where do *you* have your best ideas? Now that you've become an idea person—a basic Level 1 thinker—start noticing when and where ideas hit you, and what the catalysts seem to be. Look for patterns so that you can be ready and waiting when you find yourself there again. Put ideas on your mental agenda. Start thinking of yourself as an idea person. Which leads me to:

TOOL #2 (LEVEL 1):
Blue Slips

The most basic tool at Level 1 is a simple piece of paper that I call a "blue slip." It's just a small blue piece of paper, unlined, that can fit into your shirt pocket—smaller than a 3x5 card. Use them to collect your ideas.

When do you get ideas?

in the car on the way to or home from work

a recorder in the car?

Rx – Take one Blue Slip before going to bed for the next 21 days.

26

While we don't completely understand why, the size seems to be important (Blue Slips are not the typical 3 x 5 inch file card size, but smaller). They're just large enough to handle a single idea burst, yet they're too small to write complete sentences or long paragraphs on them. They also fit nicely into shirt pockets, better than 3 x 5 cards. The fact that blue slips are unlined has also been a real creativity booster—you're not forced to a particular size of writing.

Where do blue slips come from? We developed them as part of our long-range planning process in the Air Force. They're not at your local office supply warehouse. You simply take a piece of normal, 8.5 x 11 light blue copy paper and cut it up into eight blue slips. Any local print shop can do this for you.

You can go to almost any copy center and have them cut a ream of blue paper up into four thousand blue slips—enough for quite a few ideas!

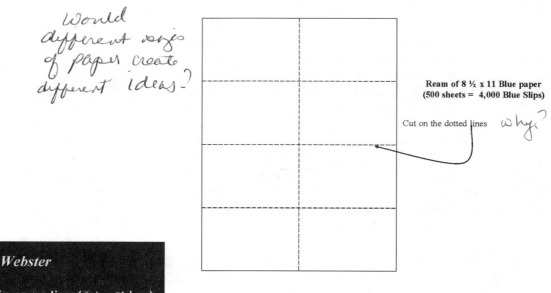

Would different sizes of paper create different ideas?

Ream of 8 ½ x 11 Blue paper
(500 sheets = 4,000 Blue Slips)

Cut on the dotted lines *why?*

The power of blue slips lies in capturing each idea on a separate slip so that you can play with it, shuffle it around with other ideas, make connections to it, or pull it out of your pocket and show someone. You can't do that as freely with a notebook or notepad. Why are blue slips blue? Empirically, they consistently lead to more ideas than writing on white paper or any other colored paper. When they are strewn across a desk with other papers, they show up well. Finally, they're distinctive enough that any time you see them they remind you of ideas and thinking.

TOOL #3 (LEVEL 1):
"What a Great Idea!"

You can use blue slips to immediately create a rapport with a customer or client. When they ask you a question or say something you find interesting, pull out a blue slip and write it down. Say "Wow! What a powerful thought." Put their name on it ("May I quote you? I always credit the people I get great ideas from."). You've just sent them a very strong message that you thought what they said was important. It's a compliment they won't forget. Want to change your life? Write down something your spouse or your significant other or one of your children says. You'll be amazed at the impact.

"But what do I do with all these blue slips?" is a question people often ask me. My response has never changed: "They aren't blue slips anymore—they're ideas!" And doing something with them, moving them into action, is when Level 1 change occurs.

27

Play with your ideas, shuffle them around.

> *"What gets written down gets done."*
> —Gord Tompson
> Vice President
> Exxon Marketing

Develop the habit of scribbling down ideas and thoughts.

Many highly creative people, inventors, and geniuses in history, were known for being compulsive scribblers. Leonardo da Vinci, Thomas Edison, Albert Einstein, Michael Faraday—were all compulsive scribblers and kept extensive journals or notebooks of some sort. Are you a compulsive scribbler? Turn your scribbles into a journal. Journalizing is a great way to give your creativity

28

a jump start. Blue slips and creative-thinking journals are among the first pieces of gear we issue people on a Thinking Expedition or in our School for Innovators. Michael Roberts, operations manager for Kentucky Fried Chicken in England and Northern Ireland and a graduate of the School for Innovators, says that journalizing helps him "keep on keeping on."

By recording ideas and insights, the rate of questions, ideas and change accelerates. The difference in two days' journals demonstrates your improving creativity. At first your approach is slow. After time you begin to make the ascent.

Ray Holbrook, Commissioners' Court judge for Galveston County, Texas, and another School for Innovators graduate, says blue slips are a breakthrough on the way to becoming an innovator. "They provide a means for preserving ideas and thoughts and also drum up those things. Journaling is more deliberate and thoughtful," he says. "Journaling is used to develop ideas and thoughts, and gives you a permanent record of progress on a project. Both practices can be invaluable if you are looking to grow personally and professionally."

TOOL #4 (LEVEL 1):
Thinking Journals

A journal is not a diary. It's a tool for regularly recording ideas, thoughts, thinking and observations on your thinking processes. A journal is about insights, introspection and reflection—not analysis and data collection. They're for deep thoughts, and in fact we call ours "A Tool for Personal Learning and Growth." And yet they're a simple tool, nothing more than a small book of blank pages. There's no right or wrong way to keep a creative-thinking journal beyond just doing it as the right thing to do. Next time you're in a grocery store pick up a small spiral notebook in the school supplies section and give journaling a try.

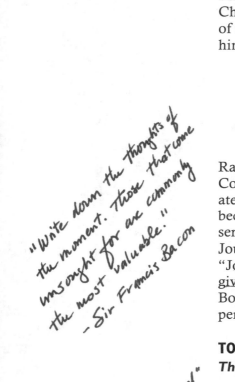

"Write down the thoughts of the moment. Those that come unsought for are commonly the most valuable."
— Sir Francis Bacon

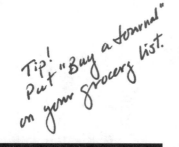

Tip! Put "Buy a journal" on your grocery list.

INNOVATION
STARTS WITH
**THINKING
DIFFERENT**

29

In November 1995 we designed and ran a Thinking Expedition School for Innovators for Johnson & Johnson's entire Executive Development Group. Gerry Kells, director of the Group, focused the expedition on exploring "the core of the core"—the critical core values that make Johnson & Johnson what it is as a company, and how to teach that in a whole new program that would become Johnson & Johnson's worldwide executive development program. The J & J team connected very strongly with the creative-thinking-journal process, its focus on Me, Inc.,® and introspection around personal values and beliefs. Since the School for Innovators, Johnson & Johnson has implemented its first version of the new Executive Development Program called "Framework for Growth"—and incorporated creative-thinking journals into it. We view the use of thinking journals as a simple Level 1 change, and Johnson & Johnson's adapting journals for their executive development classes as basic Level 5 copying and adapting. Yet for Johnson & Johnson it was clearly a Level 6 change—something no one had ever done before and very, very different culturally. Keeping a journal is not the same level of change for some people that it is for others. Background, creative style, psychological type, and culture all bring perspective and relativity to change.

What are Skyline's critical core values? Why don't I know? Ask!

Recommend to the group

MORE THINKING ABOUT THINKING AT LEVEL I

Generally speaking, Level 1 is about maintaining the *status quo*—in a positive sense. In major manufacturing companies that produce products on a line, maintaining the *status quo* means producing that widget over and over and over. The company is not about creating new stuff, it is about producing this one thing as effectively and efficiently as possible. A major piece of what goes on in any manufacturing company is doing and thinking at Level 1 and Level 2: being effective and efficient.

> *"I long to accomplish a great and noble task,*
> *but it is my chief duty to accomplish small tasks,*
> *as if they were great and noble."*
> —Helen Keller

30

See the product through the eyes of the customer.

"The rules are..."

It's vital to have Level 1 and 2 thinkers doing very structured tasks on a production line. For some people, detailed work is their passion. A Level 1 doer will complete his task to perfection but might not say anything about the defective item he passed on to the station next to him. Because that's not his job, his awareness about "ideas" like that is turned off. The Level 2 doer, however, will stop the line and raise the question, even though that may or may not be the most efficient way to run the line.

The trouble is that some people then stay at Level 1 thinking and doing. They don't move to Level 2—it's too big a change for them. It's easy to recognize people who operate primarily at Level 1. They're detail-oriented and task-oriented, structured, targeted, and conscientious. They're focused on their interpretation of what the right things are. They tend to be rule followers and black-and-white thinkers who like to gather the facts first, and they respond best to specific tasks (what) and specific instructions (how). They know their job description and will perform to the letter of it. But don't ask them to stretch outside of that job description box—they typically are not prone to that degree of innovation (which is how they see it). As a result, they may sometimes appear to be closed-minded and usually won't have an abundance of original ideas.

A while back I took a photo of three pay telephones at a gas station. A change in them really caught my eye. Two are regular height, and one is very low for drive-up or wheelchair or child use—a great example of doing the right thing: Level 1 effectiveness. It's not more efficient or a clear improvement, but it's effective and it's the right thing to do to accommodate more people and to enlarge the customer base.

Level 1 changes can be more fundamental, too, if you are redefining what is right. AT&T, the great-grandmother of the pay telephone, for instance, has been in the long distance business for decades, but as the company has changed and shifted into the global information business, it has had to continuously redefine what is right. The entire focus of the company has changed from long distance itself to information-moving over long distance—a fundamental, Level 1 change that in turn has spawned Level 4, 5, 6 and 7 changes.

"The significant problems we face cannot be solved at the same level we were at when we created them."

- Albert Einstein

ROLF'S THEORY OF RELATIVITY

All changes are relative. What's right for you isn't always right for me. Something could be a much bigger kind of "right thing to do" to you than it is to me. Different people see the right things differently.

Still, most Level 1 changes remain small, incremental changes—first order changes. With a first order change, the change occurs *within* a system which itself remains unchanged. As you move up towards Level 7, the changes typically become more fundamental—second order changes that effect the whole system as opposed to only details of the system. The area under the curve for each level of change represents the amount of energy, time, and resources the change will require, as well as the amount of resistance it will meet. It is not a straight-line projection but rather geometric. Each level of change is significantly larger than the preceding one.

31

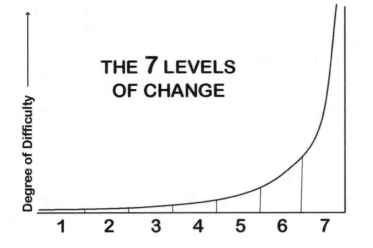

32

A   B

Pro –
immediate Change

Con –
Don't want to change

Borrowing from physics, the lower level first order changes are simple—a change of position, moving something from point A to point B. As you move toward Level 7, the changes become second order changes and complex—a change in speed, constantly accelerating as you go from point A to point B.

PROS AND CONS OF LEVEL I CHANGE

Every level of change has pros and cons. The positive aspects of Level 1 are easy to see. When you are thinking and doing and changing at Level 1, you are very focused, and results are often immediate. You learn the right things to do at your new job, and then you do them, often learning from a coworker or mentor. The right results happen. When you are doing the right things, you are helping the existing processes along, because this is a proven way that works.

Carried to the extreme—being totally focused on what's "right"—can become a negative if it closes you off to new ideas and other "right" things. The negative side of operating at this level is that generally you aren't bringing any new thinking into this level. In fact "new" or "different" thinking isn't really wanted at this level of change. You just need to do what you have been told to do, and you can become so focused on learning all the right things to do that you don't pay much attention to anything else.

Level 1 thinking can become a negative filter that blocks out other things that aren't "right" for what needs to be done.

Behind every level of change hides a corresponding level of fear.

fear (fîr) **n**. 1. A feeling of agitation and anxiety caused by the presence or imminence of danger.

Innovation is about DOING DIFFERENT

LEVEL I FEAR: PARALYSIS

At Level 1 the fear of doing the wrong things leaps out and paralyzes us. So to avoid doing the wrong things, we do nothing. My wife regularly points out to our children: "*If you were afraid of all the bad or negative things that could happen in life, you wouldn t do anything. . . you'd be paralyzed.*"

LEVEL 1 (STRESS)

In addition to fear, change can also cause stress. It can create a tension between what was (used to be) and what now is (or is going to be). The tension comes from what is expected and what actually happens.

> **stress** (strĕs) **n**. 1. A mentally or emotionally disruptive or upsetting condition occurring in response to adverse external influences (e. g., negative change)

When the right thing to do is not what you are used to doing, you are going to have to change—and that can cause stress. A basic Level 1 stress is not knowing what the right thing to do is. Once you know what the right thing to do is, not understanding why it's the right thing to do can also create stress. Sometimes a very big stress at Level 1 can simply be that *you* don't agree that the right thing to do is the right thing to do! Even worse is having to do it anyway when you don't want to.

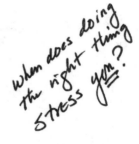

when does doing the right thing stress you?

"I don't want anybody telling me what to do!"
—Your Kids

TRANSITION TO LEVEL 2
Moving from "What" to "How"

As you master doing the right things and feel comfortable with *what* your role and your new job is, you'll begin to change. You'll find that you start thinking about *how* to do the right things right. Here you begin to transition into a Level 2 change—efficiency. Now you begin to think about *how* to do particular aspects of your job, about how to save

33

34

time, about how not to waste energy or money, and about speed, method, and process.

When doing the right things becomes second nature—reflexive—it's easy to move into Level 2 changes and learn how to do the right things right. With the right things mastered, you can begin to start noticing relationships, procedures, and processes. Your boss or mentors will point out more efficient ways to accomplish things, you'll begin to come up with some ideas as well, and you'll intuitively know you're moving on to Level 2.

THE **7** LEVELS OF CHANGE

LEVEL 1: Doing the right things
LEVEL 2: Doing things right
LEVEL 3: Doing things better
LEVEL 4: Stopping doing things
LEVEL 5: Doing things other people are doing
LEVEL 6: Doing things no one else is doing
LEVEL 7: Doing things that can't be done

ME, INC.®—PERSONAL CHANGE AT LEVEL I

At each level of change, I'm going to give you some Me, Inc.® work to do that will move you forward on the way to mentally incorporating yourself. Mental incorporation is hard work—introspective work that helps you develop a personal mission statement, take inventory of your values and strengths, determine your critical success factors, come up with 101 personal goals, and create a vision of the future for yourself.

> *"There is always hope for an individual who stops to do some serious thinking about life."*
> —Katherine Logan

Me, Inc.®, requires a major mindshift—you have to think of yourself as a new entrepreneurial business built on your personal values, strengths, experiences, and ideas. As you mentally incorporate, you'll discover your own power to focus your mission and strategy and learn how to continuously improve. You'll explore how you are unique and different and question assumptions you make about yourself.

To begin the process of Me, Inc.® at Level 1, think about yourself and the basic qualities that you have. Think about your strengths and skills and abilities, things you do well, things you know. Things that make you what you are. Make a list of them—at least one full page. In fact, go ahead and get started right now in the margin. Then examine your list and reflect on it. With this list in front of you, try to extrapolate what your personal focus seems to be—and define your basic mission, your purpose in life. Make a rough cut of it (B+) on a blue slip and plan to come back later to refine it.

> *"Life consists not in holding good cards,*
> *But in playing those you hold well."*
> —Josh Billings
> columnist and humorist
> (1818-1885)

35

Start now!

My Strengths & Skills

1. I listen
2. I support
3. I help
4. I learn

I like challenges
I like success
I create success
I problem solve

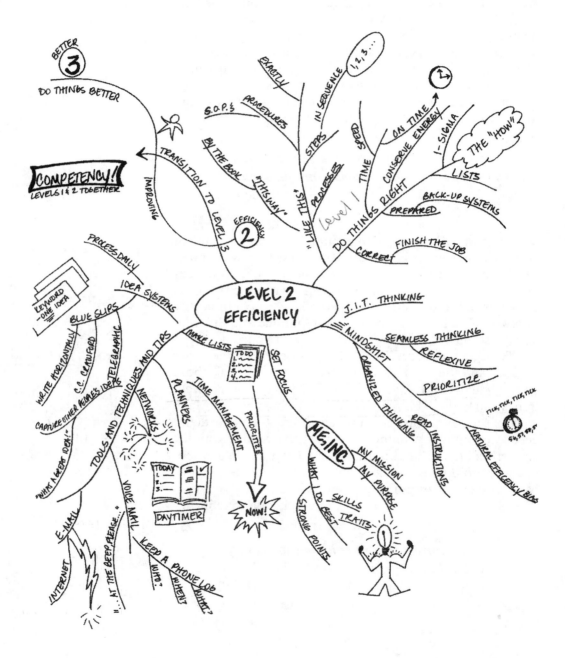

Level 2: Efficiency
Doing Things Right

UNDERSTANDING LEVEL 2 CHANGE

You've mastered the status quo, "the way things are done around here." Level 1. You're doing all the right things, you know the "what" of your new job. Now it's time for another level of change—doing the right things right. You begin to focus on *how* to do your job—the already established procedures and processes, rules, roles, efficiencies, saving time and effort, money and resources. This is Level 2 thinking, and the changes that result from this type of thinking can make a phenomenal difference in the everyday life of a company. Level 2 has a lot to do with rules, guidelines, standard operating procedures (SOPs), and time. Level 2 is all about "how."

> *"Take care of the means, and the end will take care of itself."*
> —GANDHI

People operating at Level 2 are easy to spot. They read instructions and regulations carefully, trying to get at exactly the right way to complete tasks. They ask for tips on how to do things best. When they're in Level 2 mode, they're not real big-picture thinkers; instead, they're focused and thinking sequentially, looking for quicker, faster efficiency. If you give

them a list of things to do, they'll ask you which one to do first, then prioritize the list and complete the tasks in that order. They don't often make mistakes. "Measure twice, cut once."

They like structure and organization. Buttoned-up and on time, they'll have a clean desk with sharpened pencils lined up and ready to go. In the center of the desk will be their task at hand. When they're finished, it goes in the file, and they're on to the next task—unless it's lunch time. Lunch is probably at the same time every day. So is quitting time. Time is a big driver for Level 2 thinking.

UNDERSTANDING LEVEL 2 THINKING

Level 2 thinking is efficient thinking—thinking that produces ideas with a minimum of waste, expense, energy, and unnecessary effort. Level 2 thinking generates a lot of ideas from a little thinking in a short period of time. Brainstorming, for example, is a Level 2 process. Level 2 thinking has an almost automatic aspect to it; it's JIT thinking: Just In Time.

LEVEL 2 MINDSHIFT: EFFICIENCY

The following mindshift diagram and definition illustrate the process you go through to do things right. Note that you have to focus on the right things (Level 1)

38

before moving into doing things right (Level 2) to achieve results efficiently. <u>Focusing on the right things keeps you from doing the wrong things right</u>—a not particularly useful thing to be doing.

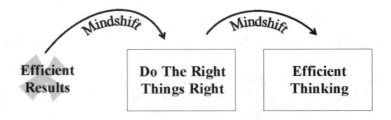

efficient thinking (ĭ-fish′ənt thĭng′kĭng) **n**.
1. Thinking effectively with a minimum of waste, expense, time, or unnecessary effort. 2. Thinking that exhibits a high ratio of output to input, e. g., many ideas in response to a single catalyst. 3. Brainstorming.

THINKING ABOUT THINKING

Level 2 thinking—efficient thinking—is still 1-sigma thinking. When you are thinking about your thinking at Level 2, you will find yourself asking, "Is my thinking right? How am I thinking about this? Am I going about this the right way?"

The ultimate check on your thinking is its effect on what you're doing, how you're working, and what results are produced: "Is this efficient?"

LEVEL 2 RESULTS
Time, Energy and Procedures

Time is what keeps everything from happening at once. Level 2 doers are great at finding ways to conserve time, energy and resources. They'll combine errands and tasks that can be completed in a logical sequence and won't stop until they find the most efficient way to do something. Then they'll make up processes, procedures and rules surrounding what they've deemed as "doing the right things right." Such as, when the gasoline tank indicator drops below a quarter tank, it's time to fill up. Or when there are only two printer cartridges left in the drawer, it's time to stock up. You'll never find a Level 2 doer scrambling for paper or supplies on deadline. They're always prepared—it saves time.

TOOL #5 (LEVEL 2):
Lists

> At the end of your day, take a blue slip and turn it vertically to make a list. Write "To Do" and the date on the top, and make a list of the things you want to do tomorrow. Then stretch a little and add the things you *have* to do tomorrow—the results you want to produce.

Lists

You've potentially organized your thinking. Is this bad? Is it anal-retentive? No, absolutely not! It's got you ready for a new day. But it can drive people who tend to operate at higher levels of change nuts—because they sometimes have difficulty with this kind of thinking. It's not their creative style, it's not in their psychological type—their makeup. Level 2 thinkers often believe they are jealous.

Yet time is one of the seven most important factors in the stuff that Americans are made of.

When I first started working with Exxon Corporation back in 1987, I became friends with Peter Hearl, an Australian on a career-broadening assignment from Esso. Peter kept himself focused and on task with an impressive little loose-leaf time-manager system. When Peter was made the manager of the Innovations Group, one of the first innovations he implemented was time-management training, a clear Level 2 efficiency change, easy and fast to put in place, and it struck a

Time management

39

40

chord with Exxon values. It was also personally valuable, and people had some choices—there were three different time management classes by three different companies—so it was easy to sell. After completing the classes, the marketing department was full of Level 2 thinking. The biggest visible change: everyone started carrying Day-Timers. I still carry mine today, and Peter Hearl and I are still friends— despite it. Since then, Peter has used his blue slip ideas and his time manager to become an executive vice president with Tricon (the triad of Pizza Hut, Taco Bell, and KFC).

TOOL #6 (LEVEL 2):
Day-Timer/Planner

> If blue-slip lists aren't focused and organized enough to suit you, go to your nearest office supply store and buy a loose-leaf planner, Day-Timer, time manager, or simple little notebook. If you *do* buy one of them, you're probably serious enough about time to even read the instructions on how to "manage" it. They're really all about the same: <u>Write things</u> down, use a <u>priority</u> system <u>to force yourself to do the most important right things first</u>. Over time, study your patterns. Notice what you do and don't do. <u>Write your personal goals</u> in it. Transfer some of your Level 1 ideas that are on blue slips into it.

Level 2 tends to focus on details and time. If Level 2 folks aren't on time for meetings, they're five minutes early and are religious about using their time manager or calendar. If they've agreed to a thirty-minute meeting with you, at twenty-nine minutes, watch out! They're already putting away their file folder because they won't need it for your closing comment (not comments!). And details . . . if you give them a proposal to look at and ask for comments, before you get feedback on content, they'll tell you there's a misspelling on page six and give you all of the punctuation errors. They're <u>great copy</u> editors.

Level 2 uses rules heavily. The first tool I gave you back at Level 1 was blue slips. Using blue slips is doing the right thing—capturing ideas. And using blue slips in specific ways is doing the right thing right (e.g., lists vs. ideas). Blue slips are an adaptation of a technique developed in the 1920s by C. C.

BIG Change

Do you realize...

...how much time it takes to adjust to BIG changes?

Crawford, a professor at the University of Southern California. Referred to as the "Crawford Slip Method" (CSM), he used shoe boxes and slips of paper cut to the right size to fit in the shoe boxes. Crawford would gather groups together, such as aviation mechanics, ask them questions about early airplane maintenance procedures and techniques, capture their answers on slips, and publish a manual in very short order.

I began using blue slips (smaller than Crawford's slips) in the U.S. Air Force to engage people in interactions during conferences and meetings, and to facilitate strategic thinking for long-range planning. It's an incredibly simple way to capture ideas and an efficient way to facilitate JIT (Just In Time) thinking and to focus idea gathering in meetings. Using blue slips in groups and meetings has some immediate advantages. It's anonymous and naturally suspends judgment by the group, so it creates a fearless atmosphere that prompts out-of-the-box ideas to come forward. It helps you avoid the drawback of "groupthink" and yet involves all of the group's participants.

TOOL #7 (LEVEL 2):
Rules for Blue Slips

Right things right—there are five basic rules for how to use blue slips:

1. Write horizontally, not vertically, on the rectangular blue slip. While it can be argued that horizontal is best for ideas and vertical for lists (see Level 2 tool #1), the real reason to do this is that it makes sorting and grouping the blue slips easier if all of them are oriented the same way. Over time, I have discovered that people develop ideas more easily when working on a horizontal plane. I don't why that is, it just is.

2. Start every blue slip by writing a keyword (your focus or category for the blue slip) in the upper left hand corner. This gets your mind focused on the thinking or idea that you're putting on the slip. The keywords can also help you group ideas later by keywords related to a central question or problem.

3. Only write one idea per blue slip. Don't try to economize or save paper. Don't write two or three ideas on a blue slip. This isn't to limit the number of ideas you

Tip! Blue Slips are THE Big Tool for becoming an "Idea Person"

42

can have, but rather to keep each idea separate so you can "play" with it easier, try it out with other ideas. This will also help you sort and process the blue slips later.

4. Ideas and thoughts on blue slips should be in brief, telegraphic style, a phrase, keywords, or an incomplete sentence. And no more than one. In other words, write the way you think—in short bursts of information.

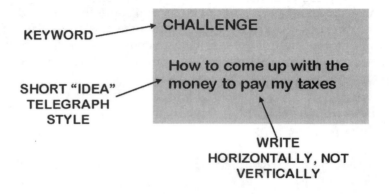

KEYWORD ⟶ CHALLENGE

SHORT "IDEA" TELEGRAPH STYLE ⟶ How to come up with the money to pay my taxes

WRITE HORIZONTALLY, NOT VERTICALLY

5. Finally, watch out for cacography! Write legibly. It will increase the likelihood of idea connections and help you to more quickly understand and process ideas later on.

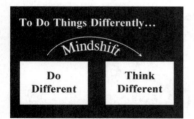

To Do Things Differently...

Mindshift

| Do Different | Think Different |

cacography (kə-kŏg′rə-fē) **n.**
1. Bad handwriting; illegible script. 2. Bad spelling.

Carry blue slips and a pen or pencil with you at all times. Plan to have some ideas. The first thing I do every morning when I get dressed is pick up the stack of blue slips I had next to the bed the night before, put them in my pocket, and put my pen in my pocket. I know I'm going to capture some great ideas each day. Yep, Sundays too. Take them to church with you. It might be a great sermon.

☑ TIP!

Use blue slips to immediately create rapport with a customer or client—or a family member. When they say something you find interesting, pull out a blue slip and write it down. Say, "What a great idea!" Write their name on the blue slip too (I always credit the people from whom I get ideas). You've just sent them a very strong message that not only were you really listening to them but also that you thought what they said was important. It's a compliment they won't forget. Want to change your life (this is a Me, Inc.® tip)? Write down something your spouse or one of your children says. Whip out a blue slip during a dinner conversation. You'll be amazed at the impact on them.

"But what do you do with all these blue slips?"

TOOL #8 (LEVEL 1):
My Blue Slips

Here are my "rules" for doing something with all my blue slips. At the end of the day, I try to sit down and sort through my blue slips. I make a stack of ideas that can be converted quickly to actions. This stack is my hot, "do it *now*" list. I also make a second stack of interesting ideas that I don't know what to do with—but they're still kind of hot. Then I create a third stack that is interesting, but . . . they're long-range ideas. The first stack I convert into a list of changes to be made or things to do, then toss the blue slips. The long-range ideas go into a basket in my office to be acted on later. The random ideas go back in my pocket with my blank blue slips. Eventually, other ideas will come along and connect with these, and they'll be converted to action or relegated to the long-range plans. It works for me. You need to develop a personal system of your own that works for you and your ideas.

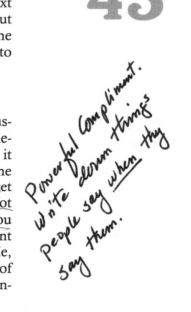

Powerful compliment. Write down things people say when they say them.

44

ONE new Rule?

LEVEL 2 AND RULES

Rules aren't just about "can't"; they're also about smart ways you "can" do things. How do you see rules? What were the rules at home when you were a kid? What rules do you remember the most? How about today—what are the "can" and "can't" rules in your home?

If you were going to make *one new rule* to improve things at work, what would that new rule be? Why would you make that rule? What's the thinking behind your thinking?

If you are naturally a structured person who is a rule-follower, check your rule-following index with speeding. Doing the right thing is obeying the speed limits. In fact, it's the law, which means it's really right! But . . . how much over the speed limit do you drive? If you are at the other end of the scale, very unstructured, breaking the rules may be doing the right thing. You may consider speed limits guide-lines, or even ridiculous (like they do in Montana), while the more structured person would be horrified and consider breaking the speed limits a Level 7 change—the impossible.

For more details on rules and thinking style, see the chapter on "Getting Ready for Change." And by the way, just how much over the speed limit do you drive?

∾

Another form of Level 2 change is <u>delegating</u>. Delegating can apply at any level: in your personal life, at home, at the office, in companies large and small. If there are too many things to do and too few people to do them, get help from others; reach outside. Delegating saves time and opens up time that can be used for thinking creatively.

I like to rock climb. Climbing is first and foremost about safety, and safety is about rules—doing the right things right. In rock climbing you delegate a lot of things to your belayer, your partner, so you can focus on the climb. You delegate safety and protection largely to your belayer. It's an efficient way to deal with worry and risk. But it's also built on the more basic aspects of Level 2 change—doing the right things right (which is *not* just about efficiency). You can't just tie knots in your climbing rope or your anchor system, you have to tie the right knots for that particular function—and you have to tie the right knots right.

The figure eight is the first knot most climbers learn and the most widely used. It ties them, personally, through their harness, into the end of the rope. If it's not right, you can fall a long way. The figure eight on a bight is used to clip in to the middle of a rope or for connecting into anchors. You double check the knots you tie and then your belaying partner checks them. Then you check your ropes and anchors. That's doing the right things right. It's all pretty focused Level 2 doing. Finally you use very specific commands to communicate in question-answer mode:

> Q: "On belay?"
> A: "Belay on!"
> Q: "Climbing."
> A: "Climb on."
> Q: "Belay off?"
> A: "Off belay."

Double-checking is doing the right things right. It takes time. It may not feel efficient. But it's the right thing to do right. And that is what allows Level 2 thinking to be seamless, almost non-thinking, so that you can do what you want to do in the best possible way. When you're rock climbing, you're not only very focused on what to do but also on how to do it. You're thinking about trying to keep your weight balanced over your toes and feet so that your hands are free to move smoothly over the rock to steady you and explore future moves. You try to conserve energy in movement and effort. When you make a move, you focus on doing the right things right, efficiently, over and over, until you get to the top. Similar to Level 1, you are very much in the moment, in the "now" of the one-inch squares, the crystals and protrusions on the rock, moving efficiently and effortlessly up on the network of safety and trust you and your partner have built into the rope.

Creating and using networks is another right thing to do right, and it can help you be extremely efficient. Within a company, develop your own network by getting a feel for who are the key people who have skills in various tasks that you don't, or who can do some special thing very well indeed. When you hit a deadline crunch, draw on your network to get things done fast. I always make it a point to get to know the graphic artists, video folks, and photographers. They're

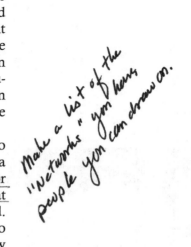

Make a list of the "Networks" you have "people you can draw on.

45

46

★ Not appropriate for Customer Service

always fun to work with, have a great eye for different, and can really work unusual magic for you. Technology has brought us some tremendous level 2 networking leverage.

TOOL #9 (LEVEL 2):
Voice Mail

Don't answer the phone!

If used intelligently, voice mail can bring incredible efficiency and time savings to you on a daily basis. Technique is an integral part of voice mail: use voice mail deliberately, not accidentally. Accidentally is when you call someone and get their voice mail. Deliberately is when you call at a time when you *know* you're going to get their voice mail. Leave details, specific questions, requests for specific information, etc., with the full intention of their calling you back and leaving you a voice mail as well—with the answers you need. Get in the habit of not answering the phone in periods where you're typically productive and efficient. Unplug it! You don't have to answer it—those days are gone. If it's unplugged you won't be tempted, and it'll roll into your voice mail system.

TOOL #10 (LEVEL 2):
Phone Logs

Study the patterns in your phone calls — incoming and outgoing

Keep a phone log. Record the time when a call came in, who it was, their company, phone number, topic, actions agreed to or asked for, and how long you talked. Periodically go back and analyze your patterns and the patterns of people who call you. You'll make some surprising discoveries that you can use.

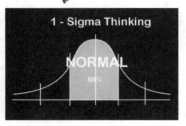

1 - Sigma Thinking

NORMAL

68%

Some time back I noticed that I had three clients who, if I called them shortly after 5:00 PM on a Friday, were always there. They always answered their own phones, and they always gave me new insights. These were three different people with whom I had been working for a long time. That led me to further analyze both my own and my major clients' telephone patterns even more closely—and I discovered some very, very helpful patterns tied to personality type and creative thinking style (for more on that read the "Getting Ready for Change" chapters towards the back of the book). We built on that knowledge to develop a completely different approach to marketing (now "connecting") our "Thinking Different" work with the sponsors and backers in companies and organizations.

47

TOOL #11 (LEVEL 2):
E-Mail

This is one of those interesting tools that fits at several levels. It is the "right" (Level 1) tool for many forms of communication, but it can easily become more trouble than it's worth if it is not used correctly (at Level 2). And there are a number of approaches that significantly improve its usefulness (i.e., take it to Level 3). We assume that all of the "basic rules" of E-mail are being followed, e.g., you run active virus scanning, you do not return or acknowledge junk or unsolicited mail, you do not use "cc" frivolously, you write as though the E-mail message will never be able to be recalled, you keep E-mail short with an appropriate subject line. The ability of E-mail to cross geographic and time zone boundaries is one key reason why we all put up with its frustrations.

So how can you move E-mail from a necessary evil to a tool that has real utility for you and your organization? Some of these are rules that require cooperation among your correspondents to make them work—but can really extend the utility of E-mail. Several examples:

➤ Respect the recipient's time. Keep E-mail short and to one topic, because it's likely to be deleted before anyone gets to topic two or three.

➤ Where possible, put the entire message in a few words in the subject line followed by <eom> to designate "end of message." There *isn't any message*.

➤ Use keywords in the subject line to provide a heads-up for the recipient. In a worldwide workgroup at Exxon, we agreed that a keyword of "BlueSlip" in the subject line would invoke an immediate read by the recipient and a 1–2 line reply within a few minutes. Used sparingly, this

[handwritten margin note: Email — One Topic Use subject line]

48

can be the electronic equivalent of overnight delivery worldwide, except it happens in minutes.

➤ Combine E-mail with audio conferences. I have run worldwide five-minute meetings (see Level 3) electronically while at Exxon and for the Network Applications Consortium. Used as virtual blue slips, this approach can provide many of the advantages of physical blue slips.

➤ Leverage the filtering and filing of your E-mail application on your computer; many provide a rules-based processing option to preprocess your E-mail according to rules you specify.

☑ TIP!

As soon as you finish reading this, ". . . go through all your E-mails that are still in 'in' and handle all the less-than-two-minute ones! Same for your to-read stack. For those kinds of things it's time to be made of Teflon." (source: David Allen, *Getting Things Done*).

Learn how to do this ⟶

Take Allen's E-mail tip one step further to his wonderful JIT Two-Minute Rule: "If there's anything you absolutely *must do* that you *can do* right now in two minutes or less, then *do it now*, thus freeing up your time and mind tenfold over the long term."

STOP! ⟵
Put this book down and go do a "MUST DO" NOW!

MUST DO → CAN DO → DO IT NOW!

To think about Level 2 changes in action, consider the military term "standard operating procedure" and visualize an F-14 fighter getting ready to take off from an aircraft carrier. Everyone is in their place and acting in sequence. The choreography must be perfect. The aircraft is cocked and ready. Brakes are on. The crew is off to the side, having pumped in the fuel. Signals are given to the pilot in the cockpit. The catapult engages, the crew moves back and kneels down out of the blast. It all happens like clockwork. The same way every time. This is Level 2—all the right things being done right. Even Woodrow Wilson once said: "To do things exactly the way you did them yesterday saves time."

MindShift

mind·shift \ 'mind-shift \ *vb* (1993)
[ME *gemynd-shiften*] 1 : to alter one's point of view 2 : to enhance one's capacity to innovate

mind·shift *n* (1993) : the process of altering one's mental approach

49

Actually, a navy carrier deck scene like that is one of the most creative and innovative scene I can think of. No two carrier launches are the same and no two recoveries—carrier landings—are the same. Things start out right, being done right. Then little things go different, or sometimes even wrong. At that point all Level 1 and 2 stuff goes by the wayside. They have to improve (Level 3) on what they learned to do. Then when that doesn't work, they have to stop doing things they've learned that always worked before (Level 4). They think back to other situations similar to this one, to something that worked then, and they duplicate it—they copy it (Level 5). Maybe it works and maybe it doesn't. When it doesn't work, the crew has to think, think fast, and think very creatively. They suddenly have a situation that is really different Level 6 change, or worse, Level 7 change: "This can't be happening!" They innovate literally "on the fly"; they come up with ideas they've never had before, and they implement them almost as they're thinking them, building on the right things (Level 1 and Level 2 training) and hoping they'll work. They usually do. Come back to this when we get to Level 6 . . .

ROLF'S THEORY OF RELATIVITY

Level 2 is far more definite than it is relative. Americans are so biased toward saving time and working efficiently that when I talk about saving time and effort and resources as doing the right thing right, people connect immediately. Time is money in most businesses. Time is precious in most families. Somehow there just isn't enough of it; we all want more of it. There isn't any relativity about it. The Kirton Adaption Innovation (KAI) scores of almost every group we've ever worked with are biased heavily towards the adaptive side of the efficiency subscale (see the last chapter in the book, "Getting Ready for Change"). Efficiency is an underlying component of the majority of ideas at every level of change.

LEVEL 2 PROS AND CONS

Level 2 thinking and doing is almost second nature to people. It's part and parcel of succeeding, not just in business but in your personal life as well. The results and payoffs from Level 2 changes show up quickly in energy, money,

50

Reflexive thinking... is non-thinking... watch out for it.

and time, leveraged even further today by technology, a huge positive change-force in our lives.

The drawback is that Level 2 thinking can lead to stagnation of ideas. In the extreme, it can become reflexive, nonthinking, operating by rote. If you have a highly efficient operation, and everyone is simply doing what is known to be the most efficient way to operate, they don't have to think. All they have to do is *do*.

Why do we do it that way? On the rules side of Level 2, there's another downside: tradition and corporate memory. Stanford Business School professor Jeffrey Pfeffer says that

> the memory of "how we've always done things around here" substitutes for "doing things the right way around here." The root, again, is fear. People don't want to make mistakes, and the best way to avoid making a mistake is to continue doing things exactly as they've always been done. Companies get trapped in a kind of circular logic: "We do what we do because it's the best thing to do. And it's the best thing to do because it's what we've always done."

> After a while, what was originally adopted as a means to an end becomes an end in itself. . . In company after company, the human resources department puts into place a whole bunch of policies that undoubtedly started with good intentions. But in time, those policies, which originally were just means to an end, become ends in themselves. And nobody remembers what outcome those policies were actually intended to produce. What you end up with are sacred cows—things that you take for granted; processes, practices, and rules that you think will help you get things done. In reality, all they do is get in the way of getting things done.

One of my favorite "because" stories is about ham.

A mother and daughter were preparing a holiday meal, and the mother was showing her daughter how to fix the ham. "First you trim the ends of the ham off, like this . . ." She said, ". . . and then you sprinkle brown sugar and orange juice on it to glaze it."

"Why do you cut the ends off like that?" the daughter asked.

"That's the way my mother taught me how to cook a ham," her mother replied. "So I've just always done it that way."

The grandmother was sitting in the living room watching TV so the daughter went in and asked her: "Gramma, why do you always cut the ends off the ham when you're fixing it?"

Gramma told her: "The pan I used to cook hams in was too short for the hams to fit in, so I had to cut the ends off. But I got a new pan and I haven't had to do that for years."

NECESSITY → HABIT → TRADITION → "BECAUSE"

When something works a certain way because of some condition, it makes sense to do it that way. You're competent doing it that way. When you are operating at Level 1 and Level 2 simultaneously, you are highly competent, so there is a tremendously strong bias against change. Why would you want to become less competent? "If it ain't broke, don't fix it." Finally, a preoccupation with Level 2 can create a sense of urgency that totally overshadows what is important.

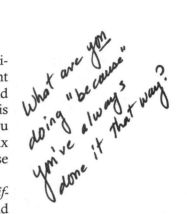

Efficiency may drown us! Everett Rogers, author of *Diffusion of Innovations*, points out that since 1990 E-mail and the internet have exploded as one of the most rapidly diffusing innovations in the history of mankind. By 2002 more than 450 million individuals were using the internet, and the rate of diffusion worldwide is increasing and accelerating— i.e., it is only going to get worse and get worse faster. *USA Today* points out (January 2002) that "in the three seconds it takes to read this sentence, more than a half-million E-mails will land in in-boxes. By 2005, nearly that many will land each second. The E-mail avalanche knows no rank." It's additive. Plus, it follows you home. Consider the Black-Berry, a wireless device that displays E-mail remotely at the same time it lands on your desktop machine. The exploding use of wireless E-mail devices is behind the coming swell of more E-mail. According to BWCS Consulting, 75 percent of corporate E-mail subscribers will be transmitting via wireless devices by 2006. Even more efficient connectivity.

The thinking behind efficiency and the way we're doing things now, soon to become the way we've always done

52

things (the rules), can be huge obstacles to transitioning to any other level of change.

LEVEL 2 FEAR: INEFFICIENCY

The fear of doing things wrong and the fear of wasting time are Level 2 fears.

> *"There is no right way to do the wrong thing"*
> —Anonymous

Unfortunately, at Level 2 the fear of doing the right things wrong can become a vicious cycle. To avoid doing the right things wrong, we constantly ask for directions, which in turn make things take longer, more time. Surprisingly, the fear of breaking the rules doesn't seem to be a Level 2 fear!

LEVEL 2 STRESS

Fear and stress are pretty closely coupled at Level 2, and stress can come in fast with Level 2 change.

- ➤ Not being sure that you've done something the right way.
- ➤ Worrying about doing things wrong.
- ➤ Not doing things right. Making a mistake.
- ➤ Having somebody else tell you exactly how to do things—and what not to do.
- ➤ Having to follow someone else's stupid rules, guidelines or procedures while knowing that they're wrong!
- ➤ How about having to stay within the lines when you color? How simple little things are done (or "should" be done) can cause big stress.
- ➤ Consider something as simple as this: What's the correct way (the how) to put on a roll of toilet paper—paper coming over the top of the roll or from underneath the roll? You'd be surprised how strongly people view this little "rule." Check it out at home. Turn all the toilet paper rolls around.

Don't forget the impact of time.

- ➤ Having a deadline. Having someone else impose an unreasonable time deadline on you.

New Levels of Thinking
"The world
we have created today
has problems
which cannot be solved
by thinking
the way we thought
when we created them."
- Albert Einstein

> Having things that *demand* your time and that build up out of your control causes major stress.

"I m late I m late, for a very important date . . . no time to say hello goodbye I m late I m late I m late" . . . *"Oh, my ears and whiskers, how late it s getting!"*

—The White Rabbit
Alice in Wonderland

> E-mail!!! How far behind are you in answering your E-mail? Consider the impact of E-mail on your life. Remember the statistics earlier?

> How much time are you wasting reading E-mail?

> How about the stress of having someone else waste your time? Or *waiting!* Waiting for someone else.

> Being late.

> Being late because of someone else!

"The hurrieder I go, the behinder I gets."

TRANSITION TO LEVEL 3

When you are effective and efficient, and you can do the right things and do the right things right simultaneously, you can focus your thinking and practice JIT thinking. You know the process and procedures, you're competent. *But* things still go wrong—and you have to move to a higher level. To Level 3—beyond competency. To improve, you have to move away from the minutia and look at the big picture, the connective processes. Level 3 is about better.

.You don't ever leave Level 1 and 2 thinking behind. All along the 7 levels of change, as changes are implemented, you return to Levels 1 and 2, redefining what is right and then perfecting it. When you move to performing and thinking and operating at Level 1 and Level 2 change simultaneously, you've become fully competent. And with that you are ready to move into change at Level 3.

53

LEVELS OF THINKING

1. Focused Thinking
2. Efficient Thinking
3. Positive Thinking
4. Refocused Thinking
5. "Seeing" Things
6. Lateral Thinking
7. Imaginative Thinking

ME, INC.® CHANGES FOR LEVEL 2

The Me, Inc.® work for you at Level 2 is not about efficiency, it's rather about the underlying concept of Level 2: Doing the right things right. Take a blue slip and quickly make a list of your strengths and skills—what you well and do right. Do it now. Don't be stingy with your positive comments about yourself. Tip! Write the comments about yourself in the third person; for some people depersonalizing your strengths and skills make this easier:

> Bob is good at . . .
> Bob is great at . . .
> Bob really knows how to . . .

Think about what you do well, what you do better than those around you, what you are best at—the right things that you really do right. Think about the compliments people pay you. Consider the basic qualities you have available. If you don't have a blue slip handy, write your list here in the margin.

With this list in mind, build on your strengths and skills, and try to come up with your basic mission: a Me, Inc.® Make a rough cut, then come back and refine it later. Remember, you are thinking about what your purpose is in life—what your focus is—how you do the right things right.

And keep coming back to this list of your strengths and skills—your Level 2 stuff. Add to this list whenever you can. Whenever you catch yourself doing something right really well.

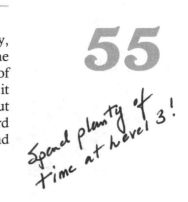

55

Spend plenty of time at level 3!

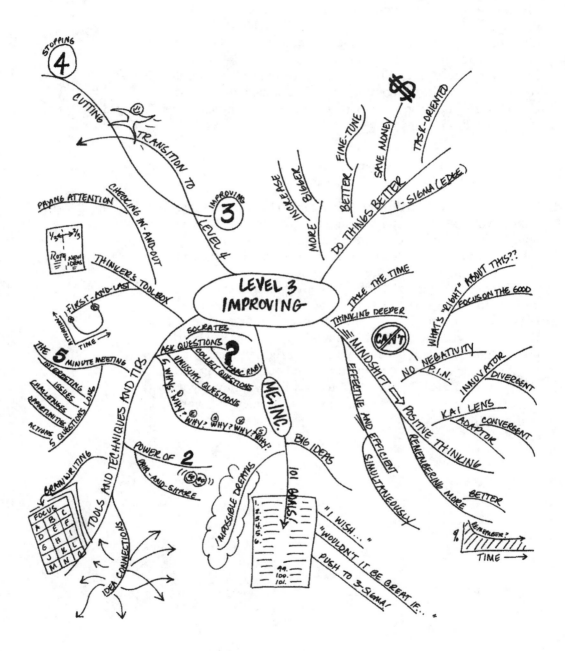

Level 3: Improving
Doing Things Better

UNDERSTANDING LEVEL 3 CHANGE

There are three key words that immediately let you know you are thinking, doing, or changing at Level 3:

1. *better*
2. *improve*
3. *more*

Start listening for those three words and you'll begin to notice Level 3 thinking. Changes at Level 3 involve fine-tuning, ways to speed things up, shorten delivery time, increase functionality, or reduce downtime. Level 3 change makes something more effective, more efficient, more productive, more valuable. At this level, "better" is a simple and constant theme. Continuing with the analogy of moving into a new job, once you've made enough personal Level 1 and Level 2 changes to be comfortable in the job, to be effective and efficient, you are competent. You know what the job is (Level 1), and you understand how to do it (Level 2). When you can do the right things and do them right, you can begin to focus on ways to improve your core activities—fine-tune them to make them better or how to simultaneously make them more effective and more efficient.

UNDERSTANDING LEVEL 3 THINKING

The thinking needed at Level 3 is better thinking that is higher in quality than other thinking. It is thinking that is more useful, suitable, or desirable than thinking that is simply efficient or focused. It is positive thinking—thinking that moves things forward in the direction of progress. It is thinking that is unencumbered by negativity or the tendency to criticize ideas.

"To make headway, improve your head."
—B. C. Forbes

People operating at Level 3 are pretty focused and task-oriented. Like Level 2 thinkers, they will be less inclined to look at the big picture and be more inclined to come up with ways to improve specific processes, particularly saving time and money. Level 3 thinkers are not as rule- oriented as Level 1 and 2 thinkers. They are still likely to be neat and organized, but they aren't quite as "by the book." They've learned "the book" and know it well, and they continuously see ways to make it better and how to use it better. If they have finished their job and done it well, they may leave the office early. If it takes all night, they'll be there to get it done, but

58

probably they'll analyze the situation that led to the late night and figure out how to do it better the next time.

LEVEL 3 MINDSHIFT

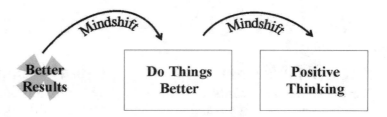

Level 3 thinking starts by reflecting on your thinking, and asking yourself "In what way might I think better?" The mindshift needed for Level 3 thinking focuses on better from a positive angle—not by trying to figure out what's wrong with something, but rather what's right—and how it could be made even better.

> *"Everything is perfect just as it is*
> *and there's plenty of room for improvement."*
> —Nisagaratta Maharaj

To get better results, you have to do things better. To do things better, you have to think better. So the first Level 3 challenge you face is how to think better.

LEVEL 3 RESULTS:

Level 3 change produces results fast. Change at this level is a straightforward build on Level 1 effectiveness and Level 2 efficiency and yields the largest number of quick, simple, and easy-to-get results of any of the levels of change. Level 3 focuses on how to change and improve customer interactions, meetings, and conferences; how to ask better questions and how to use questions to explore and drive out better understanding of problems and messes; how to generate a large number of new ideas fast with small or large groups; and how to kick-start big ideas into a go-forward plan of action. Because of that, this chapter is the longest one in the book. And since Level 3 draws on 1-sigma "normal"

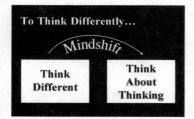

thinking, it is one of the easiest to use to get change started in an organization. Level 3 changes seem to just make good sense to people.

Changes at Level 3 are just better ways of doing things. They jump right out at you when you see them. They're very often "That's a smart idea" kinds of ideas and "Why didn't I think of that?" Often they're Blinding Glimpses of the Obvious—BGOs.

59

Spend plenty of time at level 3!

Results at Level 3—KFC New Zealand

An interesting Level 3 change is illustrated by KFC Marketing in New Zealand. Nick Sealey, the KFC marketing manager, noticed that customers would get in the queue to buy a meal during a peak business period, wait a few minutes, and then leave without buying anything. They'd go buy something somewhere else. "We love the taste, but the queue isn't worth it." Nick was going to have to improve service, do better than a two-minute wait to place an order and a twelve-minute wait for a meal. KFC was losing 15 percent of their customers. Nick organized some teams, focused simultaneously on improving effectiveness and efficiency, and improved service significantly: one-minute maximum to place an order and no more than a five-minute wait for the meal. Results: a turnaround of 25 percent increase in sales with no advertising, just better service.

Results at Level 3—McDonald's Drive-through Display Screens

On a similar note, I recently pulled into a McDonald's drive-through in Houston and was immediately impressed by the addition of a monitor screen at the part of the drive-through where you order. The screen displayed not only what you had just ordered but how (no ketchup, extra pickles, etc.) you'd ordered. It confirmed your order with you—no mistakes. Results: a faster turnaround time at the drive-through window *and* a decrease in food waste (having to throw away misunderstood orders).

THINKING ABOUT THINKING

Level 3 thinking is "normal"—pushing out to the edge of the 1-sigma range. It's about learning to think efficiently and effectively simultaneously. It's about taking time to think

60

What do you remember?

and about thinking deeply. Level 3 thinking is thinking to understand, learning how to actually listen to other people's ideas, and thinking about what they said. It's pausing to think about the thinking behind your own and other people's thinking.

Much of our thinking is governed by what we remember. Remembering provides a baseline for our thoughts. Unfortunately, people don't remember things very well, because they don't retain much of what they hear for very long. After listening to a talk or presentation or conversation, the short three-to-five-minute period immediately afterwards is the time when your retention is close to 100 percent. That's not a very long time. Within an hour it has dropped to about 30 percent, the high points only, and by the next day it's down near to 10 percent. After that it gradually dissipates to nearly nothing. Usually, however, at the end of a class or a talk, we immediately get up and leave, losing the three-to-five-minute

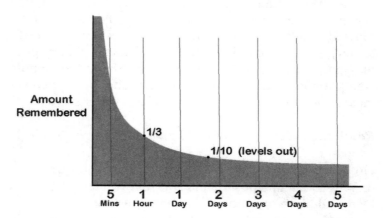

Amount Remembered

- 1/3
- 1/10 (levels out)

| 5 Mins | 1 Hour | 1 Day | 2 Days | 3 Days | 4 Days | 5 Days |

opportunity to retain nearly 100 percent.

Studies have shown, and smart students know, that the first and last things said in a conversation or presentation or class are remembered best. Advice to speakers has always been: "Tell 'em what you're going to tell 'em (first thing), tell 'em, and then tell 'em what you told 'em (last thing)." Listeners quickly learn to check out during the "tell 'em" part and check back in at the "told 'em" ending.

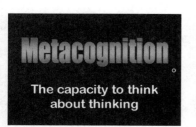

Metacognition

The capacity to think about thinking

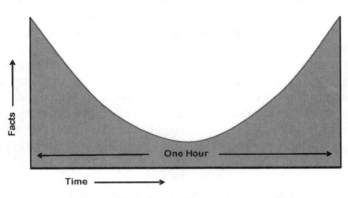

Facts

One Hour

Time ⟶

First and Last Facts are Remembered Best

Finally, consider the fact that people don't pay attention to other people very long. People mentally begin to check out of the process of listening after a relatively short time, fifteen to twenty seconds, and begin to think about or focus on something else. They check back in when the subject changes, when it's their turn, or there's a pause, or when something new that catches their mind enters into the conversation or talk or class. They operate the rest of the time in a state of in-and-out listening.

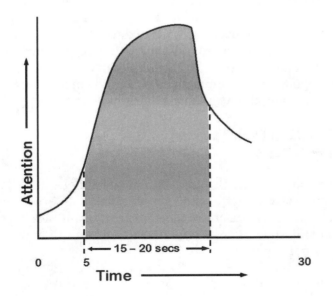

Attention

← 15 – 20 secs →

0   5   30

Time ⟶

62

So how do we use all this? Instead of beating people up for not remembering, for not listening, and for not paying attention, encourage them not to. They're not going to anyway. But show them how they can use that fact to remember a lot more and think a lot better as a result. Different people have different cycles and patterns of listening and paying attention. The key is to capitalize on that. By becoming aware of the fact that you check in and out while you're listening, and having a feel for what your own cycle of listening or attention span is, you can increase your retention.

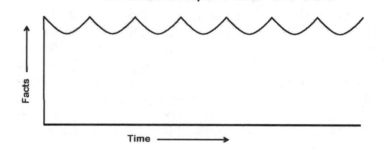

First and Last Facts are Remembered Best

... Create Multiple "Firsts" and "Lasts"

When you feel your attention wandering, check out and begin writing down the new thoughts that are coming to mind that are not necessarily related to what you were listening to. After doing that, your mind is uncluttered, and you can much more easily check back in and reconnect to what is going on in your meeting or seminar or lecture. Here are some tools and techniques to help you do that:

TOOL #12 (LEVEL 3):
Thinker's Toolbox

Have You Ever Thought About The Way You Think?

This is a JIT, Just In Time, thinking technique that can significantly improve both your retention of information and your ability to make idea connections. It builds on remembering right away—primary recency—and in-and-out listening.

Use the thinker's toolbox to do that. The toolbox itself is simple to make. Simply draw a line down a regular 8.5-by-11-inch sheet of notepaper, dividing it into two sections lengthwise (one-third and two-thirds). The left-hand side, the one-third, is for making rote-learning notes while you are paying attention. Not sentences, notes—keywords and short phrases—chunks of information that capture the essence of the subject at hand. By leaving the right two-thirds of the paper open, you leave room for future idea connections and other thoughts. Most note-takers do not plan ahead like this for lateral thinking. It's an improvement to the more typical way of taking notes.

① Rote learning

As your attention wanes and you feel yourself checking out, move over to the right-hand side of the paper and write down whatever you are thinking about now. Draw on other things you know. When you do that, you are creating new knowledge—connecting your wider knowledge to what you've just heard. Try moving back to the left-hand side and try to reflect on what you *did not* write down. Then try to make connections between what's missing, other information you already know or have previously learned, or perhaps connections between several different ideas you've already written down on the left-hand side of your paper.

Reinforce your connections by drawing arrows or lines to connect your thoughts on the left and right sides. This visual emphasis increases your ability to remember information.

② Creating New knowledge

64

TOOL #13 (LEVEL 3):
The Thinker's Position

When you complete a class, talk, session or meeting, go into a JIT (Just In Time)-think. Assume "the position"— lean forward, elbow on your knee or the table, chin on your writing hand, and for three minutes reflect on the notes you have taken and the idea connections on your thinker's toolbox. Do this without writing or adding to your notes. The three-minute think.

Then write down at least three more thoughts or ideas. This simple habit can nearly double your retention of material covered. Remember, after listening to a talk or presentation or conversation, the short three-to-five-minute period immediately following it is the time when your retention is close to 100 percent.

MindShift Is About **Change**

Unfortunately, when the bell rings in the classroom, most of us have conditioned ourselves to leap up and race out of there, blowing the three-minute window of opportunity to reinforce what we've just heard into new insights and deeper learning. Ah, well . . . we'll come back to this shortly.

~

In the meantime, another way to mindshift to better thinking is with questions. Thinking is inspired by questions, both in the person questioned and in the questioner. Isaac Isador Rabi, Nobel Prize winner in atomic and molecular physics, and holder of an amazing string of scientific honors, was once interviewed about how he had come to be who he was. A good son, he attributed it to his mother. He said that as a child, every day when he would come home from school— every day—his mother, Jennie Teig Rabi, would greet him the same way: "Did you ask any good questions today, Isaac?"

Her perpetual question forced him to continually think about questions, develop a questioning attitude, and ask questions in school. A good question can be an irritant—it forces people to take time to think! Questions take time. They make us pause and reflect and think about what we are doing. "The important thing," said Einstein, "is never to stop asking questions."

The average child asks 125 questions a day. The average adult asks six. All too soon, children learn to stop asking questions that Mommy and Daddy can't answer or don't want to. The same thing happens later in school with teachers. In fact, in school, we learn answers to questions we never wanted to ask. The end result is we begin to shy away from questions and lose what was once innate curiosity and inquisitiveness. Yet, questions are the primary way we learn.

The great Greek thinker and philosopher Socrates taught by asking questions, and through his questions, directed the focus of his students' thinking, making them come up with their own answers. The Socratic method can be relearned today as a tool for better thinking.

65

66

TOOL #14 (LEVEL 3):
The 5 Whys

Learn to ask, "Why?" again. As little children we asked "But why?" a lot. That powerful tool for better thinking was gradually lobotomized out of us because it pushes people's thinking so hard. Parents and teachers reach a point of frustration having to answer all those questions—questions take time—and sometimes they aren't easy to answer.

Today as part of the quality and continuous improvement process in many companies, employees are being retaught to ask "Why?" five times. In root-cause-analysis processes, the "five whys" technique essentially peels back the covering on a problem like the layers of an onion to eventually expose the underlying cause. The first "Why is that?" is usually pretty easy to answer. The second "Why is that?" about the first answer pushes the thinking deeper. The third "Why is that?" pushes the answer to the edge of 1-sigma, the edge of normal answers. By the fourth "Why is that?" people are really thinking (and getting irritated, too!) and you begin to approach the real root of things. The fifth "Why is that?" pushes the answer well into 2-sigma thinking, and usually is enough to reach the level of root cause in a problem area.

"Why?"

"Why?"

"Why?"

"Why?"

"Why?"

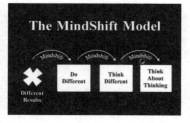

The MindShift Model

RESULTS AT LEVEL 3 +++

Mark James was a young British engineer I met in Thousand Oaks, California. He had been assigned to Exxon's Western Production Division for a three-year career-broadening assignment. But . . . this was Southern California! What could a Brit know about the oil business in southern California (despite the fact that Mark had been in international oil production operations all over the world)? So he didn't get a real job. Instead Mark was told his job was to "go make money"—roam around, ask questions, learn things and "make money." Mark took it seriously. He began to use the five-why probe—"Why? Why? Why? Why? Why?"—to dig into things deeper. "Why are we doing this?" or "Why is that?" and "Look, I'm just a simple Englishman. Why do you do this that way?" And then he'd come back with an idea. At first he would get hit on the head and beaten up badly by old thinking. Then he would come back again with another idea or a solution to a challenge—and for every three or four ideas of his, one might work. He was quite an idea-generator with a pretty high KAI score. In his short three years he personally accounted for well over $10 million in savings and cost reductions. Pretty soon, when Mark talked, people listened. Mindshift: ". . . maybe some of these ideas might work."

5 x Why? x 3 years = $10 million!!!

We interviewed both Mark and his boss and shot a short "home video" of each of them talking about innovation and ideas: Mark explaining how he'd gotten into the job of "making money" and what he'd done with that license, and his boss, Ron Bowen, talking about Mark and his ideas, and how his freedom to question things had impacted operations. We began including a clip out of the video in the one-day innovation think-shops we were running all over the company and got some interesting spin-offs: "Loose cannonball on deck" became a frequent Big Idea in a number of other divisions and organizations. Leverage a new hire's fresh perspective and lack of NIH thinking—turn them loose with the charge of "go make money. Find stuff to fix." as their first assignment.

TOOL #15 (LEVEL 3):
Good Questions

Start collecting questions. When someone asks a good question, or one that's particularly thought-provoking and causes you to become thoughtful and reflective, write it down on a blue slip (and tell them that's what you're doing, that you collect great questions). Develop a set of interesting and stimulating questions.

Pick a favorite question and begin asking it of people in places where you don't normally ask questions. Practice

68

with it for a while at home with your family or at conferences and meetings. For instance, three of my favorites are:

"What's something you don't know?"
"What's a thought you've never thought before?"
"Huh?"
They really make people think and think diff/erent.
I believe that questions are perhaps the most important creative thinking tools there are. And they are invaluable

Technique:

Start keeping track of any questions you notice that you ask habitually, the questions you are most comfortable with. These are the questions that direct your focus, and surprisingly, they direct how you think and how you feel. Notice and think about the kinds of answers they generate, and how those answers affect the quality and focus of thinking—and through your thinking, your life.

☑ TIP!

This is also an important technique to use with your Me, Inc.® process. The next time someone asks you a question that really makes you think, or one that you immediately recognize may be leading into a very important conversation, stop, pull out a blue slip, and write it down. Say "That is a great question!" Write their name on the slip with their question. Tell them you collect great questions. Several things have just happened:

> ➢ you have had time to think about the question before answering it;

> ➢ you have given the person a powerful compliment;

> ➢ you have added one more great question to your collection;

> ➢ you have had time to think about the question behind the question, and the thinking behind their thinking.

Now you can take this a step further by answering their question with a powerful question of your own.

"Do you mean . . ?"

collect good questions

We want to be HERE

Diff/erent Results

It can help you, a group, or a team explore a problem or "mess" and get tremendous clarity on it (A mess is a system, a collection of inter-related issues, problems, opportunities, challenges, history, and background).

69

> *"To understand a system, you need to understand the system it fits into and is part of."*
> —Howard Odum

TOOL #16 (LEVEL 3):
"Do You Mean . . .?"

To begin, each person writes down a "mess statement" describing the problem the group is working on (Rule: the statement should be five-to-nine words in length. See "The Magic Number 7 ±2" on page 12). Pair up everyone in the group and one partner in each pair begins the process. The first person reads his mess statement to his partner (and reads *only what is written* on the blue slip). From that point on the first person can only answer "yes" or "no."

The technique is to continue the process of paraphrasing until each person gets three "Yes" answers. This technique works best if the questioner actually first writes down the paraphrased statement before reading it to his or her partner (that way there is a written record of all the statements at the end of the process).

"Do you mean... ?"

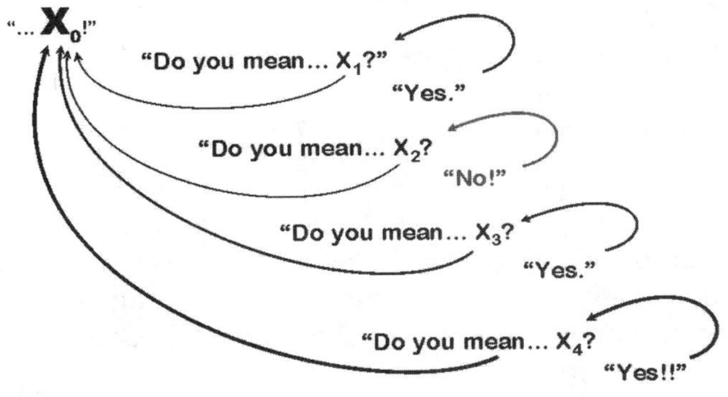

"... X_0!"

"Do you mean... X_1?"

"Yes."

"Do you mean... X_2?

"No!"

"Do you mean... X_3?

"Yes."

"Do you mean... X_4?

"Yes!!"

70

After three "Yes" answers, the roles are reversed. (Note: several "No" answers may occur before reaching three answers of "Yes"). When both partners have finished, each pair in the group chooses the one statement which best captures the essence of the problem out of their eight (each person has an original statement plus the three that got "Yes" answers). These are then called out and written on a flipchart and the entire group then uses nominal voting or some other process to converge down on and decide which statement really is *the* problem statement.

The process is intended to open up the mess as widely as possible and discover the variants tied to it. It feels like a game, and that is the trick to facilitating or guiding it—keeping the process fun. "Do you mean . . ?" is one of the most basic tools we use on Thinking Expeditions and one which we teach very early in our School for Innovators.

Use this at home to get clarity in important discussions

～

Back to questions. When your child comes home from school, or conversely, when you come home from work, the typical conversation tends to be a series of "standard" questions and answers:

"How was school today?"
    "Okay."
"What did you learn in school today?
    "Nothing."
"What did you talk about in school today?
    "Nothing."
Well . . . what happened today in class?"
    "Nothing."
"Do you have any homework?"
    "No."

There is a point at which you need to stop asking questions in order to make progress, to change things. If you keep asking questions, you'll continue to be uncertain, and only doing certain things will produce change. Change your methods and try:

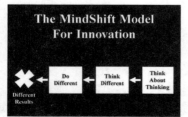

"Do you mean . . ?" followed by:
"Tell me more about that."

71

TOOL #17 (LEVEL 3):
"What Did You Learn Today?"

Instead of going down that path again, stop and sit down with your child and make a thinker's toolbox ("Oh, no! We're not going to do this again are we?"). The trick here is that initially *you* do all the writing. Then start combining several Level 3 tools and techniques into something new. You are first getting your child to mentally assume the position and reflect; you are secondly helping your child develop important remembering skills and reinforcing that by writing down what your child remembers; third, you are using questions to move the thinking process forward; and fourth, when you move to the right-hand side of the toolbox, you and your child are creating new knowledge together—moving from rote memory work to synthesizing and real learning.

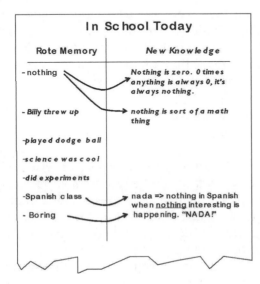

72

There is a point at which you need to stop asking questions in order to make progress, to change things. So you introduce your child to the thinker's toolbox. If you keep asking questions, and getting nothing as an answer, you'll continue to be uncertain, your child will stay uncertain, and nothing will change. Only doing certain things will produce change. The thinker's toolbox can certainly produce a change in learning patterns, in the way we think about things.

At some point you have to stop questioning and thinking and start doing. The question at that point is: "What action could I take now to get started? What can I do to improve things *right now*?"

Consider meetings. People hate meetings. They churn and churn without doing. And meetings have been shown to eat up more time than any other single thing in business. An effectively and efficiently run meeting is a real anomaly.

> *"Thank you for coming to this meeting that has no purpose."*
> —Dilbert cartoon

If you can build a better meeting, not a better mousetrap, the world will beat a path to your door.

How often have you been in a meeting, conference, training session or class where great ideas and thoughts came up but then were lost or forgotten, never to surface again? Where actions were delayed or maybe never even realized because of a lack of timely follow-up? The best time to evaluate or make things happen as a result of a meeting is right at the end. Tip! Use blue slips!

TOOL #18 (LEVEL 3):
The Hot Washup

The hot washup is a blue slip (or 3 x 5 card) technique we used in NATO at the end of any major war game exercise. The process can be used to evaluate, almost instantaneously, what just went on. And the results provide the initiative to make things happen or set the agenda of the next session. Below are three basic questions that can be asked at the end of a meeting, conference, training session, telephone conference call, etc.:

LEVEL 1
Effective

Doing the Right Things

1. What did you like or what went well? [Key Words: *liked* or *well*] This question should always be asked first to get the participants to focus on the positive aspects of the meeting or conference. Even if the proceeding had a definite negative flavor, always "force" the participants to think positive first.
2. What was the value to you personally? What did you learn? [Key Word: *value*]. If there was no value to you, or if you learned nothing, why even be there?
3. What would you like to have seen done differently? (If you could run this meeting over again . . .) [Key Word: *different*] This is a negative question that should be used last to avoid biasing their previous two questions.

    The above questions are always asked as part of the hot washup. Below are two other questions that I also like to substitute, depending on the situation, or if I am attempting to get the group to think about their thinking:

4. What did you realize about the topic? What became clear to you during the session? [Key Word: *realize*]
5. What insights did you have during the session? [Key Word: *insight*]

After you have led this process, have everyone pair and share; then collect all the blue slips, and use them to evaluate what went on and to provide a framework for action or set the agenda of the next session. You should storyboard and summarize the blue slips and feed them back to the group as soon as possible, ideally by the next day.

73

How to recap and summarize a meeting.

TOOL #19 (LEVEL 3):
Pair-and-Share: The Power of Two

This is a great way to follow up a five-minute meeting or can be injected into meetings on its own to heighten the energy and creativity levels. The single largest jump an idea takes is with the changes that come the first time it is shared with another person. When pairing-and-sharing after a five-minute meeting, begin with step two.

74

1. The facilitator begins by stopping the meeting and making everyone write down some key issues, challenges, concerns, points, questions, etc. Remember: one idea per blue slip.
2. The facilitator asks the group to pair up and alternate sharing and discussing the things they have written down. Each person is allowed only two minutes for sharing his or her ideas.
3. Next the facilitator asks everyone to pair up with another person. This time they are only to share what they learned from the previous person they paired with, leaving out any of their own ideas and thinking. This time each person is only allowed one minute.
4. Finally everyone writes down one new insight or idea they got from the pairing process. Either go around the table quickly to share them with the entire group or, if the group is large, do it by table or groups of four. Collect these blue slips for summary word processing to be distributed later.

Technique:

Pairing-and-sharing can be done almost anywhere using whatever is available to write on—even a paper napkin. If there is nothing to write on, then just have people pair up and talk. It's a great way to break up and liven up a long speech or presentation and to engage your entire audience both while you go along, and at the end to lead into a lively Q&A discussion.

When we launched the Office of Innovation in the Air Force in 1986, one of the first areas we tried to innovate was meetings. Everybody hated meetings. They were seen as time wasters and one-way non-communication.

The more boring the subject,
the longer the meeting will run.

EFFECTIVE

The "classic" meeting seems to have some universal characteristics:

- ➤ Heavy on opinions
- ➤ Short on facts
- ➤ Dominant personalities
- ➤ Limited team play
- ➤ Little bias towards action
- ➤ Focus on why an idea won't work
  (if an idea is brought up)

Wouldn't it be great if we could run a meeting in five minutes? The better meeting! So we came up with a process for doing that and began to teach it to new lieutenants and new sergeants so they could make an immediate and valuable change as soon as they reported for duty in a new assignment.

☑ TIP: SOME THINKING FOR DUMMIES

The Importance of Sharing Ideas: Discuss ideas with others. They can build on your ideas, offer new ideas to work with, and help you think of new ideas. Develop an effective way to share ideas. Have a coffee group where each day at a set time you share ideas. Use communication software on your computer. Make time each day with your spouse to discuss nothing but new ideas. [Paul Devlin]

TOOL #20 (LEVEL 3):
The Five-Minute Meeting

This is a powerful change to save time and to get people focused fast. By its design, it is simple, effective (Level 1 change), different, and for most people very efficient (Level 2 change). It really connects well for people subconsciously on the lower levels of change. But it really is a Level 3 change; it improves meetings significantly. You can start a meeting with a five-minute meeting or

76

you can insert a five-minute meeting into the middle of a longer meeting that's dragging and get it refocused. It becomes more effective and efficient.

The five-minute meeting format is like no other meeting people have been in. There is no discussion, no rambling. The basic five-minute meeting is designed as an "Interrupter" to be inserted in the middle of a bogged-down, boring meeting. Through the use of five questions combined with blue slips this very structured process stimulates thinking and promotes the generation of ideas and action. It builds on the premise that in any meeting, no matter how bad, some interesting ideas have been raised. Also, there are some key issues and challenges either on the table or under the table, and buried in the interesting ideas, the issue and the challenges, there is probably an opportunity. Finally, there is sure to be some action that needs to be taken no matter what else happens. It is on these basic contents of any meeting that the five-minute meeting builds.

In the Middle of a Meeting

To insert a five-minute meeting into an on-going meeting that has gone dead, simply say, "We need to stop this and do something different!" Then, hand out blue slips and explain how to use them. Ask everyone to write the word "INTERESTING" in the upper left hand corner, focus their thinking on what's been covered so far in the meeting, and then tell the group there will be four more questions and keywords to think about, and they will have forty-five seconds to focus, think, and write about each one (subsequent questions go on separate blue slips):

1. What are the most crucial *issues* facing us?
2. What are the most pressing *challenges* facing you personally?
3. What *opportunities* do these ideas, issues and challenges present?
4. What *actions* can we take now?

Starting a Meeting

To use a five-minute meeting at the beginning of the meeting, start by telling your group, "This is going to be

Issues and challenges are strategic drivers for change.

Level 1 is about
WHAT

different! We are going to think differently, do things differently, have different ideas, and get different results." Next, hand out blue slips and explain how to use them. The questions are a little different if they come at the start of a meeting. The operative keyword for a starting five-minute meeting is "*expectations*." Ask the group to write the word "*expectations*" in the upper left hand corner of their blue slip, and ask them to write down what they are expecting out of today's meeting. If they have more than one expectation, they need to write each one on a separate blue slip.

Next, have them write the keyword "*question*" on a blue slip, and ask them what questions they feel should be covered in this meeting (this is the equivalent of *issues* in the middle of a meeting). Again, subsequent questions go on separate blue slips. Then tell the group there will be five more questions and keywords to think about, and they will have forty-five seconds to focus, think, and write about each one.

1. What are the most crucial *issues* facing us today?
2. What are the most pressing *challenges* facing you personally relative to those issues?
3. What *opportunities* do these ideas, issues and challenges present?
4. What *actions* could we take right now?

Blue slips can be injected into a meeting at a pause or lull, when the discussion has gotten too heated, when one person is clearly dominating the discussion, when an agenda item has been covered and the group is ready to move on, or just before or after a break.

At the End of a meeting
If you use a five-minute meeting to end a meeting, your thrust is a little different. Essentially you are recapping and trying to get something to happen as a result of the meeting. The five-minute-meeting questions are an excellent catalyst, but the emphasis is on "So, what?"

78

1. What *interesting* new thinking and ideas surfaced today?
2. Based on this meeting, what are the most critical *issues* facing us?
3. Similarly, what are the biggest *challenges* for you personally?
4. What *opportunities* do you see for us?
5. What *action steps* can we take now—both near- and long-term?

There are many ways to process the ideas that come out of a five-minute meeting. Pairing-and-sharing, a tool that will be talked about next, is what makes the five-minute meeting so powerful in terms of raising a group's energy. It saves time and provides the opportunity for people to verbalize their ideas to other people, leading to new and different ideas. If you are unable to process the blue slips on the spot by using a chalk board or flip chart or reading through them, promise a typed summary of the blue slips to be distributed no later than the next day. Speed of turn-around is critical to creating a feeling of importance and immediacy surrounding ideas.

If you're using blue slips in a meeting, initiate the process by asking a question, which causes the people in the meeting to think about responses. The facilitator should limit the response time to forty-five to sixty seconds per question. This time period is deliberately short and will frustrate some people. But push on and let them know it's okay if their idea isn't finished (they'll speed up and catch up); this keeps the meeting to five minutes.

RESULTS AT LEVEL 3: MOHAWK INDUSTRIES

That was exactly what Don Mercer, the president of Mohawk Industries in Calhoun, Georgia, adopted and used very successfully with large groups of Mohawk's top dealers at their annual Dealers Conferences. He and I teamed up and gave the dealers a kind of Huntley-Brinkley presentation on "thinking differently for different results" in what we called "The President's Forum." Don billed me as the Mohawk "mind doctor" and started off by telling the dealers that I was going to help them learn how to think diff*f*erent. I then

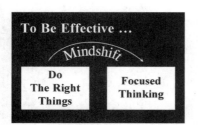

To Be Effective ...

Mindshift

Do The Right Things

Focused Thinking

showed them how to use blue slips, introduced the five-minute meeting, focused it on their businesses, paired them up to share their issues and challenges, and handed them off to "the President." Don was a redheaded ball of energy with a wild and energetic style, and engaged the dealers in some pretty exciting and very lively discussions. Using this technique, every dealer (more than five hundred of them) had a handful of blue slip issues and ideas and questions from which to talk. They left the conferences with a lot of new ideas, insights, tools and techniques to go back and use in their daily operations. Mohawk gained some tremendous big-picture insights into the real world issues and challenges facing their key customers. It was a solid Level 3 change and improved much more than just the content of the conference.

High-engagement conferences

TOOL #21 (LEVEL 3):
Conference Kick-Starts

As a result of working with Don Mercer and Mohawk, I came up with a major new idea: "starters" built around the 7 levels of change. Instead of giving keynote "speeches," I now kick-start conferences with a high energy, interactive session that "starts" things differently and mindshifts everyone *"attending"* the conference into *"participating"* in the conference differently. A starter works everyone through the 7 levels of change at high speed, shifts their thinking to becoming aware of ideas (Level 1 change), copying and adapting new ideas they hear in presentations (Level 5 change), looking and listening for different (Level 6 change), and writing everything down on blue slips (Level 1 change), with a thinker's toolbox or on So what? sheets. I also coach the conference organizers on how to engage all the participants in pairing-and-sharing (Level 3 change) in the general sessions, and how to run a hot washup (Level 3 change) at the end of each day to reinforce what everyone has learned and to get real-time feedback.

Rolling more stuff together to make a better conference.

RESULTS AT LEVEL 3: EXXON CHEMICALS
Continuing along the lines of creative conferences, while I was working with Exxon Chemicals, Randy Randol, the Public Affairs manager, talked to me about meetings. "We really know how to run regular meetings well. We have

80

rules up on the walls, process diagrams that we follow, things we check for as we go along, and we make some pretty good decisions in them. We start on time and we end on time. But . . . they're overly focused. We don't know how to have a creative meeting—a meeting where we come up with new ideas."

Albrecht's Law

Intelligent people when gathered into an organization will tend towards collective stupidity

Working with Randy, I came up with a ½-day workshop on "Creative Meetings" and idea-finding, and a new poster with Rules of Thumb for Creative Meetings—which could be used to *temporarily* cover up the other set of normal rules for meetings.

TOOL #22 (LEVEL 3):
Creative Meetings

Rules of Thumb for Creative Meetings

1. Set the stage for different
2. Don't immediately agree on what the problem is
3. Find out what's different about this situation
4. *Force* everyone to think. Ask questions—write the ideas down
5. Engage everyone in the group. Pair up and share ideas
6. Defer judgment—jump on ideas and give them life instead
7. Listen diff*erently*—keep your mouth shut and your mind still
8. Paraphrase and restate first, *then* give your ideas
9. Get at least three diff*erent* points of view from everyone
10. Stretch—in quantity there is quality

Focused Thinking

focused thinking (fō'kəs'd thĭng'kĭng)
n. 1. Thinking that converges on or toward a specific point. 2. Concentrated thinking; concentration

Great questions and blue slips are the basics needed for a creative meeting, and of course pair-and-share. When the group is larger, a very useful tool is Brainwriting with IdeaConnections sheets.

81

TOOL #23 (LEVEL 3):
Brainwriting

Taking improved thinking in meetings further and making meetings even better, consider brainwriting, a quiet and different kind of idea finding process. Blue slips are efficient but not as efficient as brainwriting, a great way to get ideas connecting. It requires a form like the idea-connections form shown here, but the forms can be hand-made on the spot with normal copy paper. Here's the process:

1. Everyone starts with an idea-connections form and defines the problem or issue at hand at the top of the form.
2. They then write down three ideas in the first row of blocks.
3. Trade papers. The next person reads the problem statement at the top, what has already been written, and then writes three new ideas in the next row of blocks.
4. They then pass the paper on to someone else.
5. You trade again and again, and in a short period of time, you generate a huge amount of ideas.
6. *Note*: It is helpful to have the first person who completes a sheet to immediately start an additional sheet and write down three ideas on it to get it started (one additional sheet for every six people involved) so that no one has to wait for someone else to finish writing on their sheet. This keeps the energy high and things moving fast.

Brainwriting engages everyone much more quickly and deeply than "brainstorming" and is typically much more productive in a very short period of time. It creates a level playing field for everyone. Quiet people tend to participate much more. Both slower and faster thinking people can go at their own pace. And people who are embarrassed to say their ideas out loud get involved. Senior people in the group and "experts" can't dominate, and the variety of ideas generated is much broader.

Much higher level of participation by everyone!

82

IdeaConnections

REFOCUS:

A.	B.	C.
D.	E.	F.
G.	H.	I.
J.	K.	L.
M.	N.	O.
P.	Q.	R.

Become Aware of Ideas

RESULTS: IMPACT WITH IMPACT

IMPACT is a professional network of young engineers in Kellogg Brown & Root (Halliburton Company's big engineering division). A forward-thinking vice president asked IMPACT to create a "top ten" list of things that entry-level employees would like to see changed in Halliburton. As it happened, we'd just led a three-day "Blue Sky Thinking Adventure" to come up with breakthrough ideas to reinvent engineering work processes and jumpstart innovation within the company—and Kim Fernandez, the chair of IMPACT and one of the founders, had been a participant. She'd connected with many of the tools and techniques used in the adventure, and had already introduced blue slipping and using hot washups in her weekly IMPACT board meetings, and had even used them to facilitate a meeting of more than one hundred people.

The list of "complaints" turned out to be larger than ten items, so the IMPACT board had members rank the items in order of importance. At that point, instead of just turning in a list of complaints, IMPACT took the request a big step further. Kim designed a new process from her "Blue Sky Thinking" experience, and introduced "brainwriting" to 110+ IMPACT folks at their next meeting. They generated over fifteen hundred ideas in ten minutes. At the end of the brainwriting, each member traded sheets with the person next to them, circled three ideas that they liked, and then combined them into a "big idea." Kim then formed the group into table teams of four or five members who discussed their big ideas, synthesized their thinking, finally chose one expanded big idea, and developed action steps for it. The ideas were collected and formatted into a report that was then passed on to the vice president. Instead of just giving the VP fifteen problems, they gave him ninety-eight solutions!

TOOL #24 (LEVEL 3):
What's the Big Idea!

Coming up with the *big* idea is a convergent process that works well with any sized group. It's a great way to close any idea-finding or brainstorming session. The process can be held to no more than eight minutes (skip steps 6–8 below). A *big idea* card is twice as big as a blue slip—it is a quarter of a sheet of card stock. Cut 8 x 11 card stock (light blue in color) into four cards; a substitute is a large 5 x 8 blue index card. Since a *big-idea* card is twice as big as a blue slip, you write at least twice as much, both front and back—and you use the power of two. This requires pairing up with a partner.

83

Converging lots of ideas down to ONE BIG Idea

84

1. *The Idea*: The process starts by having each person select one idea that they really like and think has potential to be a really *big idea*.
2. *Tell Me about It*: Each person now pairs up with someone next to them and explains the idea they have picked to their partner. This is to get fresh perspective on the idea and is a two-stage process: each person has one minute to talk while the other listens.
3. *The Big Idea—Part 1*: Each person is given a *big idea* card. They write the heading "*big idea!*" on the top of the card, give their *big idea* a name, and begin to write out and expand the idea based on the discussion they have just had with their partner. They write until they reach the bottom of the card but *do not continue on the back side*.
4. *Tell Me More about It*: Each person now pairs up with a new and different partner, and each reads what they have written about their *big idea* to them from their card. They *do not exchange cards so that the other person can read it*. It is important that the writer reads his or her *big idea* to the other person—in doing so they will naturally go well beyond just what they have written, expanding on it even more. Allow the pair two minutes for this to ensure they go beyond just what is written in their discussion.
5. *The Power of 2*: Each pair *now* exchanges their *big idea* cards. Continuing the *big idea* on the back side of the card just as if they had actually written it, the participants enhance and expand it further, completely filling up the back of the card. This gives a fresh perspective to the idea. They simply continue writing where their partner left off or write on the back of the card. (They should leave a little space on the bottom of the card for two or three more final lines to be added). Allow two minutes for writing on the back side of the card. When finished, they *do not return* the *big idea* to the person who gave it to them.
6. *Action Thinking*: Now the participants pair back up with their partner, read what they wrote on the back of the *big idea* cards, and then team up to come up with two or three action steps that can be taken to get the idea moving and into action.

Focus on Change

- Think about change
- Notice change
- Become aware of change

7. *Now What?* Depending on the size of the group and the time available, you can leverage this even further: Re-group into small teams of fours or sixes, and decide which of the *big ideas* in each team is a truly *great idea*. Collect all the *big ideas*, collect only the *great ideas*, ask everyone to take their *big* and *great* ideas with them and "make something happen," post all the *big* and *great* ideas on the wall in the back of the room. In any event, commit to word processing (summarizing) all the collected ideas and sending a copy back to everyone, publishing the summary of the ideas as minutes of the session.

85

This takes me back to Don Mercer, the president of Mohawk Industries. One day Don pulled me off to the side and said "Mind doctor, we need results! Now that you have everyone in the company writing down all these ideas, we have to get them to turn them into results. And I don't want one of those consultants that stands on the pier and yells at us to row harder. I want you to get in the boat with us and row! Find one of the mill mangers, get involved with him and his problems and his people, and work with them to turn ideas into results. I also want you to coach some of our senior leaders how to lead and think differently—and how to get results." This lead to the creation of "Think 101" and "Results 101," which are now key components of the School for Innovators.

results (rĭ-zŭlts⁄) **n**.
1. a. A favorable or concrete outcome or effect. b. A measurable success.

RESULTS: THINK 101

Don Mercer's charge led to my working much more with Larry Perugini, vice president of manufacturing operations, and Robert Wages, manager of the Calhoun, Georgia, Yarn Spinning Mill. Calhoun was at that time at the bottom of the heap and ranked fourteenth out of all fourteen Mohawk car-

86

Think 101 + Results 101
Big Ideas

pet mills in performance numbers. Larry Perugini (who was Robert's boss), and I teamed up and designed "Think 101," a workshop that taught basic out-of-the-box idea-finding tools, techniques, and processes to a select group of Robert Wage's people—all the way down to the first-line supervisors. We covered creative thinking style (the KAI: Kirton Adaption-Innovation inventory), blue slips, five-minute meetings, hot washups, brainwriting, pair-and-share, and *big ideas*. This was all pretty much level 1, 2, and 3 change and thinking.

RESULTS: RESULTS 101

At the same time we also created a new one-day workshop that we called "Results 101: How To Get Different Results." Results 101 took the output of a Think 101 session and focused it: how to converge down a large number of ideas, select and develop *big ideas*, how to take them into solution-finding, and then how to jump-start ideas into action plans. Finally we'd work on how to move the *big idea* action plans into implementation and track the results—how to measure success.

RESULTS: TURNING MEETINGS INTO RESULTS

Level 1, 2 & 3 changes: I attended and participated in a number of Robert Wages' daily and weekly meetings. We introduced the five-minute meeting and the hot washup, and with his management team we made a list of all the meetings they attended or held each week. Then we looked at how we might change things to make everything more effective, efficient, and all-around better. We developed a JIT (Just In Time) process for capturing ideas on the manufacturing line, and action plans focused on implementing the ideas in fast-forward. We worked on setting measurable goals for the ideas and action plans, and on a simple system for tracking progress on improvement in operations. Supervisors and their team leaders began using blue slips and the pair-and-share process to debrief everyone at the end of each shift change—as well as for the handoff to the new shift.

By the end of January (three months later), Robert Wages and his team had moved the Calhoun Mill's performance numbers to first place—number one. Robert left me a great voice mail in his long North Georgia drawl: "From the

**Notice Everything
Write It Down**

87

bottom of the heap to the top of the heap—the view is terrific, and I'm going trout fishing." The Calhoun Mill stayed up there in the first, second, or third position for quite a while. From a Mohawk Industries and Don Mercer's point of view, it was a Level 7 change—impossible. This couldn't have happened.

~

Ideas and suggestions to improve things are often met with resistance that draws on Level 2—the right way to do things, the way we've been doing things for a long time. Company experts and managers with years of experience developed standard operating procedures (SOPs) and regulations that spell out the way to do things around here. These are the people who coached you earlier when you were new and were learning how to do things in your new job. The experts.

"In the beginner's mind there are many possibilities, but in the expert's mind there are few."
—Shunryu Suzuki

TOOL #25 (LEVEL 3):
The NIH List

We've developed a simple tool to use when the "not invented here" (NIH) reflex automatically kicks in: the NIH list. Here are some classics:

1. "Be practical."
2. "It's too radical."
3. "It's against policy."
4. "That's not my job."
5. "It worries our lawyers."
6. "It won't work here."
7. "Management will never buy it."
8. "We tried that several years ago.
9. "We need to be careful with this."

88

Tip! Create your company's N.I.H. List and turn it into a poster

Everyone, including experts, can identify with the NIH reflex. They are good, logical, reasonable comments. Every company, every organization, every family has their own NIH List. Start noticing them, writing them down whenever you hear one. Next time you're in a meeting and the NIH reflex kicks in around the table, stop dead in your tracks in the middle of your idea that is getting hammered, and say "Wow! I hadn't thought of that. Please, everyone take one of these blue slips and write down all the phrases like that that we are going to bump up against in this company!" You've now got the data. Ask the group to quickly help you converge all of them down to the "Big 10"—the real idea-killers in your organization. Then turn those into (1) a poster for meeting rooms and (2) wallet-size cards.

From then on, anytime one of those comes up in a meeting, stop and say: "Thanks, Bob. I hadn't thought of that. That's number seven." If it's one that's not on the poster, write it on a Post-it note, stick it on the poster, and thank Bob for his fine contribution. If there is no wall poster handy, pull the small card out of your wallet, look at it and say "Yep! That's number seven, all right. Thanks, Bob." And hand Bob the card.

ROLF'S THEORY OF RELATIVITY

Improvements can be very relative. What is an improvement to one person may be a total disaster to another. Especially if the Level 3 improvement is very focused, often it overlooks how it interrelates to what's going on in the rest of the company. It could start a snowball effect that may or may not be seen as an improvement elsewhere as the change rolls out.

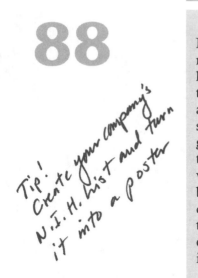

THE UBIQUITOUS BLUE SLIP

An idea-capturing technique

- C.C. Crawford
University of Southern California

LEVEL 3 PROS AND CONS

This leads us directly to the positives and negatives of Level 3. The positive side to Level 3 changes is easily measurable in time or money savings, in more sales, improved products, better processes.

The drawbacks usually show up quickly, too, when Level 3 changes haven't considered interrelatedness—the impact this change will make on the organization as a whole.

LEVEL 3 FEAR: CATASTROPHIZING

The fear that surfaces at Level 3 is the reverse of improving. It's basic worrying.

89

- ➤ Fear of making things worse instead of better.
- ➤ Fear of bad weather.
- ➤ Fear that nobody will like what you just did.
- ➤ Feat that no one will have a good time at your party.
- ➤ Fear that now something won't work.
- ➤ Seeing only the worst case.
- ➤ Catastrophizing—"We're all going to die!"

LEVEL 3 STRESS

Inside-out Stress (I Do It to Myself):

- ➤ Not being able to come up with an idea on how to improve something.
- ➤ Forgetting a short-cut that you know is a better way.
- ➤ Becoming an obsessive over-achiever.
- ➤ Being your own critic, telling yourself *"Nothing is ever good enough."*
- ➤ Not being satisfied with an improvement you've made.
- ➤ Spending a lot of time and effort improving something and then suddenly realizing it can be done a lot better in a much more efficient way.
- ➤ Not being able to stop having more and more ideas on how to improve things and simultaneously realizing you're never going to implement them all.
- ➤ Continuing to improve past the point of diminishing returns.
- ➤ Becoming a perfectionist.
- ➤ Going to extremes in doing things better (for instance, drinking too much of a better whiskey).

Outside-in Stress (Somebody Else Stresses Me):

- ➤ Having people not listen to your good suggestions.
- ➤ Being "improved" by someone else.

90

> Feeling obligated to help someone improve themselves, or do something better—because they just don't get it.

> Working long and hard on a really great improvement only to have someone else do it even better minutes later.

> Having to stand by and watch while someone else tries to figure out what you've done wrong.

> Being asked "Why?" five times.

> Having somebody tell you what you just did "better" isn't good enough.

> Plain old constructive criticism.

> Worst of all, working with someone who won't shut up, and who keeps coming up with more and more and more ways to do things better. And more and more criticism.

ATTENTION!

THIS is the chapter with all the good stuff in it. This is where all the good, easy-to-get RESULTS stuff is. If you want to liven up meetings and focus on small changes, skip the rest of the book. You won't "get it." If you already "don't get it," throw the book away or sell it used on Amazon.com.

☑ TIP: SOME THINKING FOR DUMMIES

Close your door and spend ten minutes every day thinking about ways you can improve your organization. Provide others the opportunity to share their ideas—everyone needs time to think. —Karen Crouse

TRANSITION FROM LEVEL 3: INCREMENTAL VS. FUNDAMENTAL CHANGE

We've covered a lot of change and-thinking ground up to here, perhaps without thinking about it. 68 percent (1-sigma) of all changes are Level 1, 2 and 3 changes: effectiveness, efficiency and improvements. These are also first order changes—changes that occur within a given system which itself remains unchanged. They are "local" or incremental changes. When we transition from Level 3 to Level 4 we are also moving into 2-sigma change—change whose occurrence changes the system itself. These are "global" or fundamental changes.

The most natural way to refocus is to begin cutting—looking at what you don't have to do. The operative question here is "What can I *stop* doing?" It sets the stage for moving on into Level 4.

ME, INC.®
Personal Change at Level 3

91

see pages 223-226 (what's next)

Where Levels 1, 2, and 3 are about focus—doing the right thing, doing it right and finally doing it better—Level 4 is going to be about refocus. Taking a look at things again. Before moving forward into Level 4, this transition point is a good place to look at your own thinking through the lens of the Kirton Adaption Innovation (KAI) inventory. The more "adaptive" style thinker will tend to look at things convergently, will focus primarily on how to improve things— Levels 1, 2, and 3 changes, and will accept most problems as stated. This person will stay primarily at Levels 1, 2, and 3 with both their thinking and their doing. The more "innovative" style thinker will tend to think more divergently, open things up, and push beyond improving things to emphasize different instead. His or her thinking will primarily start at Levels 4, 5, 6, and 7, accomplishing Levels 1, 2, and 3 changes by embedding them in or making them part of more complex ideas and concepts at higher levels of change. They are much more likely to challenge the problem as given, refocus it, and come up with a very different problem to work on.

TOOL #26 (ME, INC.®):
101 Goals

At Level 3 self-improvement is the focus, and setting goals is the next step toward mentally incorporating and improving yourself. In the School for Innovators, we launch a process on Day 1 called "101 Goals." This involves writing down 101 goals and wishes before going to sleep that night! This turns out to be quite a stretch for most people. Coming up with twenty to thirty goals, about one full page of note paper, isn't too difficult. These are the normal, everyday kinds of goals most people have. To push on up to fifty to sixty goals, two pages worth, is much more challenging and is where most people get stuck. They've reached the normal, 1-sigma boundary of "normal" thinking (theoretically, sixty-eight goals).

The next wall people usually hit is at about eighty to ninety goals, after they've included the goals that followed from "wishes" and "wouldn't it be great if" thinking. To get over this wall, people naturally shift into Level 4

92

*Push your thinking!
write out your list
of 101 Goals and Wishes.
Start Now!*

1.

2.

3.

4.

5.

AhHA!

Blue slips are a form
of compulsive scribbling

(doing away with things and habits) and Level 5 (copying, doing things other people are doing) and have transitioned their thinking into 2-sigma or "interesting" thinking.

The final stretch of the 101 Goals process moves into the area of impossible dreams, into things you could never really see yourself doing but would love to be able to do. These last fifteen to twenty goals really do become out-of-the-box wishes that, for the person writing them down, are pure 3-sigma or different thinking. Interestingly, one of the big wishes that always seems to come up is "adventure" or to go on an "expedition"—which is one of the reasons why the metaphor of the Thinking Expedition works so well.

"Be careful what you wish for" is an old Chinese admonition. My son-in-law, Grant Goldin, went through School for Innovators Expedition XXVII in September 1997. Inspired by the mountaineering and climbing metaphors, he added "Climb Mt. Everest" to his 101 goals list. A year and a half later, he was on the 1999 Everest Extreme Expedition, sponsored by NASA, Yale University, and the International Explorers Club.

TOOL #27 (LEVEL 3):
Me, Inc.® = We, Inc.

Kent Malone, a senior manager of contracting in Halliburton, and a graduate of the School for Innovators (October 2000), went home with 101 Goals and a discovered a powerful Level 3 improvement to the Me, Inc.® process with his family.

"Me, Inc. really touched off a firestorm of activity for me when I was first exposed to it during the School for Innovators," Ken reports.

I returned home from the Expedition and was anxious to share all this newfound insight with my wife. All my excitement was quickly jerked back into reality as she logically pointed out that many of my personal goals had nothing to do with her personal goals or our overall family goals. The only logical choice was to incorporate as We, Inc.

We each wrote down our personal goals—about one hundred each. Where we had commonality, we moved those to the We, Inc. column—luckily about fifty altogether. In discussing those fifty, we discovered we had different perspectives of what success in reaching those goals would mean. Realizing we could accomplish a lot more as a team than we originally thought individually, we ended up setting the bar higher on most issues and created some real goals with quite a bit of stretch in them.

Our individual goals generally do not require participation by the spouse. At first, we had to understand that we need our space and our individuality. By having those individual goals in writing, we find we are now much more supportive of each other's personal needs and desires. We put all the goals on a chart and have it prominently displayed in our home for a constant reminder of our goals and dreams. We also included a blank section to be filled in later, titled "26 Fun Things to Do."

Does it work? Absolutely! Eighteen months later, I am amazed at what we have been able to accomplish both together and individually. Many of the life goals which seemed to have a lot of stretch eighteen months ago seem very attainable at this point. Was it perfect? No, we have made minor revisions at least quarterly, but very many times we have been able to go back and focus decisions on issues, based upon our long range goals in writing. Many of the changes are the addition of new goals! Besides achieving results, it very simply generates another opportunity to sit down together on a regular basis and explore goals, concerns, and direction with each other—a real necessity in a successful marriage.

"What gets written down gets done!"

Transitioning to Level 4
1-Sigma Change (Levels 1, 2, and 3)

UNDERSTANDING 1-SIGMA CHANGE

Without getting overly mathematical or statistical, take a look back over your shoulder at where we've just been: Levels 1, 2, and 3, the 1-sigma area of the normal distribution. Most of what we do "normally"—68 percent of it—happens in 1-sigma:

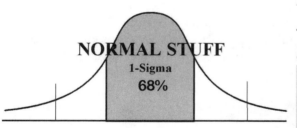

NORMAL STUFF
1-Sigma
68%

Similarly, 68 percent of changes and new ideas come from 1-sigma doing and thinking, i.e., normal changes and normal ideas. Correspondingly, the basic tools and techniques for improving things—doing and thinking more effectively and more efficiently—have been covered there: blue slips and capturing ideas, the ten rules of thumb for creative meetings, the five-minute meeting, pair-and-share, and the hot washup. Simple, but not simplistic. They work. They are also not so "normal," since most people are not familiar with them. They are the

things that can create Level 1, 2, and 3 mindshifts. And there are still a few things to think about in between Level 3 and Level 4—tools and techniques to continue the mindshift into positive thinking and to ways to improve things.

If 68 percent—a pretty solid majority—of new ideas to improve things are generated at Levels 1, 2, and 3, what happens to them?

TOOL #28 (LEVELS 3–4):
PIN

Eighty percent of new ideas to improve things don't get implemented because they are shot down by nonpositive thinking or negative thinking. They are "NIPped" in the bud.

Reverse your thinking and try the PIN approach instead to make sure ideas get a chance to develop.

P—first find something positive about a new idea.

I—next find something interesting about it.

N—last, look for the negatives.

By suspending judgment, you are cutting out the negative thinking that stops creativity and idea flow.

96

> *"The biggest quality in successful people, I think, is an impatience with, negative thinking."*
> —Edward McCabe

PIN is a simple yet powerful tool to use in meetings and the most important of the four basic rules for brainstorming and idea-finding: *suspend judgment.*

If you don't have the "Rules of Thumb for Creative Meetings" handy, start the next meeting you're in by writing "PIN" on a flipchart or whiteboard and then explaining the concept: "This is *the rule* for today. We're looking for ideas, and we're going to suspend judgment."

We've set the stage for running better meetings and running meetings better—creative meetings where we can come up with new ideas. We have a number of different tools and techniques for generating ideas: Questions, blue slips, five-minute meetings, Post-it notes, brainwriting, the power of two (pair-and-share), and the *big idea* process.

Before we move into Level 4, we're first going to look at a framework and some structure, rules, and a process that can focus and apply all the various levels of thinking and tie all the tools and techniques together to use in solving problems in meetings.

TOOL #29 (LEVEL 3):
The CPS Model

There are three stages to creative problem solving (CPS), or for that matter to *any* approach to problem solving:

1. understanding the problem
2. generating ideas
3. planning for action

In the CPS Model, each stage has two sub-stages: a divergent stage and a convergent stage. Divergent thinking opens the problem up, expands your view, and leads to a large number of ideas, perspectives, options, and solutions. Convergent thinking is more analytical and focused, reducing the problem, options, ideas and solutions to more manageable pieces or to a single answer or point of view. There is a natural creative tension between divergence and convergence.

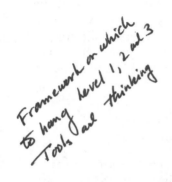

Framework on which to hang Level 1, 2 and 3 Tools and thinking

LEVEL 2
Efficient

Doing Things Right

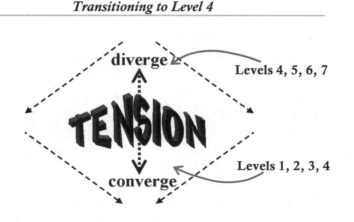

The creative-problem-solving model and the process of "CPS" is built on a repeating and complementing cycle of divergence-convergence-divergence-convergence and leverages the creative tension between them. CPS has its roots in work by Alex Osborne and Sidney Parnes, pioneering leaders in the field of creativity. Osborne, an advertising executive, fathered the concept of brainstorming (late 1940's), and Sidney Parnes, a professor at Buffalo State College, formalized Osborne's ideas as a multistage model. In our School for Innovators, we use a simple three-stage variant of the Parnes-Osborne model:

CPS model

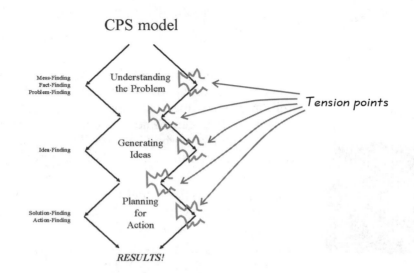

98

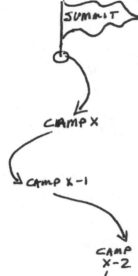

EFFICIENT

Each stage of the CPS model diverges and converges and feeds into the next. The Osborne-Parnes model defines further additional stages within the three basic stages.

1. Understanding the Problem
Opening the problem up actually has three sub-stages:

> *Mess-Finding*: Looking at the "mess"—the broader problem of interrelated issues, challenges, problems, and opportunities to find an area on which to focus: a "mess statement."

> *Fact-Finding*: Exploring knowns, unknowns, issues, challenges, missing or needed facts, and information, to expand understanding of the mess.

> *Problem-Finding*: Discovering a suitably "fuzzy" problem, full of opportunity or need for unusual and novel ideas and approaches: a "problem statement."

2. Generating Ideas or Idea-Finding

> Generating a large number of diverse and novel ideas relating to the problem statement.

3. Planning for Action has two sub-stages:

> *Solution-Finding*: Converging on a subset of ideas, refining them into potentially useful solutions, and exploring barriers and approaches to acceptance.

> *Action-Finding*: Generating and refining potential action steps to move the solutions through acceptance.

In mountaineering and climbing, our first task is to understand the problem—what mountain are we going to climb, and what does the summit look like? What other problems and challenges connected with it? Weather? Crevasses? Avalanche areas? Then we begin to generate ideas, starting at the summit and working backwards down the mountain:

> to get to this point near the top, from which we could probably make the summit, we would first have to get to this point below it (camp X);

> to get to that camp X, we would have to get to this point below it (camp X-1);

> to get to camp X-1, we would have to get to this point even further down, camp X-2;

> and so on until we get to a point at the base of the mountain at which we can set up base camp and start back up that chain of ideas (potential camps).

Then we develop a plan to put everything in place to turn those ideas into possible solutions. Then we put our climbing shoes or boots on and start climbing—we go into action. And with each move we make we go through the CPS model again and again on a smaller scale. Diverge-converge. Move. Diverge-converge. Move. Always looking for the next one-inch square to shift to and balance or grip. At each new point on the climb the climber brings into play a technique or tool that fits the situation.

At each stage and sub-stage of the CPS model the guide or facilitator similarly introduces different tools and techniques to control and focus the thinking of the group (e.g., blue slips, questions, five-minute meetings, pair-and-share, big ideas, etc.). Note that each divergent phase in each stage and sub-stage is really just some form of idea-generation—coming up with ideas, whether they be messes, facts and data, problem statements, solutions, or ideas for actions.

A CPS session is built around three components:

1. a "client" with a problem;
2. a group of people to generate lots of ideas
3. a facilitator to guide the CPS process.

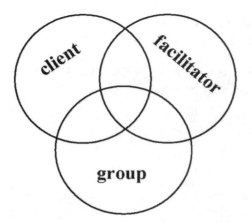

100

This brings us to "brainstorming," one of the techniques used in CPS, first described by Alex Osborne in his book *Applied Imagination* (1953). Today (2002) here's how Webster defines it:

brain•storm (brān′stôrm′) v. tr. 1. To consider or investigate (an issue, for example) by engaging in shared problem solving. 2. To think of or produce (a solution to a problem, for example) by this method.

Brainstorming is perhaps the most widely known idea-generating technique, *and also the most misunderstood and abused.* From common experience, brainstorming is simply getting a group of people together, focusing them on some issue, and having them throw out ideas as fast as they can think of them, with the ideas triggering other ideas in the participants' heads. There are two generally accepted rules which are supposed to be followed:

1. suspend all judgment until the end and
2. go for quantity—the more ideas the better.

In practice, both of these rules are widely ignored: a few ideas are thrown out, a senior person then makes an NIH comment about some of them, and the group then bogs down in discussion. CPS changes that abuse.

TOOL #30 (LEVELS 3–4):
Rules of CPS and Brainstorming

Level 2 is about

HOW

The facilitator sets the stage for CPS with Osborn's original four rules of brainstorming:

- ➤ Suspend judgment
- ➤ Freewheel—anything goes!
- ➤ Go for quantity
- ➤ Cross-fertilize

The most consistent abuse in brainstorming is not following (i.e., the facilitator not enforcing) these four simple rules. This is because the power of the rules is not well understood—by either facilitators or participants. The facilitator's job is to explain the rules, teach them to the group, lead the group through the brainstorming process with those rules *and enforce them!*

1. *Suspend Judgment.* Any comments, particularly criticism, must be held back until the end of the session or until the guide transitions the group from the divergent, idea-generating phase into the convergent, idea-selecting phase. "Negative" comments immediately dampen participation and lower the group's energy significantly.

   Suspending judgment is the single most important rule for thinking different. The guide *must* really enforce this rule ruthlessly at its first breach by any participant. This separates creative thinking from critical thinking, and the guide's job is to move the group from one kind of thinking to another.

2. *Freewheel—Anything Goes!* All ideas are accepted and recorded verbatim without any editing by the guide or members of the group. *Crazy* and radical ideas can be real sparks to moving the process toward 2-sigma and 3-sigma thinking. This is the real power of brainstorming.

3. *Go for Quantity.* Brainstorming produces very large quantities of ideas in a short period of time. The basic principle is "In quantity there is quality." Anybody can give you a few ideas for almost any problem off the top of their head (1-sigma thinking). The trick is to purge the participants of those kinds of ideas and then force them into nonnormal 2-sigma and 3-sigma thinking and new perspectives.

4. *Cross-Fertilize.* Make idea-connections, piggy-back on other people's ideas—jump on them! Once people really get into this mode, the ideas really start popping.

101

} The BIG Rule!

Now stop for a minute with all this structure and these rules. Think about it—this is just simple Level 3 stuff. We are going to improve a meeting that is going to focus on coming up with some creative ideas to solve a problem. We

102

are going to define some clear rules and roles for the process we are going to use. That's all. It isn't rocket science, it's straightforward Level 1, 2, and 3 stuff rolled together a little differently. How do we start? A CPS session is built around three things:

1. a "client" with a problem
2. a group of people to generate lots of ideas
3. a facilitator or guide to lead the CPS process

How big a group can you handle? To keep it simple, I like eight. Four pairs, or two groups of four (two pairs each). Tip: The client should be one of the eight in the group and needs to generate ideas too.

TRANSITION TO LEVEL 4

With the CPS model as your framework for leading groups into thinking different, you're ready to move on forward into 2-sigma—to explore change, thinking and mindshifts at Level 4 and Level 5. Paul Watxlawick reminds us of the differences between first order change and second order change as we move into 2-sigma:

"There are two different types of change; one that occurs within a given system which itself remains unchanged, and one whose occurrence changes the system itself."

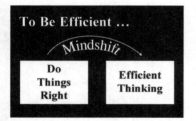

ME, INC.® CHANGES FOR LEAVING LEVEL 3

You have three tasks for yourself here.

1. With this pause in between Level 3 and Level 4, you've picked up a powerful framework for personal change as well. Start first by noticing the diverge-converge pattern in your own your thinking. Then, start applying the CPS model to challenges and problems you bump into everyday. Imbed CPS into your Me, Inc.® as a new skill, as part of who you are and how you think and operate.

2. Go back and update the rough-cut you took at your mission statement at Level 2. Try to build some of the concept of creative problem solving" into your mission, or work it into your first Me, Inc.® strategy for change. Include words like "change agent" or "innovator" and "results" and "people."

3. Finally, try CPS out on yourself right now: Using your new B+ mission statement as your "mess," do some Me, Inc.® fact-finding, problem-finding, and idea-finding before you move on into Level 4 change. How are you going to roll out your new mission?

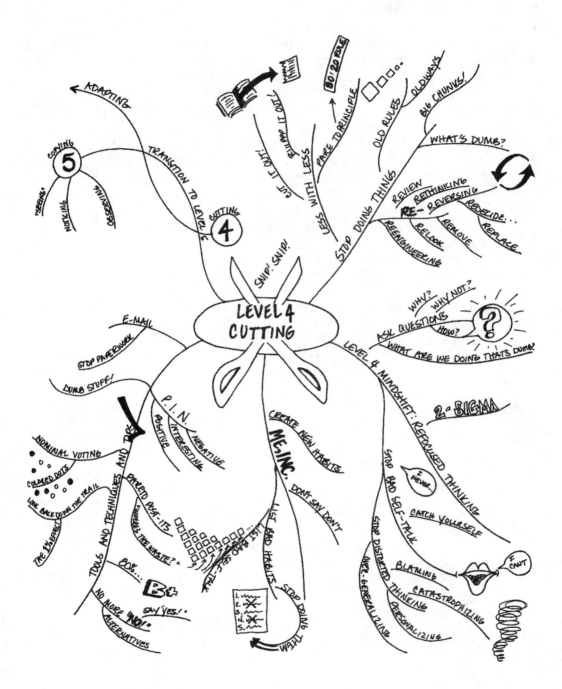

LEVEL 4 CUTTING

SNIP! SNIP!

ADAPTING

COPING
⑤
"SEEING"
NOTICING
OBSERVING

TRANSITION TO LEVEL 5

CUTTING
④

LESS WITH LESS
CUT IT OUT!
BLIMP IT OUT!
PARE TO PRINCIPLE
80:20 RULE

STOP DOING THINGS
OLD RULES
OLD WAYS
BIG CHUNKS!
WHAT'S DUMB?
REVIEW RETHINKING
RE- REVERSING REVISE...
REENGINEERING RELOOK REMOVE REPLACE

ASK QUESTIONS
WHY? WHY NOT?
HOW?
?
LEVEL 4 WHAT ARE WE DOING THAT'S DUMB?

LEVEL 4 MINDSET: REFOCUSED THINKING
2- SIGMA

STOP BAD SELF-TALK
I NEVER.
CATCH YOURSELF
I CAN'T
STOP DISTORTED THINKING
BLAMING
CATASTROPHIZING
OVER-GENERALIZING
PERSONALIZING

CREATE NEW HABITS
ME, INC.
DON'T SAY DON'T
LIST BAD HABITS
STOP DOING THEM
WATCH
1. ✗
2. ✗
3. ✗
4. ✗
5. ✗

P.I.N.
POSITIVE
INTERESTING
NEGATIVE

E-MAIL
STOP PAPERWORK
DUMB STUFF!

NOMINAL VOTING
COLORED DOTS
WALK BACK DOWN THE TRAIL
THE 1% BETTER

TOOLS AND TECHNIQUES

PARETO POST-ITS
"WHERE'S THE WASTE?"
B%...
B+
NO MORE "NO!"
SAY "YES!"
ALTERNATIVES

Level 4: Cutting
Stopping Doing Things

UNDERSTANDING LEVEL 4 CHANGE

Level 4 changes are about getting even better. If you are effective and efficient, *and* improving and doing things better, you can make large-scale improvements by moving to Level 4 and beginning to cut out things you don't need to do. Here—where you are doing away with things or stopping doing things—the payoff is incredibly high.

Everything at Level 4 ties back to Vilfredo Pareto's Law of Misdistribution, known as the Pareto Principle or the eighty–twenty rule. An Italian economist, Pareto (1848–1923), pointed out that 80 percent of the wealth is controlled by 20 percent of the people, and ultimately that 20 percent of any process really controls 80 percent of the results the process produces. Eighty percent of the value in your productivity comes from 20 percent of your effort. It follows that you can cut out the other 80 percent and do more with less. Reset your focus. Develop a Pareto mindset: Concentrate on the 20 percent and let the other 80 percent slide for a four-to-one return on your efforts.

To accomplish this type of cutting, you first have to look for the 20 percent that is creating the higher yield. Taking Pareto to the next order, applying it twice, you can get extremely focused: 20 percent of the 20 percent (or 4 percent) accounts for 80 percent of the 80 percent (or 64 percent) of the value—the sixty-four-to-four rule. So to really leverage yourself, refocus your efforts by concentrating on the 4 percent for a sixteen-to-one return.

Pareto^2

$$20\% \text{ of } 20\% = 4\%$$
$$80\% \text{ of } 80\% = 64\%$$
$$\text{The } 64\!:\!4 \text{ Rule} \rightarrow 16\!:\!1$$

Figure out where your 4 percent is and focus on it with a vengeance, with an A+ mindset. Farm out everything else you do. Hire other people to do it—or just walk away from it. On a grand scale, it's just not that important. Do less with less.

UNDERSTANDING LEVEL 4 THINKING

People who are doing, thinking, and changing at Level 4 are more likely to be preoccupied with saving money than with saving time, while they have a strong affinity for Level 2 as well, doing things right and being efficient. They are much less rule-oriented, and, in fact, eliminating old rules and long-standing guidelines will likely be a recurring theme with them. Getting rid of rules opens things up to allow them to generate more ideas and find greater savings. This is where classic "out-of-the-box" thinking starts: Changing the size of the box by getting rid of rules and customs that define the edges of the box.

*"In anything at all, perfection is finally attained
not when there is no longer anything to add,
but when there is no longer anything to take away."*
—Antoine de Saint-Exupéry

LEVEL 4 MINDSHIFT

Consider the following mindshift model to help you achieve Level 4 changes. To get better, you have to stop doing things. To stop doing things you have to refocus your thinking. To refocus, to stop doing things, you must start asking questions. Why? Why not?

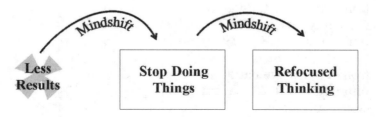

Level 4 thinking moves you into 2-sigma—out of the normal zone and into interesting thinking.

THINKING ABOUT THINKING

The mindshift at Level 4 is into refocused thinking. It's thinking about a central concept or idea *again*. It's thinking one more time about something with greater intensity. It's asking yourself "What can we stop doing? What can I stop doing?" To stop doing things you must refocus your thinking. You must stop thinking along specific, corresponding lines; stop thinking about those specific things in the way you're used to thinking about them—in your normal, 1-sigma thinking pattern.

Efficient Thinking

efficient thinking (ĭ-fĭsh′ənt thĭng′kĭng)
n. 1. Thinking that moves directly to produce an effect. 2. Thinking with a minimum of waste or unnecessary effort; exhibiting a high ratio of output to input; brainstorming

Another important aspect of Level 4 thinking is to stop distorted thinking—blaming, mind-reading, being right all the time, catastrophizing, personalizing, over-generalizing, filtering, polarizing (black-or-white). Apply the Pareto Principle to your thinking, and stop thinking about the things that don't matter in ways that are distorted. Focus where it counts (Level 1 change) and do it right (Level 2 change).

RESULTS AT LEVEL 4

Empty space—stuff is gone. Stuff you discovered that you didn't need to do. More time and resources freed up. Reduced costs. Reduced stress and frustration. Less pressure. More time to think, and to think about thinking.

Cost control, cost cutting, cost reduction and cost savings are big drivers in any company. "How can we do more with less?" Statistically, the large majority of suggestion-program ideas are aimed at saving money (Level 4), not necessarily doing things better (Level 3). You can measure the results when money is involved.

107

Distorted thinking is a handicap.

"We are very short of money so we must start to think."
—Lord Rutherford, 1921

My family achieved incredible savings with some Level 4 changes. We live in Houston, reported to be the most air-conditioned city in the world. I offered to pay my two youngest daughters, Amanda and Amy, half of the savings on the electric bill each month if they would just turn the lights out when we leave the house and turn the air conditioning down when it isn't needed. When she heard me, my wife Juliane said: "Wait a minute; I want a piece of that action too!" From 1992–1994, when we tried this, the air conditioning in our house ran only when the temperature was in the high nineties or over one hundred. Even then we only used it long enough to bring the temperature in the house down. The actual dollar savings, not just the percentage change in our monthly bills, was amazing. Juliane took that Level 4 change one step further. She used her piece of the action to lease a horse for a year, and, looking at how often we would actually be able to ride him, cut the costs by only leasing half a horse (that is, half the days available for riding).

108

TOOL #31 (LEVEL 4):
Sixty Words for Lowering Costs

Try thinking about a specific area in which you would like to lower costs. Maybe it's the highest cost area in the 80 percent. Make a list of all the cost areas within that specific area and then work through this list of sixty words to give yourself a new perspective on those areas.

Alter	Depreciate	Realign
Analyze	Destroy	Reallocate
Avoid	Distribute	Recycle
Bargain	Divide	Redistribute
Better	Drop	Reduce
Burn	Eliminate	Remove
Cancel	Focus	Rename
Cap	Hide	Reorganize
Chop	Ignore	Restructure
Clean	Lessen	Reverse
Combine	Lighten	Share
Conceal	Limit	Shift
Consolidate	Maximize	Shorten
Cover up	Minify	Shrink
Cut	Modify	Slash
Decrease	Negotiate	Spread
Defer	Optimize	Streamline
Deflate	Partial	Subtract
Delay	Purge	Transfer
Delete	Raise	Trim

TOOL #32 (LEVEL 4):
10 Percent Less

Efficiency
is about
TIME

- Quicker
- Faster
- Sooner

Another easy step to personal cutting is to ask yourself: "If I had to live with 10 percent less income, how could I do it without changing my lifestyle significantly?" What can you give up or stop doing? Consider what would happen if you put that 10 percent into a savings account or IRA or invested it somewhere it could grow or compound interest? When you make this type of thinking a habit, it's easier to get your employees thinking this way, too. Imagine how quickly the savings can grow if everyone in the company develops the habit of thinking of ways to cut.

And instead of saving money, how about time? Remember the importance of time at Level 2? Wouldn't it be great if you could buy time? How could you come up with more time to think, to try new things, to do more of what you want to do instead of what you have to do? How could you apply the eighty-twenty rule to your life to buy some time?

109

Several years ago I walked out front to pick up the newspaper one morning. It wasn't "there," and I had to look for it somewhere else. A new paper carrier had thrown it into a new spot. It took me a while to find it and got me reflecting as I read the newspaper. First, my disrupted pattern hit me. This was something I was doing every day at the same time, the same way. Second, as I flipped through the paper, it hit me that it was all bad news—negative stuff—and I was wasting twenty-to-twenty-five minutes every day reading it! Third, I already knew that early in the morning was my most creative idea-having time. So I picked up the phone, called the newspaper and cancelled my subscription. And "No, I don't want to just get the weekend papers." I figured that if anything really important happened someone would tell me. I rethought something I had never thought of as a habit. Results?

It's all BAD news!

20 x 365 = 7,300 minutes
. . . or 10+ DAYS of creative thinking time.

TOOL #33 (LEVEL 4):
Re-

Start sticking "re-" on the front of every verb that is connected with what you regularly do. Then use that to start some rethinking about it from a new perspective: Refocus. Reframe. Restate. Reword. Remove, revisit, recreate, rediscover, repay, reprint, reexplore, recapture, relook, refund, realign, recopy, remake, rewrite, reverse, redo, reform, relate. Relax.

110

Rethink. Luther Burbank once pointed out: "It is well for people who think to change their minds occasionally in order to keep them clean."

Have you ever had a lot of "stuff" in a common work area, and you were afraid to toss it because it might be needed by someone else? Ever have a hard time finding what you need because there is so much "stuff" to look through? How do you force the decision to get rid of "stuff" and still get everyone's approval? Try adding a "d" to "re-" and "red tagging" may be your answer. It's a method used by the Japanese to help set up the ultimate work environment—clean of excess. An office or work area so well ordered that it would be awkward for someone not to put something in its proper place. High-use items are close, low-use items are farther away, seldom-use items are out of sight or stored, and no-use items are history.

TOOL #34 (LEVEL 4):
Red Tagging
(Duke Rohe, M.D. Anderson Cancer Center)

Here's how it works—at your desk (start with the top drawer of desk) for each item in it ask yourself: "*Why this item, why this quantity, why this place?*" How many pencils do you have, how many do you need, are they in one spot? If any item really doesn't qualify for staying, be honest now—the item should "red-tagged" (little red cardboard tag with a string attached) and placed in a holding area for a week or two. During this holding period you can see whether or not you can do without the items. Before taking anything out of the holding area, you must be able to make a case for putting it back in the work area. Beyond that, it goes to remote storage if it is infrequently used or the trash pile. Most people only need a third of what they keep in their top desk drawer.

> ➤ Clutter corollary #1: In the empty storage space, "stuff" will grow to fill it. With that success behind you, move to the more challenging top of your desk . . .

Red Tags can be bought at office supply stores. And, by the way, Avery Dennison makes them.

Efficiency is about RULES!

➤ Clutter Corollary #2: Piles will seek out any flat surface in an office.

How does "red-tagging" work in a surgery area of a hospital? A team of nurses equipped with red tags went into their work area with the intent to cut out everything that was not routinely used. Equipment that Dr. X might use twice a year, sutures that are in oversupply, etc. *"Why is this here, how often do you use it, do you need more of them, less of them?"* Every supply item, every piece of equipment, receives this vigorous interrogation. Any item in question is red tagged. After completion, the work staff looked at all the items and questioned the harm or added work in removing the items. Usually the first time this is done, a third of the items are tagged. Again, high-use items are labeled and stored in designated places, low-use items are stored remotely in designated places more remotely and everything else in question is placed in a red tag holding area.

All workers have two weeks to preview the items in the holding area and convince others why an item needs to be placed back into the workplace (once it is out of the workplace, the burden of proof is on the side of remaining uncluttered). In this type of thinking, anything that is not being used on a routine basis is in the way of getting things done. The entire workforce has a say in where things go, and the decision to reposition or toss is a collective one. The "remains" of the holding area are returned to the vendor, made available for other areas to use, or tossed. No hard feelings, everyone has input, and the work area is now much more useful. Almost feels as good as having a successful garage sale.

However, "red-tagging" is like dusting: to be successful, it has to be continuous. When things don't have a place, everyone tends to just set things down. If everything has a designated place, then people tend to hunt for a good place for new things. Clean and orderly workplaces tend to stay that way. Trash heaps tend to just get piled higher. Appoint a monthly "red tag" SWAT team, or if you are really daring, call in someone who is unfamiliar with the area to ask,

112

"*Why this, why here, why this amount?*" Naive eyes have a remarkable way of seeing things we stumble over daily and accept. Then repeat the holding-area cycle.

This method can make the culture of the work staff take more responsibility for their environment. The Japanese say that the worst waste is that waste that is hidden. Clutter falls in this category. Red-tagging is a commonsense approach to ridding your work area of common waste. Just like blue slips, keep some red tags in your pocket or your purse, and when in doubt—tag it!

TOOL #35 (LEVEL 4):
Riiippp!

> On Thinking Expeditions, I use the example of John Keating (Robin Williams), the poetry teacher in the movie "Dead Poets Society," telling his class to rip out the introduction of their books: "Rip out the whole introduction . . . it's not the Bible. You're not going to go to hell for this." Keating then challenges his class to "learn to think for yourselves again." This scene is a powerful way to get people thinking about ripping out unnecessary habits, steps, actions, and rules in their own lives.

RESULTS: EIGHTY-TWENTY RIIIPPPING = $2.8 MILLION

Working with Hoechst Celanese Corporation on a project at its Bay City, Texas, chemical plant, I led a two-day Thinking Expedition built around the 7 levels of change to help a twenty-person team cut $2.4 million out of the project budget of $7.4 million to bring it down to $5 million. The project involved moving operations from a Bishop, Texas, plant and some new construction in Bay City. When we got to Level 4, we had a breakthrough. The biggest cost item (eighty-twenty rule) appeared to be engineering drawings. À la Robin Williams, we first tore up the engineering drawings and threw them in the air. Then, working with crayons and blank paper to really simplify things, we reengineered, concentrating only on the essentials that needed detailed drawings (20 percent). By cutting out major pieces of the contracted engineering process and instead doing it in-house, the cost of the project was

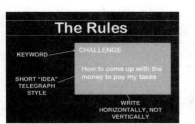

eventually cut back to $4.6 million and was approved by senior management.

"The results were incredible," said Bill Cornman, engineering manager at Hoechst Celanese, and sponsor of the Thinking Expedition. "I still can't believe it came together like that."

TOOL #36 (LEVEL 4):
Dumb Stuff

People know where a lot of the waste is in an organization. Get everyone in your company together in a big room. Put a big sign up in the front of the room and give everyone small ones like it to hang up in their offices:

> # IF IT'S DUMB
> # IT'S NOT OUR POLICY

Start off with two straightforward questions: "What are we doing that's dumb?" and "What could we stop doing that no one would notice?" Give them a handful of red tags with the "Dumb" sign printed on them, then send everybody out to red-tag anything they can find that's dumber than dirt. Try implementing just 10 percent of the things that have been red tagged, and measure and track the savings. After you total up the results, go after the remaining 90 percent

RESULTS: R & D WORK LOGS/TIME SHEETS

At Avery Dennison's research center in Pasadena, California, as a result of a Thinking Expedition, the process of all employees filling out work logs and time sheets was stopped (eighty-twenty riiiippping). Now only the managers fill out

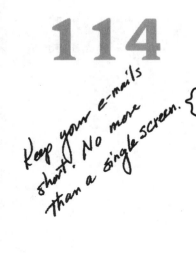

114

Keep your e-mails short. No more than a single screen.

the log for their personnel, creating a time savings of twenty hours per month, 240 man-hours per year.

E-mail was mentioned in Level 2 as an efficiency change, but it is also has an incredible ability to cut across normal hierarchical distribution and communication lines to move an organization into network mode. E-mail should be brief with any non-value-adding stuff cut out of it. It can eliminate huge amounts of paper and time spent at the copier producing the paper to hand-send out through normal distribution to be filed and clog up the system. What aspects of your job and what areas of your organization could shift into E-mail to achieve major Level 4 wins?

RESULTS: REPORTS BY E-MAIL

Avery Dennison researchers stopped distributing hard copies of technical reports. Seventy-five percent of the reports are now distributed by E-mail. Chemists have saved time spent in printing reports, making hard copies, and distributing them. Total savings of $1,600 a month in labor and materials alone.

RESULTS: DON'T BUILD ROADS

On another Thinking Expedition, working with Exxon Corporation, our goal was to reduce the construction, operating and maintenance costs on oil-and-gas-field production facilities in Alaska. Working through Level 4, we identified building the access roads to the sites as an extremely high cost item—$1 million a mile for an average of forty to fifty miles per site. The solution—don't build roads—cut them out completely! Consider, instead, all the alternative access technologies you can come up with, such as low-cost air lifting, all-terrain vehicles, sea approach amphibious access, blimps, or roads that normal vehicles couldn't use—concepts that heretofore would have been cost-prohibitive. These ideas caused major mindshifts, and a very different look was taken at proposed new production site locations with the potential for multi-million dollar savings.

TOOL #37 (LEVEL 4):
Pareto Post-its

Give everyone a pad of Post-it notes. Ask them to write down the areas where they believe there's waste in the system (more dumb stuff). Group the Post-its on a flip chart by major categories. Then stack the Post-its into columns and, voilà!—you have a Pareto chart. Focus in on the specifics in the tallest column. Ask people to develop quick-and-dirty action steps that can be taken to eliminate the waste in that column. Then do it! Start implementing the action steps. Track the results, and measure the savings.

TOOL #38 (LEVEL 4):
Convergence—Nominal Voting

Cutting meeting time can be a very popular Level 4 pastime in any company. Making meetings fun is also an asset. Introduce the concept of nominal voting to your employees to achieve both.

Nominal voting is a convenient, structured tool that helps you converge a large number of options down to a manageable few. The term "nominal" suggests that the process does not involve the typical group dynamics of discussion and consensus-building. Instead, selection of most important or popular ideas can be narrowed down with a relatively low level of interaction. The supplies needed are stick-on colored dots (the transparent type works best), some flip charts, and PIN (positive, interesting, negative) thinking.

Using brainstorming and suspending judgment (PIN), the group generates a list of problems, issues, ideas, or options that are visible to everyone on flip charts. Each item is numbered and the participants are asked to vote on the items using a blue slip *without any discussion*. Just record the item number, not the full description of the item on the blue slip. It's necessary to explain that this voting step is necessary to avoid groupthink, that is, each person individually makes choices before sharing those priorities with the group. The votes can be cast in various schemes, but the two that seem to work best are:

116

TOOL #39 (LEVEL 4):
Weighted Rank-Order Voting

This method is useful when there are a small number of options or when the group needs to come to focus upon just one or two items. Ask each person to select their top five preferred ideas and rank them in reverse order. The most preferred gets five points and the least one point. Then the members place the values next to the corresponding number on the flip chart. In small groups each member can call out the numbers and the facilitator can record the values and complete the overall weighted voting tally.

TOOL #40 (LEVEL 4):
Category Voting

This is a particularly useful method when there are a large number of items for the group to choose from or when it is necessary to converge down to a select few. At the beginning, three criteria categories are established such as "most urgent," "very important," and "important, but can wait" (or, "I personally will commit to this," "I will help some others on this," and "This is *big*—I'll play in if management does"). Each person is then asked to identify a specific number of items in each category (one-third of the total number works well). For example, with a list of sixty items, each person might be allowed to identify a total of ten:

  ➤ two that are most urgent;
  ➤ three that are very important;
  ➤ five that are important, but can wait.

Again, it is important that the group first votes individually on blue slips before placing the dots to avoid groupthink. Then, using color-coded dots, votes are placed on the appropriate items:

  ➤ red dots for urgent (two dots worth five points each);
  ➤ green dots for very important (three dots worth three points each);

> blue dots for important, but can wait (five dots worth one point each).

117

This technique is very visual—the color clusters really highlight where the energy is around the ideas and to what extent. The facilitator can tally up the votes, although the concentration of colors pretty much does the job.

After the tally, the group discusses the patterns and their reactions to them. Those items at the top of the list are ready to be worked into action plans or they can continue to be expanded and enhanced through the creative thinking process.

Remember, voting is done individually, but the voting tally needs to be a group effort. While this can be done verbally as people call out their numbers or show hands as each item is called, getting people to stand up and record their own votes generates energy in the group. It also gives people the opportunity to interact during the process.

The group's goal is to reach decisions that best reflect the thinking of all group members, that is, finding ideas, proposals, and options that are acceptable enough and have enough energy that all participants will be comfortable supporting them. The decisions may not be everyone's first priority, but everyone has had an opportunity to participate. *Consensus does not mean that everyone agrees; it means that everyone is willing to live with the decision.*

The nominal voting tool is especially effective when all or some of the group are new to each other or if the group is working on highly controversial issues and challenges. Also, nominal voting can help refocus a group that gets stuck or is in disagreement or is being dominated by an "expert."

The NATO Rule

TIPS FOR NOMINAL VOTING: THE ONE-THIRD RULE

As a guideline, allow each participant a number of choices equal to one-third of the total number of items on the list—for instance, thirty-six items, twelve choices. This ensures that a number of the items will have critical mass in terms of numbers of dots on them. With shorter lists, use fewer choices; with longer lists, use more choices.

118

WATCH OUT WITH NOMINAL VOTING: NIPPING

Just because you have used nominal voting to converge down to a few ideas does not mean that the other problems, issues, ideas or options are not important and should not be addressed. The time and place where they *are* important may simply not be at this session with this group. Because of people's natural inclination to be more adaptive and conservative during convergence (i.e., to "NIP" ideas), those items that are eliminated are often the most novel and interesting and should be explored in more detail at a later date.

TOOL #41 (LEVEL 4):
B+

"B+ing" is a way to handle the 80 percent. It may only bring in 20 percent of the value on the bottom line *but still has to be done.* B+ is a respectable grade. A B+ takes considerably less time, effort, and resources to achieve than an A+ does.

"The fear of not getting it right at every stage and all the time is probably the biggest block there is to new ideas."
—*Thinking for Dummies*

Save the A+ effort for the 20 percent that yields 80 percent of the bottom line. Statistically, everything cannot be A+. It's relative. Things follow the normal curve and only a very small percentage of things can be A+. If you can achieve A+ on 20 percent of what you do, you will have skewed the normal curve significantly.

The concept of B+ is a real mindshift!

TOOL #42 (LEVEL 4):
Look Back down the Trail

Periodically look back over your shoulder, and make a list of everything you've stopped doing since the last time you looked. This can be a real boost. Stopping bad habits often feels like a much greater level of change than achieving some new goal that you once deemed impossible. Try it right now: since the last time you thought about it, what have you stopped doing? Make a quick list and then go brag about it to someone!

MORE EFFICIENT

What can we do to be More Efficient?

...BLUE SLIP

TOOL #43 (LEVEL 4):
No More "No!"

One of the most important things you can do for yourself and your family is to get out of the negative zone and into the positive zone. Look for the positive. Start by trying to avoid saying "No!" Practice at home with your kids. Instead of saying, "No, you can't go outside and play." say, "Yes, later—after you do your homework," or say, "Give me a minute to think about it," or "Convince me." (. . . followed perhaps by, "I'm not convinced. Convince me.").

TOOL #44 (LEVEL 4):
Stop Bad Self-Talk

We pay more attention to what we say to ourselves than to anything anyone else says to us. Riiipppp out negative self-talk. Get rid of your bad self-talk list:

> "I can't . . .
> "I always . . .
> "I never . . .
> "I hate math . . .
> "I'm no good with . . .
> "I don't . . .

Catch yourself in negative self-talk, and make a note of what you say to yourself—actually write it down. You'll discover that you have some real patterns, some regular phrases you use.

I remember very clearly when the power of negative self-talk really hit me. I was getting out of my car once, already running late for a meeting, and dropping the papers I was carrying in a puddle next to the car, flailing to catch them as they fell, hitting my head on the car door, slamming the door on my coat, and ripping it badly as I tried to walk away. "This is not going to be a good day!" I said out loud. And Bam! It hit me. I was setting myself up to have a lot more of what I'd just experienced. Now when I catch myself moving towards bad self-talk, I flash instantly back to that moment on the corner of Bell and Louisiana in downtown Houston.

120

Engage your family in this—make it fun. Sensitize everyone to the concept of bad self-talk and start catching each other in it. "Whoops! Dad—that's bad self-talk."

ROLF'S THEORY OF RELATIVITY

Level 4 isn't very relative. Cutting is the clearest of all of the levels of change. There is little debate as to whether or not you are cutting something out or stopping something. This concept is very clear cut when compared to effectiveness, efficiency, improving, copying, different, and impossible. There is very little subjectivity about cutting, except when it comes to deciding whether or not cutting is the right thing to do. Cutting back on the work force may save money, but ask the person whose job has been cut whether that's doing things right. You might get a different perspective.

PROS AND CONS AT LEVEL 4

When working with change at Level 4, remember that some things are so ingrained within organizations and people's habits that rooting them out can be difficult, even painful. When you stop doing things, the effects are often immediate and large. The payoff can be very high, and people take notice.

Personally, when you cut out bad habits, you can look better, feel better, and live longer. Typically, you have to give something up that was enjoyable or at least comfortable and often you have to learn something new, which is a negative to some people. Giving things up can be hard. It takes twenty-one days to form a new habit and longer if you have to break an old habit simultaneously.

When you stop doing things, at a minimum that always frees up the time it took you to do them. You can usually use that time to do something else of higher value.

Generally your ideas for Level 4 changes irritate people. If you can't make them see the magic in PIN, of suspending judgment, they can get pretty defensive—which translates into becoming critical and attacking the change you're trying to make.

In applying the Pareto Principle, the 80 percent you are not concentrating on will suffer if it's not delegated to the right hands. There's a challenge to figuring out how much effort needs to be given to that 80 percent that is being cut out.

Competency
Thinking sumulataneously at Level 1 and Level 2

**Doing
The Right Things
Right**

Behind every change is generally another larger, unexpected change. What is gong to happen as a result of stopping doing something? Or perhaps what is *not* going to happen any longer—what else is going to stop happening?

121

WATCH OUT! What's the Change behind the change?

LEVEL 4 FEAR: HOLDING ON

➤ Fear of letting go.

➤ Fear of tradition.

➤ Fear that stopping doing something will be a mistake.

➤ Focusing on the 80 percent that only brings in 20 percent of the value.

➤ Just-in-case fear that kicks in when you're packing: "We better take everything just in case we need it."

LEVEL 4 STRESS

➤ Having to change your mind about something, having to give up an opinion or a strong belief you've had for a long time.

➤ Constantly "re-ing" everything: redoing, reassessing, reevaluating, reconsidering, rearranging, reexamining, reassuring, reworking . . .

➤ Giving up things you love and are very comfortable with.

➤ Cutting out chocolate and still not losing weight.

➤ Breaking up with someone or having to end a relationship. "*Dear John . . . after rethinking our five years together, and what our future together seems to look like, I have rethought things, and it appears as though I really don't need you in my life any more . . .*"

➤ Worry is a Level 4 stress because it is *rethinking* about something that has already transpired. You can't change it; move on—it's unnecessary thinking.

➤ Guilt stress: *Replaying* old thoughts, emotions, scenes or soundtracks in your head as a wasted emotion—it changes nothing.

122

☑ TIP: SOME THINKING FOR DUMMIES

Stop thinking! Thinking is difficult; making decisions is easy. When you think, you may not like the conclusions you reach. If you just make a decision, you normally like the result.
—Colin Crewe, KBR Barracuda Thinking Expedition

TRANSITION TO LEVEL 5: COPYING

With Level 4, you've transitioned into 2-sigma change, *interesting*. You've cut away what's unimportant, and by doing this, there may be some holes you can fill in. So you begin to move into Level 5: copying. One of the easiest ways to leap forward into clear innovation is by opening your eyes to begin noticing what others do better or differently than what you are doing and copy and adapt some of it.

LEVEL 3
Improving

**Doing Things
Better**

ME, INC.® CHANGE AT LEVEL 4

Your Me, Inc.® task for Level 4 is to take seven minutes and make a list of all of your bad habits—things you want to stop doing. Add them to your 101-goals list. Then, pick the one you feel may be the easiest to change, and make a list of *when* it is you fall into that habit. Begin to focus on the event that most often is connected with that habit (for instance, if you want to give up smoking, and you always [habit] light up a cigarette with your first cup of coffee in the morning, focus on stopping that one event only—begin to notice every time you don't do it). At the end of *each* day, pat yourself on the back for not doing it on that day. At the twenty-first-day, check to see how you're doing. When you've truly broken that particular connection, go on to the next strongest connection or event. Cut out habits in small steps, with Level 2 thinking. Use Level 2 changes to more efficiently make Level 4 work!

TIPS FOR ME, INC.® CHANGES AT LEVEL 4

> *"Faced with the choice between changing one's mind and proving there is no need to do so, almost everyone gets busy on the proof."*
> —John Kenneth Galbraith

It's easier to stop an old habit by replacing it with a new, better habit. The new habit then begins to steal time away from the old habit gradually and the old habit atrophies. As mentioned already, it takes about twenty-one days—three weeks—of doing the new habit to replace the old habit.

One final tip from Tom Peters: "Create a 'To-Don't' list that contains tasks, rituals, and meetings that you should never waste your time on again. Then stick to it."

123

Remember ... 21 Days to start a new habit of "NOT".

MY "TO DON'T" LIST

1.

2.

3.

4.

5.

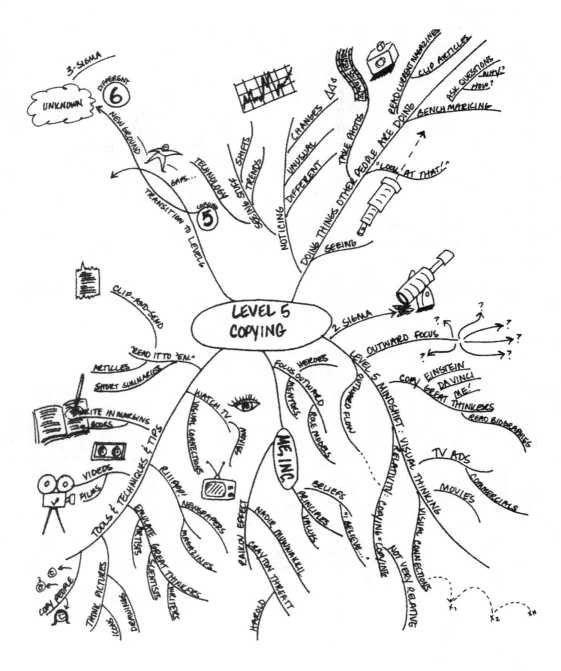

Level 5: Copying
Doing Things Others Are Doing

UNDERSTANDING LEVEL 5 CHANGE

Almost by definition, Level 5 (copying) doing and thinking, is out-of-the-box. You look over and notice something that someone else—a company, a team or a person—is doing. And you think, "That is a really good idea. Look how it is done. Wow, I could do that!" Then you copy what they are doing—only you don't do it quite the same way. Not exactly. You adapt it to your unique style or situation. By doing so, it becomes very much yours.

Copying is a great departure from what you have been doing. Levels 1 through 4 are focused on doing what you have been doing, only better. With copying, your focus shifts externally to what works for others. Here you have an opportunity to learn from their doing, seeing their solutions, and understanding their decisions, which delivered something differently.

Level 5 Changes Begin with Seeing Stuff

Seeing things—noticing—is the fundamental thinking behind Level 5 changes. No matter what you call it, whether it's copying, learning from, benchmarking, or even reverse engineering, what you notice and then make into a Level 5 change can dramatically kick-start innovation and at significantly lower costs in terms of time, resources, and effort. When you copy and adapt, you don't have to start from scratch, so it's possible to master an existing large-scale, complex process or even an entire system with the same level of effort it takes to implement a much smaller change.

Essentially, all of the hard parts are done: design, engineering, development, testing, and selling of the idea. Something that is being copied already works. It is a proven, fielded, operational concept.

Understanding Level 5 Thinking

Level 5 thinking is very visual thinking. To think at this level you have to see, perceive, notice, visualize. You have to use all of your senses and look for what's new, different, or missing. You have to scan the horizon, seeing near and far, looking back and seeing things that you missed or overlooked in the past. As Yogi Berra once said, "You can really see a lot by observing."

LEVEL 5 MINDSHIFT

To copy things other people are doing, you have to look, see and notice things. Begin noticing things that are different and unusual when compared to the things you normally notice.

Wow! look at that

126

Thinking about Thinking

Level 5 thinking is the highest level of 2-sigma or "interesting" thinking (as contrasted with "normal" 1-sigma thinking). It raises mindfulness and noticing to an art form—seeing things with your mind in a different way. It's thinking that's flexible and responsive. It's thinking that creates an image in your mind.

The more challenging side of Level 5 thinking is the mindshifts that go with it. There are two basic ways of thinking different to operate at Level 5. Copying thinking that differs in style or type from your own can be a significant stretch. Studying and emulating the thinking processes and techniques of great thinkers can be a first step in shifting or changing your own thinking. Read the biographies of great and creative thinkers.

☑ TIP!

Here are five excellent Level 5 books from which to copy great thinkers' thinking. The authors give lots of anecdotal stories and examples of style, type, techniques, habits and patterns of thinking of people such as Einstein, Edison, Gauss, Mozart, Newton, Beethoven and da Vinci.

> ➤ *The Einstein Factor* by Win Wenger (1996)
> ➤ *Fire in the Crucible* by John Briggs (1990)
> ➤ *Uncommon Genius* by Denise Shekerjian (1990)
> ➤ *Secrets from Great Minds* by John McMurphy (1991)
> ➤ *The Creative Process* by Brewster Ghislin (1952)

TOOL #45 (LEVEL 5):
Dilbert

Elvira Stesikova, a Ph.D. chemist with Conoco R&D in Ponca City, Oklahoma, related how she fine-tuned both her English and her knowledge of American management prior to coming to the United States from Moscow. "I read Dilbert." she said, "All the Dilbert cartoons I could find." This is brilliant, very creative Level 5 thinking about Level 2 thinking in order to improve yourself (Level 3 doing). Think about it: style, manners, culture, slang, and deep insights, all rolled into one package: Dilbert.

IMPROVING

Another way to operate at Level 5, seeing different, is a mindshift that first requires you to deliberately become more visual, to begin noticing things that are different and unusual when compared to the things you normally notice. It requires an opening up of your perspectives, horizons, and mental filters so that the noticing of different will come more easily. Try watching a video or TV with the sound off. When you do, you must sharpen your power of observation and seek to understand without the benefit of the soundtrack. Who knows, you may see something in the film that nobody else sees, something that's different.

Consider the mindshift diagram below. In order to do things others are doing, you have to copy things. In order to copy them, you have to see and notice things.

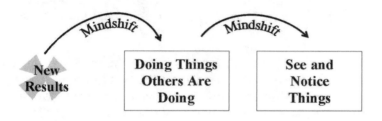

LEVEL 5 RESULTS: New behavior.

TOOL #46 (LEVEL 5):
Benchmarking

> *"One look is worth a hundred reports."*
> —Japanese Proverb

Remember in grade school when your teacher said "Everyone do your own work; do not copy your neighbors." That golden rule did apply in school, but copying is a well practiced fact of life. Benchmarking is a process legitimized by the quality movement in corporate America, and has given copying new status. In 1989 Robert Camp wrote *Benchmarking: The Search for Industry Best Practices That Lead to Superior Performance*. This was the first prescriptive book on how to benchmark, and following its publication, companies began to look at what

127

128

others did in a whole new way—as fertile ground for ideas. As with any new trend, the consulting world quickly responded with their offerings to capture the willing expenditures of companies large and small. The Houston based American Productivity and Quality Center (APQC) became a center for benchmarking for many industries. Their work helped many companies identify best practices that led to the promise of improved performance.

Benchmarking how other organizations do things and enhancing those discoveries and achievements (using Level 3, improving, thinking) is the hallmark of a successful innovator. Most often because of competitive concerns, benchmarking partners come from different walks of life, different industries. While the output of their work may be different and the customer of the

An example told during an APQC benchmarking course speaks of a hospital that needed to improve its financial performance. It recognized that an unfilled bed between patients was costly, and anything that could be done to prepare the bed for the next patient faster would benefit the patients and the hospital's bottom line. The hospital then started looking around and found there were lots of examples of organizations doing the same thing in other businesses. They looked at many industries but settled on the remarkable speed and performance demonstrated by automotive racing pit crews. While they weren't interested in fueling a car or changing its tires, they realized that to improve their chances to win, the crew must minimize the time the driver spends in pit row. With careful analysis and some conceptual leaps, the hospital modified its processes and trained its people to drive its bed turn-around time down. They copied the pit crews' processes, but not exactly, and leaped forward while shaving many hours into minutes. You never know where a great idea is waiting to be copied. The secret lies in having all of your senses tuned in to that which is around you and be willing to take what works.

Benchmarking helps you leap past the first four levels of change, which later come into play after you copy an idea. After being benchmarked, an idea can be made more effective

NASCAR pit crews

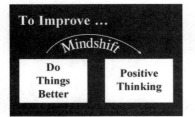

To Improve ...

Mindshift

| Do Things Better | Positive Thinking |

(Level 1), more focused and efficient (Level 2), tuned up and improved (Level 3), and aspects of it that don't quite fit or apply to you or your situation can be cut (Level 4). Copying becomes the feeding mechanism for other levels of change.

It's a fun trip. Your senses gather information from different solutions, developed with different assumptions and different considerations of risk. These solutions represents other people's knowledge of the problem developed from much of the same data and information you may have considered. But their solution traveled a slightly different journey and ended up in a different destination—all of which is subjected to a barrage of questioning whys. It requires looking past surface appearances and seeking a deeper understanding of why.

RESULTS (LEVEL 5): NON-KHAKI KHAKIS

Success draws much attention. Consider a successful fashion hit by The Gap: Khaki slacks. While the Gap was not the first to offer khakis, they certainly copied the idea from someone and with their network of stores and their brand recognition reached out and grabbed a significant chunk of the public's dollars. The broad appeal of this simple fashion statement led to copying by many in the apparel business. Soon competitor catalogs and stores alike boasted of khakis; competitors had their version with ever-so-slight variations. All saw a tremendously successful product, as simple as it was, and all quickly gravitated to this market appeal with their own response. There were khakis with pleats, flat panel fronts, and khakis with and without cuffs. Before long, their khakis began to take on other colors as well. While The Gap didn't originate the khaki, they certainly enjoyed tremendous success by taking someone else's idea and running with it. Have you ever bought khakis? Did it matter if your khakis were the "original" khakis?

"Khaki" isn't khaki any more

In the creative arts copying is a common practice. Picasso, that engine of creative energy, publicly spoke of this borrowing as a place to begin. While he had a horror of copying himself, he had no hesitation taking what he needed from a portfolio of old drawings by others. Similarly, as management guru Tom Peters has written, steal shamelessly, which is perhaps just a slightly less elegant way of saying copy something if it works for you.

130

Leaders in many companies are uncomfortable with this level of change in part because they are so inwardly focused that they are often not aware of what others are doing that's worth copying. When using the 7 levels of change as a model for brainstorming ideas, Level 5 is a predictable point where idea-finding stalls with executives. Business leaders in general simply are not very aware of what is going on outside of their own company or industry. "I don't even have time to watch TV. There's no way I'm going to have time to read stuff that doesn't relate to work. I have a hard enough time trying to keep up with my E-mail." This is something I hear all the time.

TOOL #47 (LEVEL 5):
Read It for 'Em!

When you notice something, a trend or shift, in the paper, in a magazine like *Fortune* or *Business Week*, in a new business book, on TV, or in a new movie, *make a note of it!* Then take a moment and summarize it briefly. If you can, make a copy, attach the note to the copy and send it to the busy person with something like "Joe, this reminded me of a comment you made the other day about X. Looks like you were right! Thought you'd enjoy seeing this." (1) Limit the length of your note, (2) limit the length of your summary to no more than a half page in BIG print, and (3) be selective—don't overdo reading for somebody else.

Read it for 'em is especially effective if you jump outside your normal range of reading materials. Go to the bookstore or newsstand and pick up four or five magazines each month that you normally wouldn't read. Look at what is happening in areas of interest beyond your "box." Look for things that can be useful to you from other industries or fields. Read the advertisements, editorials, and letters to the editor to see what thinkers in this realm are pondering. Innovation in any industry is often the product of transferring what is done in one industry into another. So go ahead. Go to the magazine rack and pick those rags up and see what's happening elsewhere. It may be the shortcut you are looking for to the land of different.

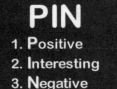

PIN
1. Positive
2. Interesting
3. Negative

131

With many companies, classic not-invented-here (NIH) thinking leads to resistance to imitating what someone else is doing. Too often, as a direct result of NIH thinking, the wheel is reinvented. Japanese corporations, however, are long-time world leaders in adapting and creatively improving upon the products and processes of others, making the best of the best even better by synergistically combining thinking at Level 3 with Level 5.

Stories of the Japanese touring production facilities of western industry are legendary—armies of them with their cameras taking pictures and asking why, why, why, why, and why till they got the glorious details they craved. The Japanese have an insatiable appetite for copying that which is useful to them. In the classic study of the automotive industry *The Machine that Changed the World,* MIT revealed that standard practices in the American automotive industry were copied by Japan, and over the years they pushed the edge, changing what they copied, innovating in ways not possible (Level 6) and drastically altering the sense of what could be done. A great example involved the time-consuming process of changing out dies in an automotive stamping plant. Traditionally, this process took a couple of weeks, idling production of a costly facility and requiring large runs of the same parts to achieve the needed economies of scale. The Japanese migrated from this traditional approach into some new stamping concepts that were not believed to be possible. The two-week die change out was reduced to a few minutes. This reduced plant downtime and allowed the Japanese to have shorter and more economical production runs. The new economics allowed the production of new car models filling more targeted, higher-margin market needs for less, driving their profitability up. Today we are all used to seeing or driving a Japanese automobile. But what few realize is that Toyota has replaced Chrysler in the "Big Three."

(like NASCAR pit crews!)

TOOL #48 (LEVEL 5):
Write in Books

If you can get in the habit of writing in books, making margin notes, or writing blue slips while you read books, you'll have fertile ground for copying now or later. Make it easy on yourself by circling, starring, underlining, or

132

highlighting so you won't miss a great idea. Use the blank pages in the back to write notes connecting what you are reading to what you are doing or can do. Look closely at the book's bibliography and notes, and follow those cues to expand on those areas of interest—old or new. The habit of NOT writing in books is an old and hard one to break. Emphasize it by telling your friends, when you loan them a book, to write in it. I am a chronic writer in books. Some pages have more of my jottings than printer's ink. When I loan a book to people they always comment on how much my notes add to the book. Tell your friend that's the only condition under which you loan books.

TOOL #49 (LEVEL 5):
Let TV Be Your Guide

Television is a great tool for getting ideas to copy. Watch it—especially commercials—with your mind, eyes, and ears actively engaged to spot something that will connect with a problem, and you'll be surprised what you can copy and adapt. Millions of dollars' worth of market research goes into those commercials. Try to figure out the thinking behind commercials, and figure out where you can put it to use in your life at home or at work. If you have cable or satellite television, watch some of the special stations like SciFi, A&E, Discovery and others where imaginations take a different path. If you see something that really tweaks your curiosity, take those thoughts and surf the Internet. See what you can find that relates to it. If you think there are some mind-stretchers on the tube, wait till you see what is on the Web. You'll soon discover that truth is stranger than fiction.

TV commercials are great sources of different thinking

TOOL #50 (LEVEL 5):
Trends Spotting

Level 5 thinkers enjoy looking for new things, discovering trends, and looking for ways to leverage the trends to specific advantage. Expand your horizons when thinking about what you are watching. Could there be possible connections between your interests and the trends in the economy, in global weather patterns, in computing, in medicine, in artificial intelligence, in bio-technology, in nano-technology, or other areas out of your normal sphere of noticing?

As you review your notes of things you have been noticing, look for patterns, connections, and trends. Identifying a trend early in its lifecycle is a matter of noticing patterns that others may not be able to see.

Many things that affect our lives in profound ways are undergoing change at a rapid rate. Identifying a trend early can lead to significant advantage if the trend is correctly characterized. There is also the possibility of influencing the trend in a manner that leads to competitive advantage. Throughout its existence, Microsoft has identified and influenced trends in desktop computing. Although some have taken exception to the methods, few would argue that it has been remarkably successful.

Watch Out!

In dealing with trends in their early stages, the lack of visibility and stability can be a trap. While the rewards of jumping on a trend in its early stages are high, so are the risks! If core components of your business are changing rapidly, you are affected by these trends whether you notice or not. The advantage of paying attention is that you will be better positioned to move with the trend, to influence the trend, or to jump off it. Caroline LaLive, an American downhill Olympic skier, pointed out: "Sports equipment evolves. You either change or get off the mountain."

Start noticing diff*f*erent, and pay particular attention to things that make you say to yourself, "Hmm, that's interesting." Write them down, add a few comments, pass them into your network, and start spotting trends.

134

TOOL #51 (LEVEL 5):
Build a Trends Network

An effective means we have found for serious "trends watchers" is the establishment of a trends-spotting network. This can be a loosely organized group of folks who are involved and interested in noticing trends. They share information about what they see so that the span of attention is broadened, and the number of intellects looking for connections and relationships is extended. As you begin to see the power of spotting trends, extend your noticing to become aware of others that are also aware. Build an informal network of these "friendlies" that are willing to exchange interesting observations, look for connections among emerging trends, and contribute ideas back into this "Trends Spotting Network."

TOOL #52 (LEVEL 5):
The "Trends Briefing"

Pick a modest number of interesting/emerging trends from several content areas. Look for (or create) some graphics or video clips that highlight something going on in each area. Be sure to include some areas that are outside or at least tangential to your organization's key interests. (Newspapers and magazines are good sources for graphics; television news programs can be good sources for video clips.) Assemble a presentation—a "briefing."

Invite a group of folks—from twenty to several hundred works well. Brown-bag lunch meetings are an easy and informal way to engage people. Distribute blue slips to the participants and go slowly through your set of trends-slides. After each trend (comprising one or two graphics or one video with brief introductory, positioning, or explanatory comments), have the participants write several blue slips. Some good questions are:

> ➤ What is a key aspect of this trend that we need to watch for or understand?

> ➤ What is one thing that you know about this trend?

Improved Thinking
- Ask for ideas
- Ask for suggestions
- Actually <u>listen</u> to other people

> ➤ What opportunities are there for us in this trend if it continues?
>
> ➤ In what way might we influence this trend?
>
> Once they have written their blue slips, have them pair-and-share with someone near them. Collect the blue slips written about each trend and incorporate them into what you collectively know about the trend. Be sure to summarize and publish results, e.g., a one-page trend description, and distribute the summary report ("The Trends Report") back to the participants within hours or a day or two after the session. You will significantly raise your organization's awareness of external factors and will recruit more interested "friendlies" for your trends-spotting network.

☑ TIP!

Be sure to include some of the senior people in your organization in the briefing as participants. They typically are far too busy with day-to-day issues to be able to stay abreast of external trends and influences. They may derive some of the greatest benefit from actual participation in your briefing.

T-N-T IMPACT WHEEL

Here's a nicely focused example of trends spotting. At a recent AMI (Association for Managers of Innovation) meeting I attended in San Diego, Steve Wiet, Director of Consumer Services for McNeil Consumer Healthcare, did a very interesting "brag" about an innovation initiative he had launched in his company: "R&D 2001 & Beyond." Steve had designed and facilitated a series of five trends and technology (T-n-T) sessions for three teams of R & D folks and assigned some readings and trends-scanning between the sessions. His focus was to look at trends to forecast new areas of substantial opportunity over the next three-to-ten years, prioritize opportunity areas for exploration, and identify bridging technologies. Steve facilitated the meetings with a variety of creativity tools and techniques, building "impact wheels" to assess consequences of future trends and events. An impact wheel is a variation of Joel Barker's "implications wheel," and the process is the same as that used in mindmapping (see tool 66 on

136

page 184). The teams produced an impressive report and a ranked summary of important trends and technologies on the longer-range McNeil landscape. Much of Steve's design, creativity tools, and thinking stemmed from Level 5 ideas he'd gotten at AMI meetings.

TOOL #53 (LEVEL 5):
Tear Out New Ideas

Before you throw away or recycle all of those magazines and catalogs that come your way, flip through them looking for at least one great idea to copy, and tear it out. Look for new products and think about the ideas behind them. How can you apply those ideas to what you do? Send the things you've torn out to your friends and coworkers or boss—"This reminded me of something you said recently . . ." or "You were right!"

TOOL #54 (LEVEL 5):
Make Visual Connections

If you get stuck looking for ideas or solutions, disconnect and try to reconnect visually. Look through a coffee table book with lots of pictures; look through your vacation photos; look out the window. Start by looking at simple images and progress to more complicated ones. Look at each image or picture for about a minute, writing down any and all ideas that come to mind. Then return to the question or problem at hand with those as a mindshift, a new point of view. Start reading advertisements like you never have before. Look at the careful crafting of the words and how they relate to the images or graphics. Madison Avenue spends lots of bucks every year to send those messages. They're terrific at pointing out why you just can't live without something. Look at the words in the ads and make a list of the ones that stand out in your mind. Let your thinking loosen up and you will start to see how an advertisement for something that doesn't seem to have *any* relationship to *anything* can suddenly take on new meaning, and Bam! you're onto something different.

Questions?

" It is better to know some of the questions than all of the answers."

- James Thurber

RESULTS: WHAT'S WRONG WITH THIS PICTURE?

Working with the Mohawk yarn-spinning mills in north Georgia, I was up to my usual practice of taking snapshots of things and people with a small point-and-shoot 35mm camera I always carry with me. When I see an idea or something unusual or interesting, I take a picture of it, or of people doing stuff. I only use slide film, and after a while I had a pretty good collection of people doing things all over the mill. I thought a slide show at the end of a staff meeting might be interesting.

I was rolling though the slides, and suddenly one of the supervisors yelled, "Stop! Back up to that last slide again." I did, and he stood up, got really close to the screen and said, "Yep. I thought so. That's a wooly-booger. Those dust balls catch in the spindles while the yarn is spinning. The yarn breaks, and production drops off until we fix that break. I'll bet that's what's been driving our numbers down." Somebody else said: "Let's go back and look at all of the slides again." We found more wooly-boogers in three more unexpected places, and we shifted into a game of "What's wrong with this picture?" We came up with a lot more other visual "wrongs" and began developing procedures to correct them as well as to hunt for and capture wooly-boogers wherever they might be. Robert started carrying a camera and using the one-inch square concept to take snapshots (35 mm slides) of operations in the mill. Then he'd bring people in to look at the slides and figure out "what's wrong with this picture?" It worked.

Carry a camera with you all the time.

TOOL #55 (LEVEL 5):
Visual Controls
Duke Rohe, M.D. Anderson Cancer Center

Remember the last time you were looking frantically around the spot where you spend the most time working, trying to find some needed information? You didn't see it anywhere so you started looking for someone who had the information, but then you couldn't find their phone number. Frustration? Stress? When you finally got the information, you probably wrote another Post-it note and stuck it on your computer monitor. In fact, back off, take a look at your desk or work areas. How many little

138

signs and notes and lists have you put up within in easy sight of where you sit or work? Those are your "visual control system."

Imagine instead a work environment that is information-friendly. No Post-it notes! Think of a place where critical information is right there, and guesswork is nowhere to be found. You know what to do and how to do it—you have the knowledge you need either in your head or where you can immediately find it. When something is wrong it's obvious to all. If you have anything less than this kind of a visual control environment, your workplace is rigged for failures. A visual control system can generally knock out a third of your inadvertent errors, and the time it saves not searching for missing information will be significant. Labs, shops, production centers, equipment storage areas, common use areas, and *your desk* are all natural places for a visual control system.

To discover the types of visuals and signage you need in your areas:

Look at your area with naïve eyes

  ➤ as if you were working there your first day;
  ➤ as if you came from another planet;
  ➤ as if you would not need to make any assumptions.

Here are 10 questions to get you started on making a work area more "visual":

1. What needs to be known?
2. What needs to be shared?
3. What do we *not* want to happen, or how do we keep it from happening?
4. Where is the best place for the instructions, information, phone numbers? Are they close to the point of action?
5. Can you make what is wrong stand out, look abnormal, be very obvious?
6. Is it public-friendly (tasteful, discreet)?
7. When something is missing or out of its prescribed place, do you know what goes there?
8. Can questions be answered with signage before they are asked?

9. Can you replace or reinforce an instruction with a picture/symbol (remember a B+ picture today is better than no picture tomorrow)?
10. Do you have expiration dates on signage that have temporal value and do you remove expired visuals to keep info boards fresh?

139

We all know how Level 5 changes work. Think about your own family. Children learn almost everything to a certain point from copying or emulating their parents. Here's how you wash the dishes. Here's how you cut the grass. Here's how you talk. Here's how you relate to other people. Children copy everything, and, by doing so, we can take them from low levels of competence to relatively high levels very fast. If you give it some thought, copying early in life is where it all started. How else would you have learned to talk?

Large companies have mastered continuous innovation by seeing what others do well and acquiring it. When a company like Exxon sees an excellent location for a gas station that happens to be owned by a competitor, it buys it and changes the sign. Similarly, you'll often see Exxon stations located next to Mr. Lube. Why? Exxon liked what it saw, acquired a major share of Mr. Lube, and now often pairs the operations, locating them next to each other. When that's the case, it's easy for the Exxon station to refer oil changes next door.

Some companies use acquisitions as their way to innovate and grow. They see something they like and buy it. Cisco, GE and Tyco all come to mind. Each of these companies have realized that small companies often are the incubators of innovation and they can move forward faster by acquiring such companies and giving them the extra resources they need to ramp up to warp speed.

RESULTS: LISTEN TO YOUR KIDS

Exxon's Western Production Division's Innovation Center decided to hold a "little idea day" and discover what the biggest little idea might be. The biggest little idea came from a high school student. One of Exxon's engineers working on a project to cool gas coming in from an offshore platform, and under a pressing deadline to finalize the contract for the

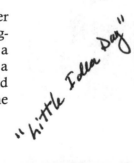

"little Idea Day"

140

project with a contractor, was describing the problem and the construction of the project at the dinner table to his family. His son suddenly said, "Dad, why don't you just put in one of those big fans that blows over dripping water like they use at the nursery to cool all the plants?" The family drove over to the nursery, looked at the setup, and the father went in and canceled the contract the next day. He copied it! A large fan was installed at a cost of $25,000 versus the contractor's proposed engineering design costs of $125,000.

ROLF'S THEORY OF RELATIVITY

The copying aspect of Level 5 is straightforward and easy to understand. However, the modifying and adapting function of Level 5 can be very relative. If I copy something and put a twist on it, it can be viewed as only a Level 3 change, because in one sense I am only improving. But if what I choose to copy was the impossible for me before, I have jumped ahead to Level 7. As soon as I copy it, it is no longer a Level 7 idea. It can be viewed as different (Level 6) or improving (Level 3). Another aspect of the relativity of Level 5 is what people choose to copy and what that reveals about their own thinking. Some people will be more inclined to copy things that make an operation more effective and efficient (Levels 1 and 2), while others will look for what's different (Level 6) or impossible (Level 7).

Back to Elvira Stesikova to make the point. After reading *The 7 Levels of Change* to meet a requirement for an executive MBA class (post-Dilbert graduate work!), Elvira invited me to come up to Oklahoma and work with her R&D group on next generation products (NGP) with the 7 levels as the baseline. When we got to Level 3, Elvira said "You know, I just couldn't read all those mind maps you have in the book, so I converted them all to a spreadsheet. Is that Level 3?" The spreadsheet is an amazing summary! But I saw it as Level 5—just copying and changing it into a different format. Then it hit me that it was really Level 6, something I had neither thought of nor done—nor had anyone else. It was brilliantly diff*erent*! Elvira has significantly improved (Level 3) this rewrite (Level 4) of the book. Flip back to appendix D and see what you think.

In the automotive industry there are countless examples of the change theory of relativity. Have you ever noticed a

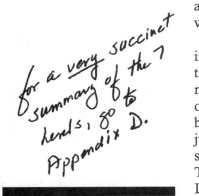

for a very succinct summary of the 7 Levels, go to Appendix D.

BETTER

What could we do Better? How could we do it Better?

...BLUE SLIP

company coming out with a new car model that turns the industry's head around? When it has been greeted by huge success, have you noticed how quickly the copycats of the industry can adapt that which is successful? If you watch as new car models are unveiled, you will see Level 5 copying in full force—copying a detail here and a sports car there. It's rampant because it works. Watch BMW as it unveils a *"new car"*—the Mini—a rebirth of a British car with legend status that was buried within its acquisition of a competitor. BMW is rolling out a new Mini; they copied this boxy little classic from the Austin-Cooper Mini in the '60s, and then let the Bavarian touch go to work. You can see the old Mini within, but it definitely ran through the levels of change as it took on a very German flavor. And along this journey BMW may well have ventured into something that was impossible for them in the past—a car that cost less that the median car in America today.

Alan Webber, *Fast Company* magazine's editor, points out that "today, the advantage that you get from out-thinking the competition lasts an incredibly short period of time. Put simply, the speed with which your competitors can copy even the best idea has increased much faster than the advantage that you get from having come up with that idea in the first place."

> *Have you ever thought about copying yourself*
> *before the competition does?*
> —Deep Thought by Ralf
> (Rolf Smith's evil twin)

THINKING ABOUT THINKING AT LEVEL 5—AGAIN

The Level 5 thinker and doer has an enormous appetite for learning. The arrival of the World Wide Web has given them the ultimate idea-and-innovation-resource engine. By pointing and clicking and navigating your way through the Web you can find a near endless supply of information telling you what other people are doing. The Web is so rich with ideas and growing at such an incredible rate that you will never take it all in. So venture out, travel around the world at light speed, and see what you will see. Companies, organizations, governments, and people are all out there sharing with you.

142

piles vs. files...

The Level 5 thinker and doer wants to know "why?" Why do we do it this way? Why do we need this? Why do they do it differently? You'll recognize the Level 5 thinker by the stuff torn out of magazines and taped to the walls in his or her office. Bulletin boards are fertile ground for them to share ideas, cartoons, articles they find interesting. With Level 5 thinkers and doers, you will start seeing more piles and less files in the office. On casual day at the office, they'll dress much more casually than the folks at Level 1 and 2, who might take off their ties. Level 5 people are good bridgers; they bridge the Level 6 and 7 thinkers to the Level 1, 2, 3, and 4 thinkers, who otherwise would have a hard time communicating. They can see the good in Level 6 and 7 ideas and at the same time bring them down to earth.

Level 5 people are outwardly focused and constantly asking others if they've seen this or heard of that. As children, they loved-show and-tell day at school. They love new! They'll drag out the end of meetings looking for ways to share all of the new ideas they have or to listen to what others have seen or heard that's new to them.

PROS AND CONS AT LEVEL 5
When working with change at Level 4, remember that some things are so ingrained within organizations and/or people's habits that rooting them out can be difficult, even painful.

1 – Sigma Change

Effective   - Doing the right things
Efficient   - Doing things right
Improving- Doing things better

Pros	Cons
Level 5 requires you to focus outward. This is a marked change from the first four levels of change, which are very inwardly focused. Level 5 changes can be very easy and can jump-start innovation.	Level 5 thinking and doing can get overfocused, isolating an idea that may not work in your own system the way it seemed to be working in the one you copied it from.
Level 5 can accelerate your rate of change, compressing the time and energy needed to leap from Level 1 to Level 7—just by opening your eyes to what others are doing well. Most great ideas already exist—go find them	Level 5 thinking can stall your efforts at originality—it's not terribly creative to copy, and if you get in the habit, pushing your own internal envelop can atrophy, so Level 5 shouldn't be over-used
You can sometimes copy something that's impossible for you to do (Level 7), and then modify it—cut some things out of it (Level 4), and make it more efficient and effective (make Level 1 and Level 2 changes to it) within your system.	"Copycat, copycat!" all the other kids chant at you.
	You might be accused of "cheating," plagiarizing, or patent infringement, or get sued because that's what everybody else seems to be doing.

LEVEL 5 FEAR: SELF-DOUBT

Fears at Level 5 crop up out of underestimating yourself, doubting your own skills and abilities (which is why your Me, Inc.® work at Level 2 is so important).

> ➤ Fear of copying the right things wrong.
> ➤ Fear of not copying the right thing.
> ➤ Fear of copying the wrong thing.
> ➤ Fear of getting "caught."
> ➤ Fear of not being physically able.

144

> Fear of being laughed at.
> Fear of criticism.
> Fear of self.

LEVEL 5 STRESS

Not measuring up seems to be the big driver of stress at Level 5. Not measuring up to expectations we have for ourselves or to expectations that we feel others have of us.

> Working very hard at duplicating what someone else is doing but just not being able to get it right.
> Copying someone else or something someone else is doing but not having it work the same way for you.
> Copying the right thing wrong and having someone else point it out to you.
> Copying the wrong thing without realizing it and having some else discover it
> Not being able to understand someone whom you are trying to copy: "I just don't understand how you can think like that!"
> Being pressured to conform to group norms.
> Finding yourself falling into groupthink in a discussion.
> Asking yourself, "Am I becoming just a copy of someone else?"
> Being prevented from copying something because of policies, traditions or bureaucratic red tape.
> Being accused of copying!
> Being copied by someone else and feeling as though they have stolen your work.

☑ TIP: SOME THINKING FOR DUMMIES

At the end of your day when you are tired, you still have room for one more thought. This quiet time will allow for some of your best thinking to occur. [Alisa Zapata]

"Always think. It will please some people and astound the rest."
—Copied/adapted from Mark Twain.

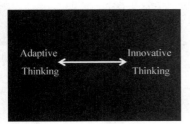

Adaptive
Thinking ←→ Innovative
Thinking

TRANSITION TO LEVEL 6

The transition from Level 5 (copying and adapting) to Level 6 (different) is also a transition from 2-sigma change to 3-sigma change—a big leap. Level 5 change and Level 5 thinking is built around being able to see other people doing something, modeling something new. It's built around copying the examples of others, using others' thinking and doing to inspire us.

> *"Where all think alike, no one thinks very much"*
> —Walter Lippman

Level 6 Is Different

At Level 6, there is no one and nothing to copy. The essence of Level 6 is about doing things no one else is doing. Level 6 is about breaking new ground, leaving new trails and footprints for others to follow and to copy. Level 6 is not about same or consistency and order. It's about leadership: creating forward motion into the unknown. Just like making the leap from Level 3 to Level 4, you can often transition from Level 5 to Level 6 by taking a step back and looking for the gaps. What's missing? Where is there a niche that's not covered?

To understand different, to value different, to think and do different, is far easier if we can identify with it at the personal level—if we can personally connect it with ourselves. Think back to all the Me, Inc.® work you've done so far. How are you different? What makes you unique and special? What unusual experiences or adventures have you had? What have you done that no one else has done? What are some of the biggest changes you've ever personally experienced? On a relative scale, how big is "different" for you? What are the boundaries, the borders, the proprieties and customs, the edges in your mind that define "different" for you? What are things that very few people know about you—the things about you that aren't same or similar, the things that make you different?

How different would others see you in the face of these insights?

This is one of the key aspects of the Me, Inc.® process: Seeing and valuing yourself as someone unique and special and different. Identifying your unique beliefs and principles. Discovering the unique set of strengths and skills that make you really you. Appreciating more fully who you are. Creating

145

Check your own "different" factor

146

a vision and mission for yourself that only you have, that no one else is thinking about and that no one else is doing.

By first seeing different in ourselves, we learn to value different, and from there we can learn to see and value different in others, in the thinking of others, and finally, in the ideas and changes that others come up with that may strike us as very, very different—as 3-sigma mindshifts for us.

LEVEL 4
Cutting

**Stopping
Doing Things**

ME, INC.® CHANGES AT LEVEL 5

Like the lower levels of thinking, doing and change, Me, Inc.® starts by focusing inward. This is an important process. Any change has to start with "you" before it can progress to "them." It's a little like conjugating a verb. From me to you to them. It's crucial to first become personally aware of a change in order to get others to buy into that change. At Level 5, Me, Inc.® begins to focus outward.

The Me, Inc.® process at Level 5 involves looking outward as you define your own principles and beliefs. Generally your principles and beliefs start with the people around you: your family and friends; your role models and mentors; teachers, grandparents, authority figures. Americans believe in truth, justice, apple pie and Mom, and when you grow up that becomes part of your belief system (Level 5 change).

As you continue to grow and mature in your thinking, you learn about others' beliefs, and you think, "Gee, I believe that, too." And you copy and adapt some of them (Level 5 change) to fit you, and your Me, Inc.® Level 5 thinking and doing connects with mentors and mentoring as well.

Think about your basic principles and beliefs. What are they anyway? How do you govern your life? How have you changed how you operate? Have your principles and values and beliefs changed or shifted over time? How? Have some proven to hold solid over time? Have others fallen away?

One of the most amazing Level 5 changes I've ever seen took place during one of our Schools for Innovators in Estes Park, Colorado. Harold C. Threatt, then manager of quality for R. J. Reynolds R & D, was one of the students. Harold has a pretty strong adaptor KAI score. His grandfather, Crayton Threatt, after whom Harold was named, had been a real innovator in his time. During one of the drawing-sketching exercises we use in the School, Harold drew a picture of the Harold side of himself reaching over and putting his hand over the mouth of the Crayton side of him every time Crayton came up with a good idea and tried to say something. At that point Harold decided to become Crayton Threatt for the duration of the School. Everything shifted! He stopped judging his ideas before they came out; he suspended judgement when he listened to other people; he tried things he'd never done before; and he became a deep thinker and risk-taker almost overnight. Crayton was a wonder to behold!

147

Have you ever really thought about your basic operating principles??

148

Norma Jeane Mortenson

. . . Marilyn Monroe

Without knowing it, Harold had stumbled onto the Raikov Effect. Dr. Vladimir Raikov, a Soviet psychiatrist, developed a deep hypnosis method which he used to make people think they had actually become a great genius in history such as Rembrandt or da Vinci. Raikov found that once they had "become" that genius, they took on the abilities the genius had been known to have had and were able to draw or paint or compose or play musical instruments with astounding ability and talent, demonstrating skills totally absent from their normal lives.

Harold Crayton Threatt transformed his own thinking without hypnosis; he simply took on all the remembered innovator traits of his grandfather (Level 5 thinking) and started living his life differently (Level 5 doing). He implemented much of his Me, Inc.® transformation on-the-spot in Colorado. When he returned to Winston-Salem, he changed his voice mail and answers with "This is Harold Crayton Threatt." Today, if you want focus, convergence, action and a quick response, leave a message for Harold; if you want new ideas and out-of-the-box thinking, call and ask to speak with Crayton. Tip! Copy Harold Crayton Threatt.

☑ TIP!
Start Listening Differently.
When you're around other people, keep your mind open, quiet, and empty. Roll around what they're saying in your mind; play with it. Don't bog down in thinking about whether or not you agree or disagree with them; look for ideas in it. Paraphrase it back to them. Then pull the stuff that works for you out of what they said, and copy or adapt it!

∾

CUTTING

In the film *Finding Forrester*, Sean Connery plays a famous author, William Forrester, whose sole novel won him world acclaim. Jamal Wallace, played by Rob Brown, is a gifted teenager—a prodigy trying to rise from a low income neighborhood to pursue a better life and the realization of his dream. As Brown struggles to write in the presence of his mentor, Forrester pulls a manuscript from his files, an old essay he had written decades ago for the *New Yorker*. He tells Brown, ". . . start with my words and when you feel your words coming write them down." Forrester used the classic teaching strategy of the art of copying as a gateway to find one's own expression.

PUSHING INTO DIFF*f*ERENT

We've reached the edge of 2-sigma, the end of the known and "interesting," and we're about to transition across the frontier into 3-sigma—diff*f*erent and the unknown. Get ready! A good way to transition your thinking from Level 5 to Level 6 is to focus on yourself as someone who is in fact different. Be different. Become different. Go get your expedition boots or shoes and put them on, and your expedition hat . . .

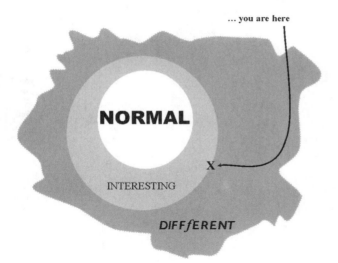

Transitioning to Level 6

BIG, URGENT AND DIFFERENT MESSES

Your boss has just handed you the biggest job you've ever been given in your life. It's not only big, it's urgent. And it's messy. It's also something that's never been done before, and *"they"* are looking for some very different solutions. You have to come up with something *different*, a totally new idea that isn't like anything you know of. The challenge is you're stuck—you don't know what to do or even how to get started. Nobody else is doing or has ever done anything like this before. But . . .

> *"If you continue to think the way you've always thought, you'll continue to get what you've always gotten."*
> —source unknown

DOING THINGS NO ONE ELSE IS DOING

This is going to take you someplace you've never been, and the chances are no one else has ever been there either. It isn't like any of the other levels of change we've pushed through so far. It's *different*.

Executives and managers are often faced with unique, challenging, and urgent tasks. More often than not, a team is formed on short notice to tackle these— to solve a problem that has not been attempted before. The team is chartered to create a new or different product or process, to achieve this with urgency, and to approach the problem creatively. However, most teams are ill-equipped to jump into these types of adventures. Although motivation and professionalism are unquestionable, the team members may not have an adequate grounding in team dynamics or the innovative and creative techniques necessary to produce results. This is increasingly the case as teams are becoming more diverse with a mixture of company, contractors, consultants, experts, and mixed backgrounds. The team doesn't know how or where to get started to move into different and Level 6 thinking.

UNDERSTANDING LEVEL 6 CHANGE

Generally speaking, Level 6 changes involve significant commitments of time, effort, cost, and resources. They're not typically changes that can be made immediately. Statistically, there are not many of them. They're rare and unusual. And they're radical.

The majority of change and change ideas come from the lower levels— primarily Levels 1, 2, and 3. These are smaller, more incremental changes that don't fundamentally affect the entire organization. Level 4 and 5 changes make a bigger impact. Level 6 changes transform. Level 1, 2, and 3 changes keep a company

152

moving along the road of continuous improvement. But when an organization is stuck, is no longer making money, or is losing market share, it's time for something diff*erent*, for a move into Level 6—into the unknown. It's time to go "on expedition."

WHAT *IS* AN EXPEDITION?

ex•pe•di•tion (ĕk′spĭ-dĭsh′ən) *n*. An excursion, journey or voyage made for some express purpose, as for exploration, to investigate unknown regions to gain insight or knowledge of something previously unseen or unknown.

Thinking Expeditions are out-of-the-box approaches to unusual and urgent problems. They use a very diff*erent* problem-solving process to lead groups into areas of unknown thinking. Typically used on the front end of a project to form up, focus, and unify the team, they generate an initial out-of-the-box idea set and give team members a wide range of creative tools—techniques for achieving innovative results.

Thinking takes time. The length of time required for an Expedition is driven by the scope of the problem and the size of the project team. From three to six days in length, they start early and end late with few or no breaks. The intense format stretches a group significantly.

A Thinking Expedition rapidly moves individuals and teams to new levels of thinking, accelerating the mindshifts needed to discover new and diff*erent* results. To get diff*erent* results, managers and executives today must *do* things diff*erent*. However, before they do things diff*erent* they must first *think* diff*erent*. And before they can begin to think diff*erent*, they must *think about the way they think*— they must examine their basic thinking processes. Thinking comes before doing, and *thinking about thinking* comes before thinking. This triple mindshift is critical to effecting any change aimed at getting diff*erent* results:

This is 3-Sigma. We're at the 4%-5% level, 1 out of 25 ideas...

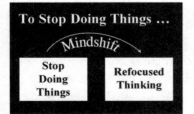

To Stop Doing Things ...

Mindshift

| Stop Doing Things | Refocused Thinking |

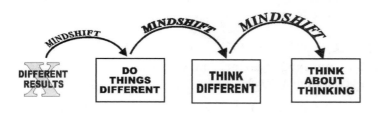

The Mind*Shift* Model

The concept of the Thinking Expedition is to deliberately move individuals and teams through this triple mindshift to new levels of thinking—and to provide them with the tools, techniques, and processes needed to make some challenging changes in their thinking.

A Thinking Expedition has four driving requirements. All four must be present or it won't work:

1. ***Results***—Is the backer or sponsor truly looking for diff*erent* results and 3-sigma ideas? Is a significant level of change needed, and is the desired outcome a product or process that must be very different?
2. ***Urgency***: Is there any urgency? *A sense of urgency is the most critical element.* Real urgency is the need to start the effort *now*, immediately or very, very soon.
3. ***Unusual***—Is the challenge unusual? Unique? Difficult?
4. ***Backing***—How important is this? Is there a senior backer or sponsor for the expedition? Are they willing and able to *commit* time, visibility and personal involvement?

How does a Thinking Expedition work? No two are the same. Each Expedition is designed to attack an unusual problem with its own unique challenges. Yet all follow the pattern of a classic expedition, and the flow of that process can be charted, even predicted. Specific discoveries, time-lines, and results on expedition, however, cannot be predicted, as the following example will show. A group at Procter & Gamble Co. was given a dramatic challenge: double the company's revenue (to $70 billion) by the year 2005. They recognized that they had to think differently in order to make this type of change. The team went "on expedition," and the article about their adventures was written by

154

FAST C☾MPANY Magazine
January 2000

*Change expectations
immediately and set the
stage for different*

☑ **TIP!**
*Look different. Set up the
room so that the moment
people walk in, "different"
hits them in the face.
Visual impact is a power-
ful mindshifter.*

Sometimes innovation
may just be a matter of
getting rid of something.

an "outside stretcher" from *Fast Company* magazine who
joined the team.

LEVEL 6: THE THINKING EXPEDITION

Fast Company Magazine, January 2000
by Anna Muoio, Senior Writer

"This is not a meeting. This is not a training session.
There are no exercises. It's all real work," declares Rolf
Smith, who is standing before the Face 2005 Team—22
chemical engineers, biologists, and project leaders from
Procter & Gamble Co. with a mandate to develop new products that will redefine the future of cosmetics. "This is an
expedition. No whining. No sniveling. No excuses."

If Smith speaks with military authority, that's because
he spent 24 years in the U.S. Air Force. His military career
has included working with the Electronic Security Command, becoming an expert in artificial intelligence, and
launching the air force's first Office of Innovation. (Indeed,
by the time Smith retired from the air force in 1987, after
declining an assignment at the Pentagon, he was known
throughout the ranks as "Colonel Innovation.") But Smith
doesn't just talk the military talk.

He walks the walk. His baggy, khaki-colored cargo pants
are zero fashion and all function. The dozen pockets of his
safari vest are filled with gear. As flute music from the Bolivian
Andes plays in the background, Smith paces around a room
that's cluttered with tents, backpacks, and climbing ropes. Outside, a narrow path stretches toward the Potomac River.

The P&G people are puzzled—and on edge. They are
about to embark on a long, arduous, and potentially rewarding expedition. A Thinking Expedition.

The genuinely exciting news about the new world of business is that there is more room for creativity than ever.
Smaller and smaller groups of smart people can do bigger and
bigger things. Just ask the people who developed the first
Netscape browser when they were kids just out of college, or
the pair of Stanford graduate students who started Yahoo! as
a way to postpone writing their Ph.D. dissertations. Now the
sobering news: You're only as good as your last great idea.
The half-life of any innovation is shorter than ever. People,
teams, and companies are feeling the heat to think up new

155

products, services, and business models. What's the reward for one round of successful innovation? Even greater pressure to revisit your success, and to unleash yet another round of innovation.

That's precisely what these 22 P&G employees from Hunt Valley, Maryland, are facing. They are part of P&G's high-stakes effort, dubbed Organization 2005, whose goal is to double the company's revenue (to $70 billion) by that year. Cathy Pagliaro, 34, an energetic associate director for P&G's cosmetics-product- development department and the woman responsible for launching this expedition, explains the challenge that her group faces: "Our CEO, Durk Jager, has declared that Organization 2005 is about three things: stretch, innovation, and speed. The challenge for our small group is to help make those words a reality. My department has a charter to do new and different things to help fulfill our revenue goal. But to do that, we can't think about things the way they've been thought about inside P&G for the past 162 years. The only way we can change is if we start to think differently. I don't know exactly where that will take us, but I do know that it looks different from where we are now."

Through his Virtual Thinking Expedition Co., based in Houston, Texas, Smith has guided teams from some of the country's largest organizations—IBM, DuPont, Ford, Exxon—on expeditions driven by the human desire for a sense of adventure in the pursuit of the next big thing. "Americans instinctively understand the concept of an expedition," says Smith. "The history of the world is built on one expedition after another. It is part of our makeup and our psyche."

A Thinking Expedition combines creative problem solving with challenging outdoor experiential learning—similar to an Outward Bound boot camp for the mind. "It's an accelerated unlearning process," Smith explains. "The days are intense, full, and demanding. There are no scheduled meals, no scheduled breaks. We deliberately design the expedition to push people out of their 'stupid zone'—a place of mental and physical normalcy."

"Metacognition (see the mindshift model) is the first step in the process of change," Smith argues. "But to take this step, individuals or organizations first have to overcome a major obstacle—an overwhelming fear of thinking."

Use banners, African music, jungle tablecloths, tents, maps on the walls, boxes with EXPEDITION stenciled on them.

The Rules? All normal rules are suspended. Level the playing field for everyone on the team.

156

"Thinking is the hardest work there is, which is probably why nobody engages in it."
—Henry Ford

phre•no•mo•pho•bi•a n. An abnormal and overpowering fear of thinking.

"Come to the edge," he said. "No," they said. "We are afraid."

"Come to the edge," he said. They came. He pushed them . . . . . . and they flew.

—Guillaume Apollinaire

Refocused Thinking
refocused thinking (re-fo′kəs′d thing′king)
n. 1. Thinking that converges on or toward a central point again; to concentrate once more with greater intensity.

If you listen carefully to Smith's ideas about how companies can prosper in this change-or-die environment, you realize that he almost never summons the two words that are used incessantly by every other guru in his field: "creativity" and "innovation." "Among businesspeople, I've discovered that the word 'creativity' can derail a conversation in one second flat," he says. "It's too touchy-feely. It isn't about results. In the air force, I learned that the word "innovation" scares people. It implies too dramatic a change—the kind of change that threatens to leave people behind."

So Smith developed a different way of thinking (and talking) about the nature of change and the process of unleashing new ideas. His central proposition is deceptively simple. Although not all change is the same, there is one common element—thinking. When you break down the process of thinking into a manageable number of steps, you reduce the perceived risks associated with change. These levels of thinking, Smith is quick to stress, require seven corresponding levels of action—the doing that creates change. *"Being creative is when you think different,"* Smith says. *"Being innovative is when you do something with your ideas."*

Smith's goal for every Thinking Expedition is to move a team along this continuum.

Smith has incorporated another crucial piece of his worldview into Thinking Expeditions. Breakthrough ideas, he believes, come from the edge—that uncomfortable point at which levels of stress, tension, and exhaustion are pushed beyond the comfort zone. "People are more creative when they're on the edge," explains

Smith, who often works with teams well into the early-morning hours, guiding them into new creative territory. "People like to complain that they don't think well when they're tired or hungry. I take those people aside and tell them, 'That's the whole point. We don't want you to think well. We want you to think differently!'"

Don't Clean Up This Mess!

"You are not who you were yesterday," Smith tells the members of the P&G team, who are now outfitted in safari vests with the logo "THINK Expedition" stitched across the front pocket. The first day of the expedition, which ended at 11:30 PM, is now behind them. They have been briefed on the mission, the ground rules, and their roles. The main objective, Smith insists, is not to solve the specific product-development challenges that the team faces—no one is going to invent a new mascara or face cream in the next five days. Rather, it is to define and refine the challenge itself— or, as Smith likes to call it, "the mess" that the team faces as it tries to invent new products. Quoting Albert Einstein, Smith says, "The formulation of a problem is often more essential than its solution." Even though it's early in the morning, and breakfast hasn't yet been served, this statement perks some people up. "Most people are convinced that they already have the solution to every problem," says Smith. But invariably, he tells the group, after a few days on an expedition, the nature and depth of everyone's understanding of the so-called mess change significantly.

Smith and the P&G team began working on the mess long before they arrived here. Each participant had filled out an Expedition Visa, a detailed questionnaire with open-ended and fill-in-the-blank questions. The visa serves two functions. First, it gives Smith a richer understanding of the creative challenge from the perspective of the entire group, as opposed to how his initial contacts at the company see things. Smith and his team leaders then use those insights to design the overall flow, timing, and route of the expedition. They read each visa like detectives reading clues, gaining deeper insight into how each person thinks. "By the time the team walks through the door, we know enough to bond with people very quickly," he says. "The secret to guiding is to establish trust—fast. From there, you have to learn how to read the group in terms of all the different personalities, types, and styles that members bring with them."

No one needs a visa to read Jeff Leppla, 37, the idea man behind a breakthrough technology for one of P&G's innovative (and still highly secret) beauty-care products. Leppla has enough energy to power a locomotive—and to run his own horse-breeding and racing operation in Lexington, Kentucky, on the side. His enthusiasm is infectious. At dinner the night before, he rallied the people at his table like an indefatigable football coach. Referring to Smith, Leppla boasted, "Guys, we're going to break this dude in!" But even he recognizes the scale of the mess that he and his colleagues face. "There has to be a crisis to push us to take a risk. But often we lack a sense

157

Mess: A whole bunch of inter-related issues, problems, challenges, opportunities, ideas, background and history

www. thinking-expedition. com / visa.html

"When trust is high, precision can be low. But when trust is low, precision must be high."

—Chris Argyris

158

create and generate URGENCY!

Thinking Expeditions both compress and accelerate time.

LEVEL 4 CHANGE

STOP

What can we Stop doing?

...BLUE SLIP

of urgency. And in a company as big as ours, urgency can be a difficult thing to feel."

Indeed, *generating a sense of urgency* is one of the main design principles behind Thinking Expeditions. That's why Smith had advised Cathy Pagliaro to begin creating—through a flurry of cryptic emails to her team—a sense of mystery and anticipation weeks before the expedition. "I didn't tell anyone what we were doing, where we were going, or what to expect," she admits. "All I told them was to block off several days to go off-site. It was a huge risk to keep people in the dark. A lot of them couldn't handle not knowing. But you want to nudge people out of their comfort zone, because that's when real growth happens." She then adds, with obvious satisfaction, "I sure pissed off a lot of people!"

Smith plays his part like a master puppeteer. From the moment you walk into his staging room, you are imprinted with a sense of both urgency and difference. Contact with work or home is not prohibited, but it's strongly discouraged. Days run far into the night, and nights run into the early morning. And throughout the expedition, Smith and his team rely on an ongoing stream of multimedia props to spark and energize the flow and ideation—and to maintain the feel of a real expedition.

For instance, film clips from movies and videos are used to show the orchestration of expeditions—how teams are formed and how they prepare for the leap into the mapless unknown. Scenes in which panicked scientists avert disaster by making a lifesaving fix from whatever is on hand is shown to illustrate Smith's Level 7, doing-the-impossible thinking. Slides, photographs, and music—from Mozart to the Gypsy Kings—are used to shift mood and thinking direction.

And then there is the staple of any Thinking Expedition: blue slips—Smith's tried-and-true tool for capturing ideas. Smith is adamant, almost to the point of obsession, that a fresh supply of blue slips always is on hand. The key to capturing an idea, he stresses, is to write it down.

In fact, Smith believes that in both work and life, the only things that get done are those that get written down. So the hundreds of blue-slip ideas that the Face 2005 Team will generate over its five days are gathered to create the "Trail Ahead Travel Log." The log is divided into sections that list the team's discoveries, results, vision, and concepts of operations, as well as what to do to keep the sense of the expedition alive when people return to P&G. "I wanted to make sure that we not only had a different experience but also discovered and created a tangible output," says Pagliaro.

Smith also knows that it takes smart, thought-provoking questions to inspire the kind of thinking that generates breakthrough ideas. So a slide appears on the screen at the front of the room: "The average child asks 125 probing questions a day. The average adult asks a mere 6." So during an expedition, Smith asks a lot of questions. Some are focused on specific problems; others are intentionally vague, open-ended—and even, on the surface, a bit silly. One of his favorites: "What's a thought that you've never thought before?"

Smith recalls that during one of the first Thinking Expeditions that he led—this one for Exxon Corp. in 1994—one of his obtuse questions ended up saving the company millions of dollars. A team of engineers assembled to focus on several of Exxon's offshore oil-production sites. "Most engineers live in a world where projects are done efficiently, effectively, and with slight improvements," says Smith. But he had a different agenda. "Several sites were in the ice, in the middle of nowhere. At that time, building roads to the sites would cost roughly $1 million a mile. I wanted to push those engineers into a higher level of thinking. We asked team members to think of a completely crazy idea—something that they believed couldn't be done or wouldn't work. You know, one of those stupid ideas."

One engineer came up with a dumb idea with radical implications. "Let's stop building roads to the sites altogether!" he declared. It was a complete mind shift for the team. After elaborating on the idea, the group discovered a more innovative (and cost-effective) way of reaching offshore locations—a "dumb" idea that had the potential to save Exxon $50 million per production site.

The Long Climb to Creativity

The day is hot, humid, and overcast—the kind of day that frizzes hair and dampens spirits. Everyone hopes for rain. Some hope that it will bring relief from the heat; others pray that it will postpone the day's agenda—rock climbing. Harnessed, helmeted, and with all the appropriate legal waivers signed, the Face 2005 Team starts hiking down a narrow

Blue Slip

Write Ideas Down!

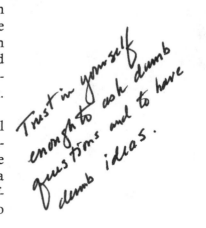

Trust in yourself enough to ask dumb questions and to have dumb ideas.

160

path in Virginia's Great Falls Park toward the Potomac River—and toward a sheer rock face at the water's edge. Admittedly, the P&G crowd looks more like the grown-up cast from *The Bad News Bears* than like a team of scientists on a serious expedition.

It turns out that climbing is also an integral part of Thinking Expeditions. Mike Donahue, 53, founder of the Colorado Mountain School, introduced Smith to the power of climbing in 1991: He guided Smith, along with Smith's family and partners, up Longs Peak, a 14,255-foot mountain in Colorado. Since then, Donahue and Smith have been guide partners. They complement each other perfectly. Donahue is tall and trim, with a face that looks like it's been weathered from the outdoors. Where Smith quotes Einstein, Tom Peters, and Margaret Wheatley, Donahue prefers to emphasize his points with more personal references or ancient quotes. He's particularly fond of one Himalayan saying: "When the explorer is ready, the guide will appear."

For Donahue, the power of climbing is that it's a perfect metaphor for work and life. "Climbing is an ongoing process of making decisions and moving forward," he says. "One of the easiest ways to change is simply to alter your position—to focus on the one-inch square in front of you and put one foot in front of the other. But to go forward—on a cliff, on a project, or in your career—you sometimes first have to take a step sideways, or even a step back."

But getting to the top is just the first of two main objectives in climbing; the descent is equally important—in real climbs as well as during a Thinking Expedition. It's also just as challenging. "It's just as far getting down a mountain as it is going up," Donahue says. On an expedition, the "long trek home," as the descent is called, represents the work required to turn the big ideas that were generated at the summit into pragmatic action items that can be implemented when the team returns. "On an expedition, the driving force is the summit," Smith explains. "Once it's reached, the focus then becomes getting back down. But this direction reversal is one of the most dangerous points of the expedition." It's during this leg of the adventure that Level 7 hypoxia (when the body's tissues are deficient of oxygen), as Smith calls it, can set in. Team members are tired, they want to get home, and worse, they stop thinking. *The danger is that*

LEVEL 4 CHANGE

Streamlining

they return to their organization with the "high" of climbing but without the "how" of getting things done differently.

Smith looks at his role this way: The guide is connected to each person on the expedition by an invisible rope. His job is to keep the right amount of tension on those ropes, so that everyone is right on the edge of stress. But guiding is a delicate business. "Sometimes," he says, "we'll pull the group a little too hard, and we'll have to go in and fix things."

And sometimes those ropes snap. At 11 PM on day two, the invisible rope connecting the Face 2005 Team did just that. It was late. People were grumpy. And Smith was orchestrating yet another think-fest, placing individuals at tables for an exercise. Participants at each table had to come up with a list of their strengths, and they had to determine which skills the group as a whole lacked, those that might be needed when implementing product ideas later on.

That's when the "troublemakers," as they came to be called, started flying high. This team insisted that it lacked no skills. Team members listed everything from technical savvy, to packaging design, to project priority setting, even to psychic abilities. But their confidence was starting to disturb some of the others—and finally long-buried tensions exploded. There was crying, pouting, yelling, finger pointing, and even some door slamming.

"Our team truly felt that it could dream up and make anything happen," explains Jeff Leppla, one of P&G's project leaders and also a hair-on-fire troublemaker. "And if we didn't know how to do something ourselves, we knew others who could help us. We could get funding, write business plans, conduct market research, and come up with product, packaging, and process design. All we needed was a lawyer. But I realized that our confidence provoked an enormous defensiveness from the rest of the group. I see now that we must have come across as a bunch of know-it-alls."

It was a major blowout that served as a perfect lesson—one that Smith could not have planned better himself. In fact, it granted department head Cathy Pagliaro one of her biggest take-aways. "The 'troublemakers' had no idea how they were being perceived," she says. "And the rest of the group was pissed off because they felt unvalued, cut off, and unappreciated. This stuff happens all the time in the real world of work. For me, there was no clearer way to demon-

161

> *"It is more important to know the right questions than the right answers.*
> —James Thurber

Personality type and thinking style started to become obvious...

162

strate the power of differences among teams. And once you understand that power, you can leverage it when forming teams or tackling a problem. When you experience it as we did, it drives the lesson home as no lecture ever could."

Anna Muoio is a Fast Company senior writer and was a "stretcher" on the P&G Thinking Expedition

∽ end of *Fast Company* article ∽

Where do we go from here? "On expedition" across the 3-sigma frontier into the unknown of Level 6.

The Pareto Principle
[The 80:20 Rule]

80% of the results come from 20% of the efforts

ME, INC.®—ON EXPEDITION!

At this transition point to Level 6, your Me, Inc.® task is to turn your life into an adventure. Here are some tips you can use to accelerate the process.

TOOL #56 (LEVELS 5–6):
How to Turn Your Life into an Adventure

> ➢ Start now.
>
> ➢ Wake up every morning "on expedition"—before you open your eyes.
>
> ➢ Imprint yourself as an expeditioner and adventurer: Look like one!
>
> ➢ Carry foreign coins in your pocket to constantly remind you of where you've been or are going.
>
> ➢ Feng Shui: Turn your office into your base camp.
>
> ➢ Play expedition and adventure music in your car and your base camp.
>
> ➢ Keep an expedition journal. Write expeditionary thoughts in it.
>
> ➢ Recruit a teddy bear or stuffed animal—carry it with you as a companion.
>
> ➢ Expeditions move forward "on foot"—one foot in front of the other, one foot at a time. Take a step.
>
> ➢ Get some "expedition shoes"—wear them places.
>
> ➢ When you walk, walk a little faster.
>
> ➢ Reimprint yourself everyday.
>
> ➢ Do something else—not what "they" are doing.
>
> ➢ Eat exotic foreign foods and strange stuff.
>
> ➢ Take risks.
>
> ➢ Say "Surprise me!" when you order a meal in a restaurant.

163

164

- Expect the unexpected.
- Get lost somewhere.
- Don't carry an umbrella.
- Buy an "expedition hat"—wear it.
- Get rid of your briefcase and use a backpack instead.
- Carry unusual expedition supplies in your backpack.
- When things go wrong, realize you're about to have an adventure.
- Quit whining. Stop sniveling.
- Realize that whatever happens on expedition is what's supposed to happen.
- Laugh out loud at yourself.
- Explore yourself—discover who you really are.
- Find your boundaries, your edges—then push them!
- Break some rules.
- Start exploring and discovering more.
- Do diff*f*erent. Be diff*f*erent. Make diff*f*erent happen.
- Read about great expeditions and adventures.
- Learn key words and survival phrases in at least seven different languages.
- Dream up a great adventure you'd love to have.
- Start telling people about it.

➤ Map out an expedition you've always wanted to go on.

➤ Hang a framed picture of it on your wall.

➤ Tell people you're going to go do it.

➤ **Do it.**

165

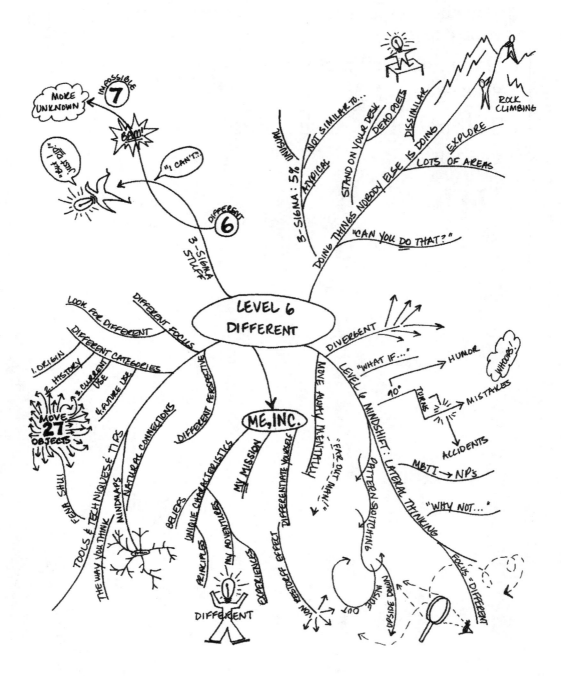

Level 6: Diffferent

The essence of this book is thinking diffferent

Thinking different isn't just important, it's a matter of life and death.

> *"It is a different type of battle. It's a different type of battlefield. It's a different type of war. And that in itself is going to be a real challenge for America."*
> —George W. Bush September 2001

Moving into Level 6 is *really* different. It isn't like any of the other levels of change we've worked with.

UNDERSTANDING LEVEL 6 THINKING

At Level 6 three is a deliberate choice to think different, to do different, to be different. To move beyond average, beyond normal, beyond interesting. To shift into and explore 3-sigma.

At Level 6 there is a deliberate move away from the conventional wisdom and structure, from guidelines, rules, regulations. There are deliberate moves across accepted channels of thought and cuts across patterns instead of movements up or down with them. Level 6 thinking approaches a problem or concept or task from a different perspective or point of view, including backwards and inside out. Your thinking leverages your creativity and transforms your ideas into non-normal, unorthodox, and unusual results.

All this makes Level 6 thinkers easy to spot. They stand out. They're often habitual or unconscious rule breakers. They generate lots of ideas, and many of the ideas are so far out there (out in the 3-sigma area) that it causes most people (Level 1, 2 and 3 thinkers) to view them as nuts. They aren't nuts, they're just way out there. And many of them tend to blurt out their ideas before they are fully formed so they don't sound very good to other people.

At the other end of the scale, Level 1, 2, and 3 thinkers are more circumspect—they edit and reedit their ideas before they are willing to let other people hear what they have to say—and sometimes they stifle their ideas by keeping them inside too long. Unlike the lower level thinkers, Level 6 people don't seem to really care what you think about their ideas—it's more important for them just to share them with you.

168

UNDERSTANDING LEVEL 6 CHANGE
Doing Things No One Else Is Doing

"The significant problems we face cannot be solved at the same level we were at when we created them.
—Albert Einstein

The large majority of change and change ideas come from the lower levels—primarily Levels 1, 2, and 3. These are smaller, more incremental changes that don't fundamentally effect the entire organization. Level 4 and 5 changes make a bigger impact—they change the existing system of which they are a part. Level 6 changes fall on the edge of or outside the existing system; they can transform and sometimes destroy existing systems. Level 1, 2, and 3 changes keep a company moving along the road of continuous improvement. But when an organization is stuck, it's time for something diff*e*rent.

Why different? You're effective and efficient; you've improved and cut out waste. You've copied the best and adapted it to fit. You've expanded your thinking and pushed out into the known as far as possible. Where do you go now? You have to come up with something diff*e*rent, a totally new idea that isn't like anything you know of or like anyone else knows of. Dissimilar. Distinct. Unusual. You can't find ideas like this because they don't yet exist—*you* have to come up with them yourself. You have to move from the known into the unknown with your thinking.

Generally speaking, Level 6 changes also involve significant commitments of time, effort, and cost of resources. They're not typically changes that can be made immediately. Statistically, there are not many of them. They're rare and special. And they're radical.

THINKING ABOUT THINKING

Level 6 thinking is diff*e*rent thinking—thinking that is unlike in style, type, form, process, quality, amount or nature to anything else. It's thinking that reverses basic assumptions and accepted logic or reasoning. It's thinking which is distinct or separate, particularly in style and process. It's unusual thinking. It's strategic thinking.

The Pareto Principle
[The 80:20 Rule]

80% of the results come from 20% of the efforts

169

In a group, Level 6 thinkers and doers are the "stretchers." They'll pull the lower level thinkers past their normal realm of thinking. When your company is moving to higher levels of change, you have to have the stretchers there. They'll push the idea count way up, the volume, and others at lower levels of thinking will be able to piggyback onto their ideas and refine them. And if the group can control itself and suspend judgment (PIN), they'll see the stretchers produce some diamonds in the rough.

"And those who were seen dancing were supposed to be insane by those who could not hear the music"
—Friedrich Nietzsche

How are Level 6 people different? They generally have broad and varied backgrounds, lots of different interests. They've traveled, either to foreign countries or into foreign kinds of knowledge. They'll be aficionados of something or maybe a number of somethings. They may be musical. If so, they probably play a couple of different instruments, one well and the other not particularly well but well enough that they enjoy it. Their offices will reflect their interests. They'll tend to like different, more abstract art work. Their desks, shelves, and filing cabinets will be covered with piles (not stacks) of information. They often never look inside their filing cabinets. With them, out of sight is out of mind.

piles, not files, "messy" organization

They don't want the furniture that everyone else has in their office. It's not that they want something more prestigious, just something diff*e*rent. They might bring in something from home like an old rocking chair or an antique clock with Westminster chimes. When you come into their office, you'll have to clean something off to find a place to sit down.

And when you sit down they start hitting you with new ideas and insights. They cannot *not* share them. "Have you seen this?" "Did you hear that?" You won't find them sitting down and reading a book from cover to cover like a Level 1, 2, or 3 doer. Instead, they'll have several books going at once and will skip around reading a few pages, or sometimes chapters from each, not necessarily in any particular order.

If there's a casual day at the office, the Level 6 folks will be real casual with wild shirts and socks. Even on a noncasual day, their socks or ties will give them away. Think: playful. If

170

there's a new trend in dress or electronic equipment or sports shoes, they'll be on to it.

Even when I was in the air force, my Level 6 traits managed to leak out. The air force would periodically test uniforms with a defined test group somewhere in the world. Wherever it was, I would manage to get it. I loved being "out of uniform" different. When I worked with NATO, the British forces had a really sharp-looking uniform sweater and I managed to get hold of one. I put my Lt. Colonel's shoulder boards on it and got away with wearing it during NATO exercises, because I told everyone it was a new U.S. Air Force uniform test item. Amazingly, several years later we actually adopted a modified version of the British sweater.

THE LEVEL 6 MINDSHIFT

The mindshift at Level 6 is into a whole new way of thinking.

> *"The problems we have created today cannot be solved by* **thinking** *at the same level we were at when we created them."*
>
> —Albert Einstein

With Level 6 you shift to lateral thinking—moving away from where you were, disconnecting, moving off to the side and thinking about something from a completely different angle— changing perspective completely, looking at things out of the corner of your eye, standing mentally on your desk, and constantly looking at the world from different angles in diff*f*erent ways.

> *"All behavior consists of opposites . . .*
> *Learn to see things backward, inside out, and upside down.*
>
> —Lao-tzu

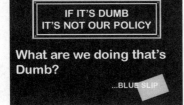

IF IT'S DUMB
IT'S NOT OUR POLICY

What are we doing that's Dumb?

...BLUE SLIP

Consider the following diagram and definition. To get diff*f*erent results, you have to do things different. To do things no one else is doing, you have to do diff*f*erent. To do things diff*f*erent requires lateral thinking.

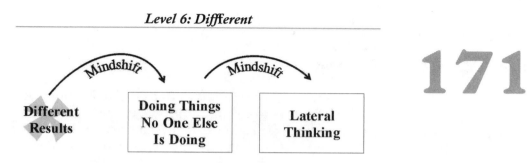

diffferent thinking (dĭff'ər-ənt thĭng'kĭng) **n.**
1 Thinking which is unlike in style, type, form, process, quality, amount, or nature; dissimilar. 2. Differing in thinking from all others, unusual. 3. Thinking which reverses basic assumptions and accepted logic or reasoning. 4. Weird thinking.

Do you really want to think different?
Do you really want to do different?
Do you really want to be different?

HOW DO YOU GET STARTED AT LEVEL 6?

Change. Different is about change. Consider that the simplest form of change is change of position. Moving something from point A to point B. Now things are different. The something isn't where it was, it's somewhere else. Things have changed. Things are different. Do one thing different each day, think one thought different each day, and *notice that you did*.

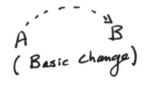

"When you come to a fork in the road, take it."
—Yogi Berra

172

$$3 \times 3 \times 3 = 3^3 = 27$$

TOOL #57 (LEVEL 6):
Feng Shui

Feng Shui is the oriental art of placement for harmony. If you really want to change, or if you are stuck in a rut or an unpleasant situation, if you can't get to different, move twenty-seven objects in your home that have not been moved in the last year. This will enhance your ability to move forward harmoniously in life, to change smoothly. By making twenty-seven small, seemingly nonsignificant changes in your life, which afterwards you notice on a daily basis, you will have raised your own awareness of the need for change and that things are easily made diff*e*rent. Simple stuff. Watch out! This can also drive some people in your home slightly mad.

Suppose you have the challenge of introducing a new a major change (a Level 6 different kind of change) to a group of people in your organization. Where and how do you start? Go back to Feng Shui, but differently. Change twenty-seven things in your office. And every day shift a few more around. Then start "moving" people, but slowly—start with the meeting where you are going to begin introducing "the big change."

TOOL #58 (LEVEL 6):
Change = Move!

The power of a group of people is their diversity—different backgrounds, experiences, expertise, age, sex, skills, adventures. The real trick is how to combine this diversity so that everyone "meets" everyone else over the course of the session. Force connections. In any large meeting (sixteen or more people) that lasts longer than thirty minutes, *make* people change seats—help them shift their locations and perspectives, their connections with the people next to them. Instead of moving twenty-seven objects in the room, move twenty-seven people! To make it smoother and appear more orderly, count the number of tables in the room (or divide the room up into "areas" if it only has chairs in it). Then have everyone

LEVEL 5
Adapting

**Doing Things
Others Are Doing**

"count off" by the number of tables or areas, and have the people move to the table with the number corresponding to their "counted off" number. This really shuffles them up. A variation: number, "letter" or color code everyone at the beginning. Then use those to reassign people into new combinations as the meeting unfolds. For most people at a meeting, this will be like going to church and having to sit in a new pew on the other side of the church.

Move? They won't like it. They'll hate it. They'll resist. They'll say that if they stay where they are and everyone else moves, it's the same effect. They'll say they don't want to move. They won't move. And at the end they'll say "The best part of the meeting was meeting and talking to so many different people."

TOOL #59 (LEVEL 6):
Diffferent Focus

If you want to achieve breakout thinking, focus on what's diff*erent* about previous experiences or solutions, not what's similar. Start keeping a list of things and thinks that strike you as diff*erent*. Take a blue slip, turn it vertically, label it "My Diff*erent* List" and every time you run across something that catches your eye differently, write it down. Every time *you* do something different, write it down.

"A great thought begins by seeing something differently, with a shift of the mind's eye."
—Big Al Einstein

TOOL #60 (LEVEL 6):
Diffferent Perspectives

In the movie *The Dead Poets Society*, Robin Williams (as John Keating the poetry teacher) stretched his students' thinking by climbing up and standing on top of his desk. "Why do I stand up here? I stand upon my desk to

174

get up right now, shut the door, and stand on your own desk — TRY IT!

constantly remind myself that we must look at the world in a different way," Keating said. "You see, the world looks very different from here. You don't believe me? Come see for yourselves." And the whole class climbs up on the desk and begins to see things in a different way. On Thinking Expedition, this is a tool that has produced great results. We have everyone stand on the tabletops or on their chairs to get them to physically, deliberately look at things in a different way. It's dramatic, different and energizing. For adults in business, it's crazy. People laugh and have fun with it and break out of their normal thought patterns immediately. And they get the beginnings of breakout ideas.

> *"Think left,   and think right,*
>
> *and think high.*
>
> *think low*
>
> *Oh, the thinks you can think If only you try."*

—Dr. Seuss
Oh, the Thinks You Can Think

Commit these four lines from Dr. Seuss to memory. Stop reading and try it right now (no one is watching you). Read it out loud once, then cover it with your hand and repeat it from memory. Now you can recite poetry to legitimize what you're doing. Buy a copy of *Oh, the Thinks You Can Think*. Pull it out and read from it when you're ootching a group into thinking different. Make them memorize it, too. It works.

TOOL #61 (LEVEL 6):
Humor, Jokes, Laughter, and Ninety-Degree Turns

Why are fun, humor and laughter important to thinking different? They lead to breakouts because they come from breakouts. Humor and jokes lead you down one line of thought and then WHAMO!—there's the punch line that takes you off at ninety degrees in a completely different direction than where your head was going.

COPYING

Right out of the box. Get people to make up jokes and punch lines about the problem they're working on as catalyst for new ideas. You may be surprised to discover how many people have *never* made up a joke! Give them something easy to get started: "How many X does it take to change a light bulb?" (X is "kind" of people they are working with, or that they themselves are, e.g., engineers, nurses, school teachers, physicists). Then have them tell each other their jokes.

Here're two more catalysts to be aware of: accidents and mistakes. When you are intending to do A, and B happens instead, when you are traveling down one path with your thinking or doing, and an accident turns you ninety degrees into another—there are opportunities for Level 7 ideas to break through. Many of the truly great scientific discoveries came from accidents and mistakes and experiments that went "wrong."

Reese's Peanut Butter Cups—have you seen the old commercial? Two guys sitting on a bench eating their lunches. Another guy gets ups off the bench; it tilts up like a see-saw, and Bam!—the chocolate bar slides down the bench, falls into the peanut butter jar and . . .

Hmmm . . . if you deliberately cause an accident is it really an accident? If you try to fail and succeed, which is it—have you made a mistake?

TOOL #62 (LEVEL 6):
Categorically Diffferent

We all tend to notice things in terms of categories that we have personally developed and become comfortable with over time. These categories then function as lenses in terms of *what* we see and how we see what we see. To raise your awareness of diff*f*erent, to notice more diff*f*erent things, or to notice them diff*f*erently, create new categories and begin looking at objects "through" them. Win Wenger, in his book *The Einstein Factor*, suggests four such categories:

176

1. Origin
2. History
3. Current use
4. Future use

When we see something, normal thinking sees it in its current use. "Origin" moves backwards in time and raises the question of how the object was made or where it came from. "History" might look at how long it has been this way or who has used it or how it was used. "Current use" brings in today's realities and applications. "Future use" moves your thinking into new possibilities and opportunities.

Often something really new and different is simply created out of something old and not-so-different, or out of combinations and synthesis of lots of lower levels of change. By looking at things you and your competition have in "current use," some things neither one of you is doing that's different, and cutting some things out you hadn't thought of—making some pretty normal things categorically different—you sometimes get some interesting results. Jasper Johns, the artist, explains it:

> *"It's simple. You just take something and
> do something to it, then you do something else to it.
> Pretty soon, you've got something."*

RESULTS: KFC-PIZZA HUT HYBRID KITCHEN

In New Zealand, KFC and Pizza Hut, at the time both members of PepsiCo's fast food family, realized that the kitchens in both restaurants were different but similar. What if—the different in each could be adapted to the other (Level 5 change—copying), the same could be combined and reduced (Level 4 change—cutting), and it could all be done in a single KFC-Pizza Hut restaurant, a new hybrid (big and more—the number three driver for Americans), with more choice (American's number one driver) and more efficiency (America's number four driver)? Bam! Same kitchen, two different restaurant concepts, all under the same roof.

BOOK

The Stuff Americans Are Made Of
7 Cultural Forces
That Define Americans

1. Choice
2. Impossible dreams
3. BIG and More
4. Time
5. Mistakes
6. Improvise
7. What's new

—Joshua Hammond &
James Morrison

"A great thought begins by seeing something differently, with a shift of the mind's eye."

- *Albert Einstein*

PepsiCo had been dabbling in this for some time, but the idea hadn't gone anywhere. New Zealand KFC pulled together some folks into a fast forward innovation team, went through a creative-problem-solving (CPS) process, came up with some completely different tangents (Level 6 change—different thinking), designed some new technologies (no rocket scientist stuff), and began running the highest volume in the world for Dual Concept restaurants.

In the end, it was almost all common sense, a BGO (Blinding Glimpse of the Obvious). The Pizza Hut and KFC teams hadn't just used a lot of School for Innovators thinking tools, they'd actually started listening to people with an open-minded "no bad ideas" approach. They didn't reinvent the wheel; they just changed the shape of it and adapted things other people were doing. They carefully visited all their competitors who were doing "gold standards" things in service and products. Then they copied the competitor's best ideas (Level 5 thinking) and adapted and improved them (Level 3 thinking) to fit KFC/Pizza Hut operations and concepts.

Their first big finding was that they couldn't service their consumer needs under the current restaurant design they had. They pulled a team of staff and mangers together, brainstormed, and used CPS again to come up with new breakthrough, flexible-adaptable floor plans, and kitchen flow designs.

Then they pulled in more teams from both KFC and Pizza Hut and had them each independently generate their ultimate vision for a restaurant (Level 7 thinking). They analyzed the new concepts jointly, looked at what the similarities and differences were. And then they reversed roles and had the KFC gang design the Pizza Hut of the future, while the Pizza Hut folks designed the KFC restaurant of the future (Level 6 thinking-doing). The result: some really great, different perspectives and new ideas.

The old dual concept had two separate management teams and two sets of cooks under one roof, and never the twain would meet. Just a bigger restaurant serving two different kinds of meals. The New KFC-Pizza Hut New Zealand concept moved to one management team, one staff team, and lot of modification of standard KFC and Pizza Hut processes and procedures (Level 1 and 2 effectiveness and efficiency changes) based on staff/line input (Level 3

177

178

thinking—improvements and *big* Level 4 changes—stopping and cutting). The big idea was starting at the back of the restaurant where the very different kinds of raw materials came in, then progressively moving forward from the back, blending and synthesizing more and more of the functions and operations. To accomplish this, they modified a lot of the standard hardware (equipment, technology) and software (procedures, rules, people skills—and thinking). In the end, they were able to put the dual operation under one roof the same size as the traditional restaurant (Level 6 change—different!).

RESULTS: THINK RED

Level 6 ideas are like those transformer action figures—they keep building and changing. In 1990, a Level 6 Exxon service station owner came up with an idea to sell Supreme, the new high octane fuel. It was a simple slogan: Think Red. Prior to then, Exxon stations had two-hose pumps. One was blue, the other was green. The blue had always been high-test. To handle the new supreme, they installed new pumps with three handles, and the third one, the highest octane, was red.

The station owner created a sticker for the pump: Think Red. And buttons for his cashiers: Think Red. His customers started asking questions and soon learned about supreme—the ninety-eight octane designed for high-performance vehicles like BMWs and Porsches. Supreme sales jumped more than 30 percent in a very short period of time. Exxon eventually bought the rights from the owner and took the idea to Houston where it was tested with a full blown campaign: Red hats, T-shirts and more. Exxon hooked up with Big Red soda and with a local radio station, K-RED. The idea was tremendously successful. Big Red sold more soda during the test quarter than in the previous year. Credo's listeners, young and high octane themselves, fed a new market of young Exxon credit card holders that obviously liked diff*f*erent and a high octane image, and Exxon never would have thought about tapping them.

THE *WASHINGTON POST* AND WORD POWER

Consider the power of words like "red" or "expedition" or others that conjure up an immediate mental picture. A word is a sound or a combination of sounds, or its representation in writing or printing, that symbolizes and communicates a meaning. Words are powerful and play a big role in creative problem solving. Have you ever tried your hand at making up new words and new meanings? The Washington Post's "Style Invitational" asks readers to take any word from the dictionary, alter it by adding, subtracting, or changing one letter, and supply a new definition. Here are some past winners:

> *dopeler effect*: the tendency of stupid ideas to seem smarter when they come at you rapidly.

> *intaxication*: euphoria at getting a refund from the IRS, which lasts until you realize it was your money to start with.

> *sarchasm*: the gulf between the author of sarcastic wit and the recipient who doesn't get it.

> *vaseball*: a game of catch played by children in the living room.

> *oootch*: To shift up increasingly steep slopes from level to level in small increments.

TOOL #63 (LEVEL 6):
Create New Words

Start spelling important words another way. Make a list of the most important verbs and nouns that are associated with the mechanics of a problem on which you are working. Then use the add/subtract/change one letter rule to create some new words and come up with a new definitions for them. Use your new words to reframe the problem, to approach it laterally from a totally different perspective.

For example, I am engaged in rewriting this book right now, and I keep getting distracted or pulled off by normal day-to-day business interruptions, phone calls, shiny beads, etc.

"I don't give a damn for a man that can only spell a word one way."
—Mark Twain

179

180

Problem:
How do I stay focused on writing and editing?

write	republish	examples
words	remove	email
time	phone calls	edit
stories	normal	distract
shiny beads	mindshift	business
sentences	interruptions	book
rewrite	focus	add

> ➤ *depublish*: to remove a book from the mind of the publisher

> ➤ *premove*: to remove or sideline text before it has been written

> ➤ *xedit*: to strike through thoughts about to be thought and before they have been written down

> ➤ *focuss*: focusing so hard that you become profane

> ➤ *foocus*: to focuss one's mind on one thing much longer than is normal

RESULTS: FOOCUS!

I started foocusing and by xediting large numbers of new ideas and interesting stuff, the book immediately came together.

> *"When I use a word, "Humpty Dumpty said,*
> *in a rather scornful tone, "it means just what I choose*
> *it to mean—neither more nor less."*
>
> —Lewis Carroll,
> *Through the Looking Glass*

WHY TRENDS?

OPPORTUNITY!

... Every Trend Has An Opportunity

RESULTS: ARCTIC THINKING

You usually have to climb to a Level 6 change by moving through lower levels of change first (ootching). Several years ago, I ran a thinking expedition for a joint ARCO, BP and Exxon task force to look at ways to reduce the costs of producing and exporting LNG (liquid natural gas) in the Arctic. One of the three joint project managers contacted me and asked us to design an out-of-the-box-thinking workshop that would make the joint team comfortable with divergent thinking processes and 3-sigma ideas. We created a Thinking Expedition built around the 7 levels of change—a metaphorical push into the unknown of Arctic field operations in which all normal operating rules would be thrown out.

The Thinking Expedition was split into two three-day operations, two months apart. Stage I was used to form up the team, shift their thinking, train them in innovation tools and techniques, and then push forward into the unknown by slowly diverging and exploring up through the 7 levels of change. Major breakthroughs began occurring as early as at Level 4—stopping doing normal things, and cutting out processes and procedures that had been the industry standard for years. The potential for very large cost savings, which this level of thinking uncovered, surprisingly pushed the team's thinking first *lower* into Level 3 and the exploration of general technological improvements in a wide range of areas; we looked at things that now would function under Arctic conditions but which previously would not work there (i.e., technology changes over time had shifted possibilities). We looked backwards down technological shifts into some black holes of traditional engineering.

From those insights, thinking rapidly *shifted back* into considering wide ranges of new and different technologies and work processes that were not being used or even considered (Level 6) in the Arctic by oil companies—but which other kinds of companies were using and operating with under severe conditions. The Level 3 and Level 6 technologies and processes were then forced into impossible combinations to solve impossible problems in ways that wouldn't work or couldn't be done (Level 7).

TOOL #64 (LEVEL 6):
Divergent Convergence

The Thinking Expedition was then resumed two months later with Stage II after the team had some time to work through all the ideas, research the more unusual areas, and flesh many of them out into an operating concept or technical approach. Stage II took on a very different "non-focus" compared with a normal project of this

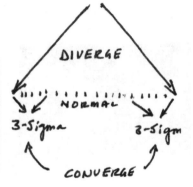

DIVERGE

NORMAL

3-Sigma   3-Sigm

CONVERGE

181

182

nature: divergent convergence. Instead of focusing on developing the "good" ideas that had come out of Stage I—the ideas that clearly would work or that management would buy—the team went for the "out there" ideas on the fringes. We focused (foocused?) on developing strategies and action plans using only the 3-sigma, highly divergent ideas—the Level 6 and Level 7 concepts and changes.

The breakout results for the three companies were conservatively estimated by the sponsors to be changes of 30 to 40 percent in operating costs with long-term potential savings in excess of $5 billion.

Sometimes you have to clearly define your mess, your challenge—build your mountain and *see* it—before you can begin to climb. Often when you generate all the interrelated issues, challenges, obstacles, opportunities, ideas, and history associated with the mess that is your challenge, and integrate them visually—the mountain—the solution begins to emerge as a trail to the top through the mess. The following story shows the way this works.

Steve Weichert, an Exxon manager at the Benicia Refinery in the Bay Area and a 1989 graduate of one of our very early School for Innovators sessions, called us in 1995 with the idea of running a Thinking Expedition focused on the turnaround maintenance cycle at Exxon's Benicia Refinery in San Francisco. Benicia is essentially a single-thread operation; when major periodic maintenance is scheduled, the entire refinery must shut down and production stops. Huge numbers of contractors descend on the facility in barely controlled chaos. Steve's objectives for the Thinking Expedition were to significantly reduce the time required (Level 2 and Level 4 changes) for the maintenance operation or to find a way to perform the critical maintenance functions without completely stopping production (Level 6).

TOOL #65 (LEVEL 6):
Mountain Building

Two key elements of every Thinking Expedition focus on "building the mountain" out of blue slips and then "route-finding" up the right mountain. This is done by

WATCH

What trends should we be Watching?

...BLUE SLIP

generating all the inter-related issues, challenges, obstacles, opportunities, ideas, and history associated with the mess that is the exploration area of the Thinking Expedition, or the focus, usually starting with a five-minute meeting and then following it with some heavy-duty mess-finding questions. The group is then broken up into table teams of four or six people, grouping similar styles and types together (KAI & MBTI scores), and they start integrating and synthesizing their individual collections of blue slips into a coherent whole—the mountain. It was during this part of the Benicia Thinking Expedition that the major mindshifts and breakout thinking occurred in the team of engineers. Clarity around the complexity of the problem leaped out as the route-finding through the mountain range uncovered the chain of events that would have to happen before any compressed turnaround objectives could really be achieved. The Aha! effect was profound (Level 6 thinking), and *big ideas* started popping up everywhere. The major results of the Thinking Expedition were tied back much more to the engineering mindshifts, and resolution of the problem definition, than to actual solutions and action plans.

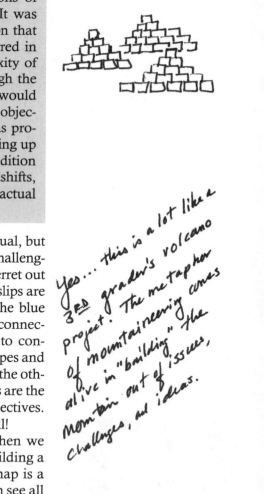

Building mountain ranges is very messy, very visual, but also very kinesthetic (the "building" part) and very challenging work. Heavy point and counter-point argument ferret out the crux points and most difficult areas, and the blue slips are initially in a heavy state of flux. People rearrange the blue slips constantly to show different relationships and connections among the ideas. Then the discussions begin to converge. Since each Table Team is made up of similar types and styles, each Table Team's work is quite different from the others in its thinking and its approach to the mountain, as are the end results. We end up with a wide range of perspectives. Mountain-building highlights different extremely well!

Seventy-five percent of learning is visual, so when we need to communicate big ideas, a visual tool like building a mountain or a mindmap is often the best. A mindmap is a visual representation of your thoughts where you can see all of them about a particular topic on one page. Mindmaps use no sentences; instead they rely upon icons and key words to help carry concepts further. They spread out like a spider

Yes... this is a lot like a 3RD grader's volcano project! The metaphor of mountaineering comes alive in "building" the mountain out of issues, challenges, and ideas.

184

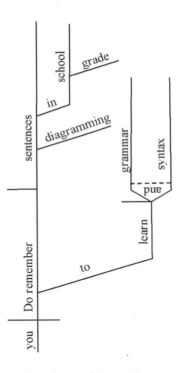

web. Mindmaps actually have tremendous structure even though they may not appear that way. They are a flow of consciousness. They're never finished because your thinking is never finished.

Mindmaps develop the way you think. You have an idea; it sparks something new. Your train of thought jumps around creating new branches to the mindmap. Caution: mindmaps can be stressful for highly structured people, but often can be used to stretch them to a higher level of change.

Mindmapping is different. It originated with Tony Buzan, who developed the technique based on research findings that showed the brain fundamentally works with key concepts or "chunks" of information and ideas in an interrelated and integrated way. Your brain doesn't come up with ideas in a linear fashion—it jumps around. Mindmapping accommodates that and allows you to use your whole brain—both your creative and analytical sides—by freeing you from the constraints of linear thinking.

TOOL #66 (LEVEL 6):
Mindmaps

How do you mindmap? Start with a blank sheet of paper. Set the focus either by drawing an icon in the middle of the page or writing down the topic or subject you want to focus on, then circling it. Begin brainstorming with yourself by thinking of major aspects of the topic. Draw a leg outward from the center and write the thrust of one of the major aspects along the leg. Print the keyword describing it in all capital letters. Continue brainstorming and bring some connecting points off the main leg as smaller legs or points that connect with—expanding or refining—the main leg. Capitalize the first letter of these words or phrases. If further expansions or refinements occur to you that are related to these, bring a third-order leg off them and print the words or phrases on this leg in lower case letters. Headline your ideas. Limit them to one or two key words as much as possible.

Do you remember "diagramming sentences" in grade school to learn grammar and syntax?

Gertrude Stein sure did: *"I really do not know that anything has ever been more exciting than diagramming sentences."*

Focus on Change

- Think about change
- Notice change
- Become aware of change

I think mindmapping might be. As you're creating your mindmap, you're likely to think of other major thrusts. When you do, immediately add them as more main legs and begin adding to them. Use a different color for each new major leg and all its branches and subbranches. This makes the mindmap even more visual. Use icons and symbols to emphasize points as much as possible—simple little stick figures and primitive drawings.

You can either brainstorm all the major lines first and then the branches on each (the more linear approach), or brainstorm a main leg and its branches and subbranches, or jump around randomly from one line to another as the ideas you're generating cause other ideas to pop off. When you have completed the mindmap, you can add "structure" to it by circling each main leg and all its subbranches and using different colors to set off each grouping. For an example, take a look at the mindmap of a Thinking Expedition in the last chapter.

TECHNIQUE: DE-MINDMAPPING

To transform a mindmap to a linear, sequential outline, number each major leg and, along each leg, number its subbranches to reflect their order, and their subbranches as well. Then follow the numbered sequences down the legs to word process it into a normally structured outline.

Mindmapping is a great tool for understanding a problem and is especially powerful in exploring the issues, challenges, obstacles, goals, and objectives imbedded in a problem, especially when the interrelationships are unclear.

Mindmapping can also be used with groups to review and refocus a topic or subject that the group has been working on for some time. Similarly, mindmaps are great summary tools in classroom situations. With groups, an approach that works well is to construct a large mindmap out of six sheets of flip chart paper taped together on a wall. Start by having two key members of the group, working as a pair, write down major legs and sublegs that the rest of the group calls out in the forms of key words. The two group members start the initial form of the mindmap going. Then they can engage everyone in writing and drawing on the mindmap, calling out key words, phrases, and ideas as they develop legs and sub-legs.

185

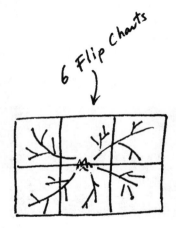

6 Flip Charts

186

TOOL #67 (LEVEL 6):
Strategic Visioning

Here's an example of using mindmapping for strategic thinking. Several years ago, working with my church's long-range vision group, we hit on the concept of using a very large 5' x 12' mindmap to engage everyone in the congregation in visioning the future. We had already identified eight major strategic interest areas, using blue slips and a five-minute meeting, and we drew on those as "starter" legs for a skeleton mindmap to spark everyone's thinking. We laid the mindmap out on three sheets of foam core board so it would be sturdy and portable, made smaller "worksheet" versions of (8.5 x 11 paper) to insert in the weekly bulletins, and planned to launch it at the annual church picnic. Our plan was then to continue using it for the entire month to give people time to reflect on it and engage in time at their own comfort level and style.

On picnic Sunday, Rick Hartmann, our pastor, opened his sermon by holding up a bulletin-sized mindmap and talked about it. He set the stage for everyone to add to the big mindmap during the picnic, made the first additions himself, and—it worked! By the end of the picnic, markers were flying, and a good-sized crowd was gathered busily around the mindmap.

The next Sunday, Tim Anderson, our out-of-the-box assistant pastor and a graduate of our School for Innovators (Expedition XVIII, August 1996), had the big mindmap moved right up to the front of the church and tied his entire sermon to it. A few weeks after returning from the School for Innovators in Estes Park, Colorado, he had already set the stage for different by giving a mindshifting sermon wearing his Thinking Expedition vest and THINK hat. We had also engaged two of the main ministry committees (Education and Children & Youth) during their regular meetings in developing their own mindmaps of what their ministry really was, what they were currently doing, issues and challenges they faced, and what they hoped to do—their part of the vision.

That was followed the next week by a church council offsite meeting, which I guided (using their KAI scores), and

---

Adaptive Thinking

adaptive thinking (ə-dăp'tĭv thĭng'kĭng)
n. Thinking designed for, suitable for, or having a capacity for adaptation; copying

which refined the big mindmap. The council members and all committee members then began adding to the visioning mindmap each week. Because the pastors, Rick and Tim, continued tying the mindmap into their sermons, the whole congregation became more and more actively engaged. Eventually we used nominal voting techniques to draw everyone into focusing and prioritizing the pathways we would follow into the future. *Big ideas* were developed with supporting action plans, and we had some pretty exciting change, ranging from Level 1 to Level 7, underway in short order at Holy Cross Lutheran Church in Houston.

In the end it wasn't just the mindmap that was a Level 6 change. From the congregation's point of view (Rolf's Theory of Relativity), *everything* we tried was different for most people.

Mindmaps are such strong visual and imprinting tools that *very often a whole map can be recalled or reconstructed without looking at it again!* Because of this, mindmaps are a powerful tool for interactions to help explain out-of-the-box ideas. The following story is an illustration of just how powerful mindmaps can be.

RESULTS: THE DIRECTOR'S BRIEFING

Anna Natsis, a senior civilian manager in the Defense Information Systems Agency (DISA), used a mindmap a few weeks after graduating from the School for Innovators in August 1994 to brief her new director, a three-star air force general, on her functions then as Chief of Quality Customer Service. She described him as a dynamo who had little time for all the managers to tell their stories. She was given only fifteen minutes.

"I knew I had to make my story stick and wanted to do it differently than everyone else," Anna says. "They had all trooped in with the inevitable military-like charts and viewgraphs, listing numbers, functions, challenges, etc." Anna decided to use a mindmap to cover "a lot in one look versus a lot of talk."

> I chose to use a small poster-like chart, approximately twenty by twenty-six inches. It was white on one side and gold on the back. I laid out the main branches: People, Issues, Customers, Initiatives, Opportunities, Challenges, and Functions. With the help of my folks

188

(who somewhat questioned my risk-taking), we laid out all the facets of these key branches, using different colors, of course. It turned out to be a great brainstorming session for us as we in essence developed our vision for the organization.

Since the director was an unknown for Anna, she was taking a big risk.

I rolled the chart up into a scroll, gold side showing, and wrapped a blue ribbon around it. (air force colors: blue and gold!) When I arrived for my appointment, there is no question that the secretary and executive assistant to the director thought something was wrong. I had no viewgraphs and would need no viewgraph machine. "Surely Ms. Natsis had lost it." When I entered the director's office, I'm sure he was wondering a bit, too. I spoke a minute or two describing what a mindmap attempts to do, and then rolled it out for him. Needless to say, he was a bit surprised! As I ran around the topics, focusing only on a few, I knew I had him when he said, "Wow." I just happened to get myself a director who was very tuned to visuals. (My luck.)

When I finished with my 15 minutes, the director said that what I had presented was not simply a mindmap, but a "Fused Picture of the Quality Customer Service Battlespace."

Fused picture of the customer or Service Battlespace..."

(Some background: Anna's director had come to her agency to leapfrog the telecommunications-and-information-systems organization into the twenty-first century. Part of his mission was to bring information to deployed war-fighters rapidly, reliably, secure, and in an understandable manner. He was championing a program designed to provide the war-fighter a "fused picture of his battle space," thus eliminating the need for many computers and massive amounts of data.)

Anna was later promoted to her current senior executive service (SES) rank, the civilian equivalent of a one-star general. She believes that the promotion has a direct connection back to how she explained her concepts to her new director using a mindmap—and her own willingness to be open to using new ideas and new tools to express them.

Adaptive Thinking
Copy
- Notice more
- Stop and stare
- Clip newspapers and magazines
- Combine and synthesize

How do you *really* learn how to think different, do different, get different results? How do you do you *really* do all this Level 6 stuff?

189

TOOL #68 (LEVEL 6–7):
The School for Innovators

The School for Innovators was created to do exactly that, to teach people how to think different, do different, and how to lead small groups of people into different—into attacking tough problems creativity to make change and innovation happen in their companies.

We launched the first School for Innovators in 1988 and began creating a cadre of innovators and problem solving facilitators within Exxon—a direct outgrowth of the Exxon Innovation Initiative. Since then, the School has evolved through a process of continuous customer-driven innovation. Students, graduates, and sponsoring organizations provide an ongoing flow of ideas for real-time incorporation into the curriculum.

The goal of the School is to transform people into skilled facilitators able to guide groups and teams in thinking different and jumpstarting innovation. Graduates return to become catalysts for faster, more effective translation of creative ideas into innovative solutions and bottom-line results.

We start with Level 1, 2, and 3 tools and techniques, the basics on which everything else is built. How to change and improve meetings. We take them though the same levels of change you've read about up to this point.

Then we start ootching them into Think 101 (how to think different) and the creative-problem-solving (CPS) model, Think 201 (thinking about thinking), and Results 101 (how to get different results)—all the underpinnings of the mindshift model. They begin to shed old habits and old thinking (Level 4), and copy and adapt new habits and new thinking (Level 5) as they practice and refine tying all the tools and techniques together with CPS. The seven or eight days of the School oootches everyone to higher and higher levels of change and thinking and deeper and deeper into Level 6.

190

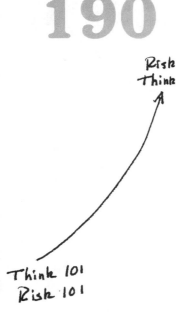

Risk
Think

Think 101
Risk 101

Working with the Colorado Mountain School and Mike Donahue, a fourth generation mountaineer, we've integrated rock climbing into the curriculum so that the metaphor of the Thinking Expedition gradually transforms into the reality of being "on expedition." Getting people to rope up in small teams to scramble to the summit of a mountain (Risk 101), or climb several hundred feet up a sheer rock face (Risk 201), pushes well into Level 7 for nearly everyone. It's so different that it's something they can't imagine themselves ever doing. They end up with a totally different perspective—not of the world, but of themselves. Level 7 suddenly becomes only a Level 6 different.

Return to normal, to who they were before the School for Innovators, just doesn't happen. They can't ever go back to being who they were. They've changed on the deep end. They've developed skills with tools and techniques that have changed how they see things, how they think about things, and how they will now work. For them to be able to go back and change the company, to lead innovation, they have to change themselves first. So that's what we focus on. That's what Me, Inc.® is all about, and going "on expedition" accelerates the process.

"The School changed my life" is probably the most common feedback we get from graduates. They return home very diff*f*erent. [For more details, see "History of Expedition XXXVII, page 299])

> *"Man's mind, stretched to a new idea,*
> *never goes back to its original dimension."*
> —Oliver Wendell Holmes

Graduates of the School go back home as innovators, thinking very different about everything, but they all have real jobs and their company has real problems they're returning to. Innovation and change are going happen as a result of the way they work, the way they integrate "diff*f*erent" back into their lives and their normal jobs and projects and the business on a daily basis. They go back and become part of their company's strategy for innovation by what they do and how they do it with what they've learned.

To Copy ...

Mindshift

| Copy Things | "See" and Notice |

Innovation is about *doing*.

**Idea
+
Creativity
+
Enhancement
+
Evaluation
+
Implementation**

INNOVATION!

Source: U.S. Air Force
Innovation Initiative, 1985

TOOL #69 (LEVEL 6):

A Strategy for Innovation

NOTE: The following is an extract from an article in *Fast Company* magazine, January 2000, written by Anna Muoio (See chapter 5/6, Moving into Different):

F&ST C@MPANY Magazine
January 2000

It was not until 1984 that Smith, then a Colonel and director of long-range planning for the Electronic Security Command ESC (now called the Air Force Intelligence Command), consciously began focusing on the process of innovation. And it was at this point that the U.S. Air Force's chief of staff made a bold request: Make the air force more innovative. "No one thought we could do it," says Smith. "A lot of people said that there's no way you can teach people to be creative and innovative. They're either born with it, or they're not."

That was the tone of the senior staff meeting on Security Hill in San Antonio in early May 1986. After the discussion on Innovation was over, General Jackson looked down the table at me and said: "Rolf, the boss (sic: The

192

USAF Chief of Staff) has *directed* us to play into his Air Force-wide Innovation Initiative. The staff is pushing back against it. Can you come up with a strategy for innovation that fits with the ESC Mast Plan?" It took us two weeks to put together and staff the paper across the headquarters. On 21 May 1986 we published Electronic Security Command Strategy Paper #3—INNOVATION and went into execution (see appendix C).

[Anna Muoio continues:] . . . But with a letter from his boss, Brigadier General Grover Jackson, authorizing him to go anywhere in the world and to do whatever it takes to "make innovation happen," Smith created the U.S. Air Force's first Office of Innovation. Its purpose? To spread innovative thinking and practices around the world—in places like the Strategic Air Command, the Space Command, and U.S. Air Forces Europe (USAFE)—and to create a global network of innovation centers in the field. "Our group had license to jump the chain of command to get things done. We were on a fast track for bold ideas.

The impact was immediate—and huge. Smith and his team received, on average, 600 ideas per year from 13,000 enlisted men and women "in the trenches" worldwide. But it was one young airman on the Kelly Air Force Base, in San Antonio, who taught Smith the most important lesson in cultivating an environment in which breakthrough ideas actually are allowed to break through. The first creation of Smith's office was something called Form Zero (bucking an air force rule that all forms had to be numbered beginning with the number one). Anyone in the force could use Form Zero to submit an idea. One day, Smith received a form from this airman: "Put speed bumps in front of the barracks," it said. "I'm on night shift and have to sleep during the day. I can't get any sleep because people speed down the street in their cars." Though admittedly this was not a breakthrough idea, it was a reasonable request, so Smith's office worked with the airman to implement a solution. He didn't get the speed bumps but the problem got fixed.

A few months later, the same airman sent in another form: "There's only one pay phone in the hallway of my barracks. Every time I talk to my girlfriend, everybody stands in the hall, listens, and laughs. Let's get a phone booth outside the barracks." Again, Smith's team worked with the airman to come up with a solution. Like clockwork, a few months later, they got yet another idea from the guy. "But the third time around," Smith says, "it was one of the biggest operational ideas we ever got. It absolutely blew us away. It solved a problem that I can't talk about—but that the air force had been working on for a long, long time." The lesson? "If you show that you truly pay attention to ideas—even the small, seemingly insignificant ones—then you'll create an environment in which people feel comfortable generating and offering them.

Anna Muoio's article highlights the criticality of setting the stage for innovation and creating an environment in which ideas are actually moved forward, turned into innovations.

THINKING ABOUT THINKING AT LEVEL 6—AGAIN!

"You can't make people be creative and innovative—they either are or they aren't!" I don't know how many times I heard that from the people I have worked with when I have been trying to spark innovation, teach innovation, or bring up systems and process to enhance creative thinking and innovation.

I find it "interesting" how often senior people will say that what they are doing is different because no one in their industry is doing it. The reality is that they aren't aware of what is going on in other industries (as you'll recall from Level 5).

ROLF'S THEORY OF RELATIVITY

Anna's story about her new director illustrates how relative Level 6 thinking can be. Though a mindmap was diff*f*erent to her director, he immediately transferred the concept to his own framework and definition base and made it familiar. Some-

194

thing is only different if you don't know about it. Someone else may have known about it for years. To them it might simply be Level 2: efficiency—doing the right things right.

PROS AND CONS AT LEVEL 6

When working with change at Level 6, keep in mind how *relatively different* "different" can be to different types and styles. Differences in KAI scores also become much more apparent when in the pros and cons of Level 6.

There is nothing to compare Level 6 ideas with...

PROS	CONS
Level 6 is exciting. It's where breakouts have their roots. When you begin working at this level, you are moving into the unknown of big possibilities, discoveries, unexpected opportunities, surprises, major transitions, and areas where all bets are off—or a WOW! with huge impact—in dollars, time savings, new markets, and totally new directions.	Level 6 is scary. Ideas at this level are different from 95 percent of all other ideas. There's nothing to compare them to or use to evaluate them to have any certainty that they will work. The likelihood of failure appears much higher to Level 1–5 thinkers.
In fact, because Level 6 is about different, you really have no idea what will happen or what you'll get.	It's much more difficult to sell ideas at this level because they are so unfamiliar and strange to normal thinking.
Being different is fun! People at this level love being "the first" and doing "the first"—breaking new ground.	Because they tend to generate lots of ideas, Level 6 thinkers often roll right over other people's ideas, and can dominate a team.
The risk is high, but the potential rewards are enormous. Level 6 ideas, if implemented, usually have fundamentally different results than any other level.	Different always gets attention (and not always positive attention. If you hook up with folks who don't like different, your life is not going to be a lot of fun.

2 – Sigma Change

Cutting   - Stopping doing things

Copying - Doing things other
              people are doing

PROS (continued)	**CONS** (continued)
Different always gets attention. When different connects, it really connects and it really sells. If you are in partnership with someone who is not a Level 6 thinker, who perhaps works very well at Levels 1, 2, and 3, whose style and type is very different from yours, then the two of you can go higher and farther and faster than any other team out there. Drawbacks to Level 6 are myriad. When I started listing cons, the list ran onto another full page. So I stopped listing them. Level 6 thinkers see them as positives anyway!	"It isn't easy being green" sang Kermit the Frog on *The Muppet Show*. And Level 6 Thinkers are definitely green. Lonely is the road of the innovator . . . This can seem to be a waste of time because so many ideas will clearly never be used. Without realizing it, Level 6 thinkers can cause a great deal of stress for others by stretching them more than they can handle. Level 6 changes can be very expensive. Most ideas come from people who are big idea-generators, not implementers. And sometimes Level 6 thinkers get so enamored with doing something different that they do it just for the sake of doing it.

LEVEL 6 FEAR: NORMALCY

- ➤ Fear of being different.
- ➤ Fear of being noticed.
- ➤ Fear of being laughed at.
- ➤ Fear of rejection.
- ➤ Fear of tradition.
- ➤ Fear of trying different things that might not work.
- ➤ Fear of falling off trying.
- ➤ Fear of the unexpected.
- ➤ Fear of getting hurt.
- ➤ Fear of exposure.

196

> "The one permanent emotion of the inferior man is fear; fear of the unknown, the complex, the inexplicable. What he wants beyond everything else is safety."
> —H. L. Mencken

LEVEL 6 STRESS

> ➤ Nothing different, everything the same, normal, boring through routine and repetition.
>
> ➤ Having to listen to boring people talk—*Blahblahblah* . . .
>
> ➤ Working with someone who is totally different from you in type and style and thinking.
>
> ➤ Being taken literally.
>
> ➤ Not being able to get an exciting Big Idea across.
>
> ➤ Trying to explain something to someone who just doesn't get it—doesn't have the Big Picture.
>
> ➤ Trying to be "*NORMAL*."

> "Nobody realizes that some people expend tremendous energy merely to be normal."
> —Albert Camus

"Water which is too pure has no fish." — Ts'ai Ken T'an

☑ TIP: SOME THINKING FOR DUMMIES

If thinking is predictable, it isn't thinking. (Duke Rohe) Ridiculous ideas can transform normal ideas into brilliant solutions. (Jimmy Cook)

TRANSITION TO LEVEL 7

When a change or idea is not only different but is so different that there is no known way to do it, when major obstacles leap out as soon as you start looking at the realities of implementation, when much of what you're looking at simply can't be done, you've shifted into the realm of impossible, the arena of magic and miracles. Moving from Level 6 to Level 7 is a transition from the possible to the improbable.

Change for Continuous Improvement		
Effective	-	Doing the right things
Efficient	-	Doing things right
Improving	-	Doing things better
Cutting	-	Stopping doing things
Copying	-	Doing things other people are doing

➤ Different . . .

➤ In what way might we . . .

➤ I wish . . . Wouldn't it be great if . . .

➤ Can't be done . . . Won't work . . . Impossible . . .

When you do come up with an idea that makes that change possible and when you've implemented it, you've reached Level 7. No, that's not correct at that point. Actually you just transformed the Level 7 into a Level 6.

Think about it.

198

ME, INC.®

Your task at Level 6 is to differentiate yourself. What are the truly unique factors and experiences, beliefs, principles, goals, and strengths that make you *you*? What's your mission? Most of the time, you'll find that your mission is unique. It applies to you and your unique vision, situation, business, and differentness. Your values, principles, strengths, and beliefs all add up to support you in carrying out your mission. Go back and finalize your mission now. Keep it to one short sentence. Whittle it down to its essence. Practice saying it out loud.

Use what you've learned at Level 6 to create a Me, Inc.® mindmap—a big picture of you that ties together everything you've come up with thus far. Each of the major areas you've worked on at the various levels of change can become a major leg. What are you starting to look like?

Your vision for yourself as a change agent and innovator should be emerging now. It isn't a question of whether or not you will be an innovator, its *how*. What does your new picture of yourself in the future look like?

"To change one's life:
Start Immediately.
Do it flamboyantly.
No exceptions."
—William James

A good friend of mine who worked with me both in the Innovation Center while I was in the air force, and later in Exxon took a very simple and straightforward Level 6 approach to Me, Inc.® When he was eighteen years old, Ronald Singleton simply changed his name. His whole name. All of it. He changed it so that his name would be his vision and his values.

He'd given it a lot of thought, he told me: "I've always felt a little weird or different with respect to the people I was around, so 'Nadir' sort of seemed to be a good fit."

"*Nadir*" means "unique."

Change

INCREMENTAL
Fine-tuning, sticking with things we are comfortable with but making small improvements.

FUNDAMENTAL
Results in a new way of doing our work – giving up some of the past which results in a quantum change in performance.

"'*Muwwakkil*' means 'trustworthy,' and I felt very strongly that I was trustworthy; however, this would remind me to always live up to that ideal."

"Being not easily upset was the part that didn't fit at all. I was something of a hothead. I remembered a high school teacher told me once that whenever you lose control, some-one else has it. That stuck with me and influenced me in selecting 'Saleem' for my middle name. '*Saleem*' means 'not easily aroused to anger.'"

Ronald Singleton is not the same person Nadir Saleem Muwwakkil is. Nadir is an innovation.

When you incorporate, you have to come up with a name for your new company, the new you. It's a chance to rename and reframe yourself, to give yourself a nickname.

"The more you're like yourself,
the less you're like anyone else."

—Me, Inc.®

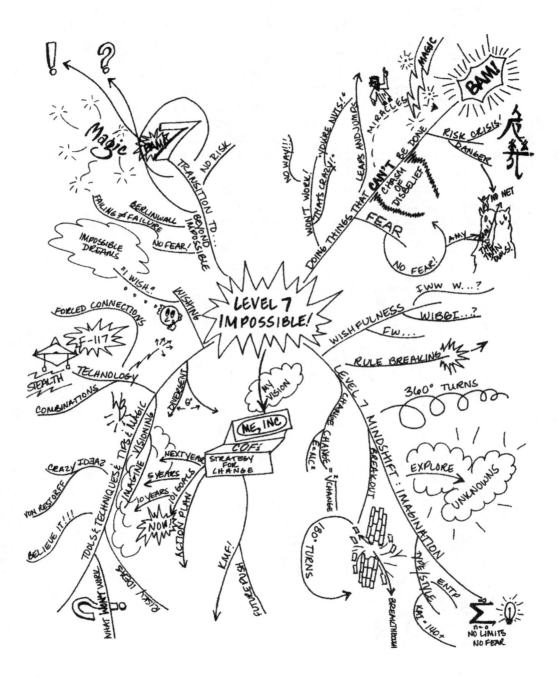

Level 7: Impossible
Doing Things That Can't Be Done

"You can't lead a normal life and be creative. You have to continually go where no others have gone."

In August 1992, while rock-climbing with my family on the Twin Owls in Estes Park, Colorado, we learned what Level 7 really meant. Some six to seven hundred feet up a sheer rock face my eight-year-old daughter Amy froze. We'd reached the end of a long ledge that tapered down to about two inches wide and sort of disappeared into a crack that went up around the corner. The rock face dropped off fast from the ledge into the valley farther and farther below. The wind was blowing, our clothes and jackets flapping. Cars and people in the parking lot we had started from look smaller than ants. Amy was tied into the rope in front of me but out forty feet on the disappearing ledge. Mike Donahue, our guide, was in front of Amy out of sight around the crack and up another hundred feet. Amy looked down, realized where she was, and saw only that it was impossible for her to move—pure Level 7. She froze. I tried everything I could think of to coach and coax her on, but she wouldn't budge. She was absolutely paralyzed, and she kept looking down at the ground six hundred feet below. Hypnotized, she simply could not move.

Nothing was working, and finally I gave up. Actually, I had a mindshift. Logic and reason wasn't working with Amy, so I tried to move into some parallel thinking with her—trying to think the way she must be thinking at Level 7. What couldn't I do? I certainly couldn't abandon her, leave here there clinging to bare rocks . . . so I did. I said, "Amy, my foot's slipping, and I can't stay here with you any longer. If you can't go up, I'm going to have to leave you here and go back down the ledge." And I took a step backwards.

202

"Jump and the net will appear."

Bam! Amy came to instant life, made the move—Bam!—made the next move, and—Zip!—shot around the corner and up the crack like a squirrel (Level 7). All grins, moving smoothly with a lot of adrenaline as Mike coached her on up. The rest was easy. We were there. She'd done the impossible. Her summit had been down below at the turn, not up at the top. Wow!

UNDERSTANDING LEVEL 7 CHANGE

There is risk to Level 7. Sometimes when there is no way to get out of a situation, it takes a leap of faith. We use rock climbing as an integral part of the School for Innovators, both literally and as a metaphor to help people think the impossible. Then when they *do* the impossible, when they reach the summit, nothing is hard any more.

Eight years later, when Amy was sixteen, she wanted to go back and climb the Twin Owls again with me, but differently. We did. It was different, but not the kind of different the first time had been. Now the original Level 7 wasn't even Level 6, it was maybe Level 5. We were just copying what we'd done eight years before. The Wow! was a lot smaller.

Change
Two Different Types

1ˢᵗ Order Change — Change that occurs within a given system which itself remains unchanged.

2ⁿᵈ Order Change — Change whose occurrence changes the system itself.

My insight: You never get a second chance at a first experience, and because of that a lot of people miss the first one. They miss the big Wow!

UNDERSTANDING LEVEL 7 THINKING

Level 7 thinking is imaginative thinking. It's breakout thinking. It's thinking which is forceful and which pushes through and emerges from a restrictive mental condition. It's paradigm breaking. It's possibility thinking. Creative thinking—in which something new is created. Childlike thinking. Naïve thinking. Magical thinking. Thinking the impossible.

THE LEVEL 7 MINDSHIFT

The mindshift necessary to think at Level 7 is imagining things that *can t possibly happen*. The single biggest mindshift you can make is to totally suspend judgment. As soon as you say "impossible" or "can't," you're judging. When you suspend judgment, anything's possible. To make this mindshift you have to be willing to play with ideas instead of immediately embracing or rejecting them.

This is the edge of the envelope—3-sigma thinking: as diff*e*rent as it gets. Breakout. The impossible, the unlikely, the uncomfortable. Consider the following mindshifts. To do things that can't be done, you have to breakout of normal patterns of thinking. To breakout, you have to think imaginatively.

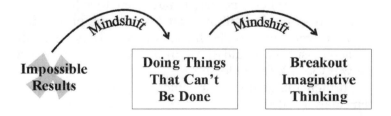

THINKING ABOUT THINKING

W. Somerset Maugham said: "Imagination grows by exercise, and contrary to common belief, is more powerful in the mature than in the young." Level 7 thinking forms a mental image of something that is neither perceived as real nor present to the senses. It deals with reality by rejecting it and

204

using the creative power of the mind—resourceful thinking. It's thinking that penetrates obstacles and restrictions in unexpected ways from unexpected directions.

RESULTS (LEVEL 7): RISKY PROSPECT DAY.

Back when I was still working exclusively for Exxon Company, USA, we ran an "innovation briefing" for Dave Lehman in the Central Production Division. This was one of the first innovation sessions outside of the Exxon's Marketing Department where my work had begun. Francesco Corona hit on the crazy idea of drilling riskier prospects as a way to overcome bottlenecks in production operations. He repeatedly wrote the idea down on blue slips from a variety of perspectives during the innovation briefing. Many of them were connected to the perception that management simply would not take risks or that management was too stubborn to try new concepts (Level 6 ideas). The more ideas Franco had about this, the more he began to focus on considering deeper and riskier plays in mature oil fields.

Dave Lehman jumped on the idea and on 30 August, one month after the Innovation Briefing, "Risky Prospect Day" became a reality. Dave's assessment of the perception (as part of management) was that to his knowledge, not a single well that had been presented to management had ever been turned down—and that they were simply not being brought to management's attention for fear of being turned down. Dave asked that a technical review, called Risky Prospect Day, be held and that management then look at the riskiest prospects for drilling that the various production geologists were aware of. He further offered to buy lunch for any geologist who could show him a legitimate prospect that was too risky to endorse.

Further, the geologists as much as possible would do their analyses at the "back of the envelope" level. Dave's five requirements for the prospects:

1. geologic map presentation describing the play concept
2. any additional data to support the idea
3. estimate of reserve potential
4. probable drill costs (optional)
5. a limit of fifteen to twenty minutes for the presentation.

Eleven risky prospects were reviewed, six were worked up for formal presentation, and one was to be worked up as soon as additional seismic data was acquired. Four prospects were in fact labeled too risky for Exxon to drill, and three of those were recommended to be promoted as farm-outs. Three lunches were bought and paid for the next day by Dave Lehman, and Risky Prospect Day was a big success. The first well drilled came in at a level that easily paid for all the rest.

The major benefits were not so much in the successful drilling but more in the creation of a forum for geologists to show their riskier thinking to management for evaluation prior to extensive workup and preparation for formal committee presentations and without the demoralizing effect of having an idea "turned down" publicly. The geologists later progressed to in-house workshops and seminars in which they shared skills and techniques for looking at risky prospects in very diff*e*rent ways, usually converting them into *not* risky prospects by drawing on the diversity of their pooled expertise.

TOOL #70 (LEVEL 7):
Ninety-Degree Turns

Aside from fear, some other big catalysts for Level 7 change are humor, accidents and mistakes. When you are intending to do A, and B happens instead, when you are traveling down one path and an accident turns you ninety degrees, when a punch line really hits you—there are opportunities for Level 7 ideas to break through.

TOOL #71 (LEVEL 7):
Can't

Think about some things that can't be done. We can't finish this project by Monday . . . we can't speed up the delivery date . . . we can't change the process. Then think about what would have to change to be able to accomplish those things. That's how you move toward the impossible. Even better, write down something that can't

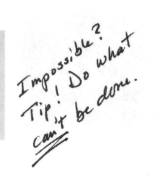

Impossible? Do what can't be done. Tip!

206

be done and give it to someone else who isn't familiar with it at all. Ask them how it could be done. They don't have the same mental blocks about it that you do (you know the facts and they don't).

Can't be done? Make something up out of thin air that would make it to possible to do what can't be done! Make up something that doesn't exist, something that isn't true. Tell the truth differently. Go to the extreme. Lie. Think about it—lying is one of the purest forms of creativity.

Nick Sealey, New Zealand market manager for KFC/ Pizza Hut and a School for Innovators graduate (January 1993) says that the tools his company has taken away from the School for Innovators have changed the way they treat ideas and things that can't be done or won't work. "We're not afraid to try things or to really empower people," Nick says.

RESULTS: KFC HOME DELIVERY

In 1994, Nick oversaw the introduction of home delivery into Kentucky Fried Chicken. He had been told that it just didn't work for KFC worldwide.

Nick had taken some time out and done some retrospective thinking. In New Zealand ten to fifteen years ago, 60 percent of KFC business was in meal replacement for families of four who would come out to eat or pick up buckets for carryout. That slipped down to 25 percent when TV dinners and other ready-made meals made inroads. Looking at some other trends and noticing some shifts in consumer habits in their stores, Nick felt his part of the world was different and had different potential, so he pushed to at least get the home-delivery concept tested in Australia. It tested very successfully in Australia, and the Australians passed their learnings and experiences over to the Kiwis. New Zealand took that template, adapted, modified, built on it (Level 5 copying). They ran several creative-problem-solving sessions with both staff and management, focused on roadblocks to success, and began implementing the *big ideas* they came up with.

They stopped treating Home Delivery as an attachment to the store business, made it a separate and distinct business (Level 4 change—stopping doing things, and Level 6 change—

LEVEL 6
Different
**Doing Things
That Haven't
Been Done**

a different business), and homed in on people, equipment, and some low-level technology ideas. All these changes combined to be a real Level 7 change, something that had already been shown wouldn't work and couldn't be done. By 1996 KFC Home Delivery Units in New Zealand were pushing four times the sales in the United States. Nick and his folks used that same approach next to double the volume Pizza Hut was doing in New Zealand.

"The key is people, their ideas, and not constraining yourself by being judgmental, no matter how outlandish those ideas may seem at the time," Nick says.

BRAIN DEAD?

Based on my experiences, three of the most difficult systems to change are religion (dogma and tradition), the military (structure, hierarchy, and commands), and hospitals (the right way to do things).

I recently had a long conversation with my brother-in-law, Paul Eckstein, about medicine, medical breakthroughs, and innovations. Paul is a heart surgeon, an electrical engineer (MIT), *and* a graduate of the School for Innovators (Expedition XXXIV). He has given me a number of big mindshifts. Consider the public's (sic: "normal") view of the operating room during open-heart surgery. They "kill" people every day, all day long, and then bring them back to life. To do open heart surgery, they have to stop your heart. They can't accurately work on your heart while it's beating. They drop your body temperature to room temperature (way down). Then they cut the arteries to the heart, tie them into the heart-lung machine, your heart stops beating, and you're dead. Then they fire up the machine, and it pumps for you instead of your heart (which is dead). They finish repairing and fixing up your heart, the valves, or whatever, they hook the arteries back up to it, disconnect the heart-lung machine and zap you with a defibrillator. Whamo! You're alive again. Magic. Can't be done. Impossible. But . . . there you have it.

Now rethink about that procedure and our view of alive or dead (very either-or): Life or death is the brain, not the heartbeat. The heart's purpose is to keep your brain alive. When the brain loses blood flow for more than five minutes (the brain heats up), you progress into brain damage and

Thinking is life!

208

quickly to being brain-dead, at which point you are really dead, even if you're "alive" with your heart still beating nicely. So . . . the first impossible breakthrough aspect of heart surgery lies in the idea of "suspended animation," lowering the body temperature to room temperature—to seventy degrees, a 28.6-degree drop—in order to preserve the brain longer than five minutes. At seventy degrees you may have closer to ten minutes of live brain time in case the heart-lung machine blows up or breaks down while your heart is "dead" and being worked on.

On the other end of impossible, doing things that can't be done in a hospital, consider this for balance: when you're talking about human life (and its alternative, death), and you have a standard procedure—a *proven* right way to do something in a hospital or an operating room—it's medical dogma. The idea of taking a chance with something new and different and *unproven* is really pushing the medical envelope, even if it is only a Level 3 improvement to make a procedure better, or a Level 4 idea to stop doing part of the procedure, or a Level 5 copying of some other hospital's or physician's procedure that you'd like to *try* on a patient (sounds like "experiment with").

With medicine you have to go very, very slowly and incrementally because the downside is so high—human life. And attitudes have changed—there is a scientific method (the *right* way to do something—Level 2). In the old days medical literature was like a case study, one or two cases or a hunch you were following, working on. Today you only publish a mathematically analyzed, statistically accurate study—your incremental changes have to undergo scientific and peer scrutiny and statisticians. Now there is much greater and more rapid communication, and also increasing scrutiny from colleagues and the public. There is much greater scrutiny on changes with lawsuits, and malpractice claims waiting in the wings. Innovators face tremendous onslaughts of liability issues.

So what do we do? How do we bring about higher levels of change in the field?

Wish for it. Wouldn't it be great if . . .

For example, diabetes. Approximately 10 percent of the population is diabetic; further diabetes has a serious global effect on the body. Today it's epidemic in children because

DIFFERENT

209

so many children are overweight, and you have to stick yourself frequently to test your blood sugar. Wouldn't it be great if . . . we had a device that doesn't require you to stick yourself constantly—a tiny insulin pump that automatically gave you a dose of insulin when you needed it. It's just over the horizon . . .

Malpractice? Hospitals and doctors would give anything for a "retrospectroscope," a device that would look back at the procedure you are about to do before you do it to so that you can see what you should have done instead of what you did before you ever reach the "did" stage. No more malpractice suits.

Wouldn't it be great if we could just glue cuts and wounds shut (Level 7) instead of bandaging? Superglue was developed to do that. It works and now at best its a Level 3 improvement.

Prozac and Viagra . . . ?

TOOL #72 (LEVEL 7):
Make a Wish

> Wishing is a powerful way to expand your ability to think and do the impossible at Level 7. I mentioned this back at Level 6 in the context of mess-finding. Now we'll look at wishes as a Level 7 tool to achieve breakthrough. Don't be afraid to make a wish and see where it takes you. This is how some incredible products started. "I wish we had an airplane that they couldn't see and couldn't shoot down. An invisible airplane, yeah, that's what I wish we had." What would we need to have that wish come true? A new material that doesn't reflect radar. A different wing angle that doesn't reflect radar. A whole strange-looking design that radar can't see. Bam! Suddenly the impossible is possible. When you solve those challenges, you have the Stealth Fighter—The Lockheed Skunkworks F-117.

In Iraq, the Stealth Fighter flew over two thousand combat missions and came away without a scratch. Able to go in and out without being seen or shot at, the pilots could take much more time and be much more precise (Level 1 and 2 doing), and achieve significantly improved accuracy (Level 3

Stealth...
The F-117

210

doing) to produce Level 7 results. With less than 3 percent of the total aircraft in the theater of operations, they hit more than 40 percent of the strategic pinpoint targets with amazing accuracy: 3-sigma leverage.

What would be the equivalent of a Stealth Fighter in your operations? What could it do to your bottom-line results? A great question often used by Joel Barker, the futurist, is: "What is impossible today, but if it were possible it would fundamentally change the way you do business?"

After making wishes, getting a little crazy can be the next best way to solve an impossible challenge. Here's a Level 7 process tool that you can use with a group working on a tough problem (Note that it requires twenty to thirty minutes to complete, and you will need some paper clips). The facilitator or guide asks each person to focus on the "mess" as they see it—the collection of impossible issues, challenges and problems on which the group is working.

TOOL #73 (LEVEL 7):
The Crazy Idea

Step 1: Messing Around
You write out the mess as a short statement on a blue slip and label it "Mess." Now, mess around with your mess. Restate it at least three different ways. Look at it from three different angles and try to get more different with each one. Write each problem restatement on a blue slip.

Step 2: Thinking Outside the Box
Look at your four different blue slips stating your problem and think, "Given this mess, what's the craziest idea I could try?" This is an idea that if you told it to someone, they would immediately conclude you're crazy. Now, write your crazy idea down on a blue slip and label it "Crazy."

Not all ideas are good ideas. But all bad ideas aren't totally useless. Take a hard look at your Crazy Idea. On a scale of zero to one hundred, with zero being totally useless and one hundred being perfect, where does your crazy idea sit? Grade your idea and write the score on your crazy idea blue slip.

Different

different (dif'ər•ənt, dif'rənt), *adj.*
1. Unlike in form, quantity, amount, or nature; Dissimilar. 2. Distinct or separate.
3. Differing from all others; unusual.

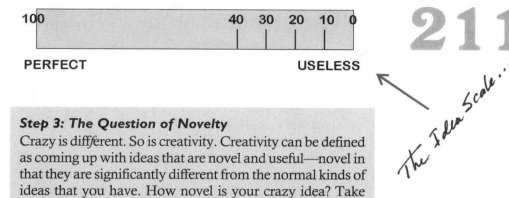

The Idea Scale...

Increase the rating on the Idea Scale.

Step 3: The Question of Novelty

Crazy is diff*f*erent. So is creativity. Creativity can be defined as coming up with ideas that are novel and useful—novel in that they are significantly different from the normal kinds of ideas that you have. How novel is your crazy idea? Take another blue slip and label it "Novel:" What elements of the idea make it significantly diff*f*erent—novel—from other ideas you've had?

Step 4: Forcing Perspective

Now take another blue slip and label it "Useful." What was it about the idea that kept you from giving it a score of zero? What small aspect of the idea is "useful?"

Take another look at your idea. It really is pretty weak, isn't it? What's missing from your idea that—if it were included in the idea—would significantly move it toward the perfect end of the scale? Write that on a third blue slip labeled "Missing." Clip together your "Novel," "Useful," and "Missing" blue slips so that they don't accidentally get mixed in with anyone else's in the group.

Step 5: The Sanity Check

At this point you may find a "sanity check" useful. Just how crazy is your idea, really? Find a partner: turn the "crazy" blue slip face down and exchange it with the person sitting next to you for their *crazy* idea. Turn your partner's blue slip over and read it. Don't discuss it, just read it.

Step 6: The von Restorff Effect

Research by a German psychologist, H. von Restorff, points out that the more bizarre an idea, the more arousing it is, the more memorable it is, and the more unique it is. It stands out. Great ideas stand out. Take a blue slip and label it "Unique" and write down what you see as

212

unique about your partner's crazy idea. What makes it stand out? Where does it have potential for greatness?

Step 7: Positive Negativity

Now, looking at your partner's idea, start first with the positive (remember PIN?). Take a blue slip, label it "Advantage," and write down a possible advantage hidden in your partner's crazy idea. Next consider the crazy idea from a "how-to-implement" angle. What limitations does the idea have that will raise questions? What roadblocks do you think it will run into? Note that this is not a negative viewpoint; it is an effort to bring positive, focused critical analysis to the idea. Take a new blue slip, label it "Limitations" and write down any major limitation you see.

Step 8: Energizing Ideas

Innovation starts with an idea and can also end there. To move from a creative idea to an innovation, there must be action. The idea must be implemented. As Peter Drucker once pointed out, "All ideas must degenerate into work if anything is to happen." Imagine that you were given the job of implementing your partner's crazy idea. Take a blue slip, label it "Step #1," and write down the first step you would take to get this idea moving—not fully implemented, just energized. Then assume that step number one has been done, what would step number two be? Write it down.

Step 9: Fast-forward Clarification

Now you're ready to have a clarifying, structured discussion. *This will be done in two stages*: first your crazy idea and then your partner's crazy idea. Choose one of the two crazy ideas (yours or your partner's) and take two minutes each to first explain what you saw as

1. unique and novel
2. what advantages you found and what was useful about it
3. what limitations the idea had and what you felt was missing in the idea

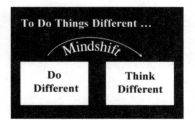

This is a listening process. While one of you is reading his or her thoughts from the blue slips, the other should try to listen as intently as possible. Don't think about what you are going to say when it's your turn. Take turns reading your blue slips and listening.

Step 10: Action Planning

When you have finished sharing all of the blue slips for *one* of the crazy ideas (yours or your partner's), discuss the possibility the idea has for implementation. Then jointly, as a team, come up with two more blue slips with action steps for moving the idea towards reality. Label these blue slips "Step #3" and "Step #4."

Step 11: The Final Touches

After you have finished either yours or your partner's idea, clip all of the blue slips for the idea together in the following order:

1. MESS
2. CRAZY
3. NOVEL
4. UNIQUE
5. ADVANTAGE
6. USEFUL
7. LIMITATIONS
8. MISSING
9. STEPS #1, #2, #3, #4 (or more).

Combining all of these Turns a CRAZY IDEA into a different concept

Take a blank blue slip, label it "Name" and come up with a catchy name that capitalizes on the novelty or uniqueness of this crazy idea. Clip the "Name" blue slip on the top of the appropriate stack. Then go back to step 5 and start the process over again with your partner's crazy idea.

You and your not-so-crazy partner have now converted two crazy ideas into concepts with shape and action plans. You've also expanded your normal thinking into the realm of impossible. Approximately 20 percent of the ideas pro-

214

duced with this technique can lead to near-term break-through improvements!

☑ TIP! (WATCH OUT)

The crazy-idea process is a real stretch for some people, particularly those who are more comfortable at the other end of the spectrum of change. Not only does the mindshift into Level 7 thinking push their thinking, having to write so many blue slips (which they see as being pretty worthless) pushes them as well. Steve Hammond, a friend of mine through the Association for Managers of Innovation, and Director of Strategic Planning for Zurich Life, used the process with a group of their insurance brokers as part of a strategic thinking session he was facilitating. One participant begged Steve to stop the process and actually became physically uncomfortable with it before it was finished. Nonetheless, the final crazy idea turned out to have some very good, not-so-crazy thinking wrapped around it.

And here's an example of what can happen when you stick with it all the way through to implementation.

RESULTS (LEVEL 7): CRUSHING WITHOUT CRUSTING
Battelle National Laboratories

In 1995, I ran a Thinking Expedition for Battelle National Laboratories, which does R & D contract work strictly for the government, addressing the problem of disposing 3 million tons of napalm which the navy had stockpiled in Southern California. The napalm was stored in aluminum containers, and the navy contract required them to be crushed. The project was behind schedule. We laid out the detailed end-to-end engineering design and process flow on the wall with Post-it notes (the engineering design group had previously come up with "The Solution") and then we assigned the "wrong" people to work on each stage (i.e., people who had no expertise in that particular aspect of the engineering or operation). Then we used the crazy-idea process. One crazy idea got it back on track. *"Don't crush them."* In what way might we crush the containers without crushing them, without having to make the machinery that pounds them flat? Impossible. Yet the cylinders could be "crushed" by evacuating the air out of them. When you suck out all of the air, atmospheric pressure crushes the

Different vs. Similar

If you want Breakout Thinking, focus on differences, not similarities, with previous experiences or solutions.

cylinders. Basic physics. This idea and several other engineering design ideas accelerated the project by some four months and helped put it back on schedule.

ROLF'S THEORY OF RELATIVITY

This is the shakiest level of change when it comes to relativity. It's the one you will most likely hear arguments about, because everyone's level of knowledge is different, and because of that, their interpretation of what is impossible is different. Also depending upon whether someone is a strong adapter (Level 1, 2, or 3 thinker—effectiveness, efficiency, improving) or a strong innovator (Level 4, 5, 6, or 7 thinker—cutting, copying, different, impossible), their perspective of and beliefs about impossible will be different. An impossible change to a Level 1 person may be only a Level 1 or 2 change to a Level 7 person. A lot of "Impossible!" is tied up in not knowing—in the unknown. The relativity here has a lot to do with the following question:

> *How do you know what you don't know*
> *if you don't know what you don't know?*

PROS AND CONS OF LEVEL 7

216

PROS	CONS
When you have a Level 7 idea and it comes to fruition, it often carries with it brilliance, the mark of genius. The positives are incredible change—you've achieved the impossible and with it can come fame and wealth and incredible success.	There's a lot of risk to Level 7 ideas because beyond Level 6 (different), you're in new territory. There's no historical perspective. Frequently you are going against long-established and well-proven ways of dealing with something. The biggest road blocks are not in the technology challenges but in the perception of what is possible. You're shattering something a lot of people have believed in. That's a powerful mindshift, and some people can't handle that. There'll be fallout. There's a fine line between genius and insanity! You may have to generate fifty ideas to get one breakthrough—and Level 7 thinkers often do. Despite the breakthrough, people will still remember those fifty crazy ideas. You can't look crazy if everyone around you isn't suspending judgment. Your ideas may eliminate people's jobs. People may quit because the change is so radical. The impact of change at this level is huge and has the potential to be unmanageable. You're on the far side of 3-sigma—different thinking. You're on expedition. You're exploring. You're moving into the unknown and some people won't want to come along. Others are sorry they went . . .

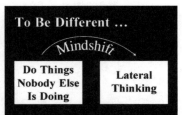

To Be Different ...

Mindshift

Do Things Nobody Else Is Doing

Lateral Thinking

LEVEL 7 FEAR: DISBELIEF

➤ Fear of the known . . . you don't want to believe it.

➤ Fear of the unknown.

➤ Fear of not having a basis of comparison.

➤ Fear of problem size.

➤ Fear of believing.

➤ Fear that I *can t* do that.

➤ Fear of a fault, a weakness in the safety system below you.

➤ Fear of total failure.

➤ Fear of the point of no return.

➤ Fear of death, of not coming back alive.

➤ Fear of others dying.

Level 7 is the sum of all other fears below it.

LEVEL 7 STRESS: NOT KNOWING

➤ Who is watching me?

➤ Who is judging me?

➤ Am I nervous because I stand out?

➤ What if I end up all alone.

➤ What if I "get a little crazy" because I really am?

➤ Will I find someone to share my dreams of the impossible?

A basic Level 7 stress is not knowing. Emergencies. Having to invent something from nothing. Stressing because your mind is racing but unable to fill in any possibility.

Hammering away at all this is not being able to "un-know" something—you *know* it and you can't get rid of it, you keep thinking about what you know, and it stops you cold. For instance, stress replaces fear when you are about to rappel off a cliff and you *know* you only have eighty-three feet of rope but the distance down looks like at least one hundred feet. Jump out of a plane at 12,500 feet—*you know you have a parachute . . . but you also know you're at 12,500 feet*!!! Putting your hand in the garbage disposal to get something out—you know it's turned off, but the consequences if it

217

"If you were afraid of all the bad or negative things that could happen in life—you wouldn't do anything . . . you'd be paralyzed."

—Juliane

" The more you know, the less you understand."
— Tao Te Ching

218

automatically turns itself back on. Trying not to know what you know when you're doing creative problem solving.

A Level 7 stress often comes from being around someone who is impossible to be around. Listening to someone who can't be understood, or who can't understand. Sometimes people have deep-seated, fundamental beliefs that make understanding something different irreconcilable. "I don't understand how you can think like that!!!"—"Do you think you ever could?" This is a stress caused by impossibility.

☑ TIP: SOME THINKING FOR DUMMIES

Trash Bad Ideas: When you come to a meeting, bring with you a small trash pail and place it just outside the door. When you have a crazy idea that you know is crazy, write it down and throw it out in the trash pail outside the door. Encourage all participants to write down their crazy ideas and throw them out as well. At the end of the meeting, take the pail back to your office and read as many of the crazy ideas as you can. Clean out the pail for the next meeting. Transcribe and storyboard these crazy ideas, distribute them back to the team after the meeting. (Michael Zeitlin)

TRANSITION TO WHAT'S NEXT

So what happens beyond impossible? Where do you go when you've done what you didn't think you could do? If your goal is continuous improvement, you start the whole process again back at the beginning. You take the impossible, your Level 7 idea, and you implement it because it's the right thing to do—effectiveness, Level 1. Then you do it more efficiently (Level 2); you improve it (Level 3); you do away with parts of it you now find you don't need (Level 4, cutting); you look outward and copy things other people are doing that can make it better (Level 5); you make it diff*f*erent (Level 6); and now you're back to impossible (Level 7).

Of course, every idea won't go through each level, but you can easily see how once you've done the impossible, you have to start over somewhere if you are going to continue to be innovative. Breakthroughs don't stay breakthroughs very long.

Lateral Thinking

lateral thinking (lăt'ər-əl thǐng'kǐng) *adj.* 1. Of, relating to, or situated at or on the side. 2. Shifting perspective so as to view or consider something from another direction, including backwards.

Here's a new mindshifting insight for me: Level 7 change *only exists in your mind*. Once you bring it out of your head, out of your Level 7 thinking, and *do* it, it isn't a Level 7 change at all. Because you actually just *did* it. A Level 7 change does not ever exist; the *idea* of a Level 7 change exists as Level 7 thinking.

Think about it.

219

220

Me, Inc.
[today's date]
My Big 3 Lifetime Goals
1.
2.
3.
Next 3 Years
1.
2.
3.
6 Months to Live…
1.
2.
3.

Breakthrough

Doing something so different that it cannot be compared with any existing practices or perceptions.

ME, INC.® CHANGES AT LEVEL 7

By going through this process of mentally incorporating, you can emerge with a new attitude towards change. Mentally incorporating yourself changes your thinking about yourself. Now you can aim toward the future—your vision of yourself. Think of the impossible. Push your own mental envelope and really stretch. Make a wish. Make some more. Take a relook at your 101 goals. What do you want to become in ten or twenty years? Grab a blue slip and start a short Me, Inc.® list that will really get you focused and thinking *different* (Tip! Write small and keep them all on one side of the blue slip):

What Are Your Big Three Lifetime Goals?

Then bring your forward thinking back a little closer:

What Are Your Big Three Goals for the Next 3 Years?

And then get very, very focused. What would your Big Three Goals be if you discovered that you only had six months to live?

6 Months to Live: My Three Big Goals

Share this with your family. Keep it in your wallet so that you have it with you all the time.

And use them to get serious. Sketch out a personal vision of the future, *your* future, five-to-ten years from now. Describe it: What will you be doing, what will have happened? How will your values and principles have played into that future? What will have changed?

With your vision, mission, values, principles, and goals clearly defined, the challenge becomes how to make them all an integrated, connected reality—how to make it all happen. There are a number of underpinning elements, things that must be in place, that will be absolutely critical if you are to succeed. These are your *critical success factors* (CSFs)—things that either *must* or *need* to be in place for you to succeed with your mission, vision, and purpose. There should be no more than eight total (without the word "and" in any of them) and each should contain either the word "must" or "need" to be complete. Paired comparison analysis (PCA) is an excellent tool to use to think your CSFs through.

Finally, consider some broad strategies to follow in carrying out your mission, for accomplishing your goals, for leveraging and applying your strengths, values and principles to move you toward your vision. Write them down on some blue slips so that you can rearrange them in an order that makes sense to you.

221

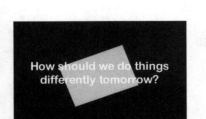
How should we do things
differently tomorrow?

What's Next?

Every ending is also a beginning. If you are going to succeed at continuous improvement, you have to be continuously innovative, and that means continuous change. Change doesn't start with a new beginning. It starts when you let go of the way you used to do something—the ending.

What do you do when your wish comes true, when you achieve the impossible? You can't stop, because you can bet that someone is already copying (Level 5) you right now. You've done the impossible—suddenly it's not impossible. You can't just stop changing if you are truly going to be innovative.

When you've achieved the impossible, you need to come up with a new vision to carry you forward. Think about the Berlin Wall. I remember talking to my wife's uncle, Horst Hirsch, a Berliner, in 1989. He'd been a sixteen-year-old during the fall of Berlin in World War II and had watched the Russians take the city. He later saw the Russians put up the Berlin Wall, and he knew it was a permanent reality. It would never come down. He knew that the Soviet Union would never let that happen. *"Nicht möglich."* Impossible. From his point of view, the wall would always be there. Germany would never be reunited. The Soviet empire would last forever. Two months after our conversation, the wall came down. Today that's all old news—it's "So what?" stuff.

The entire Eastern Bloc is busy reinventing itself beyond impossible. In fact there isn't any Eastern Bloc anymore—East Germany and West Germany are back to being Germany, and Hungary, Poland, and the Czech Republic have joined NATO. The rest of the old Eastern Bloc and a lot of other countries on the sidelines of NATO are now members of the Euro-Atlantic Partnership Council (EAPC)—a multilateral forum where NATO member and partner countries meet on a regular basis to discuss political and security-related issues and develop cooperation in a wide range of areas. Estonia, Latvia, Lithuania, Bulgaria, Romania, Ukraine, Georgia, Uzbekistan, Turkmenistan, Tajikistan, Kazakhstan and Azerbaijan—just to name some we never used to be able to even name. At present, there are forty-six members and rising continually: nineteen NATO member countries and twenty-seven partner countries. What was impossible isn't. It's just different now. Think about it!

☑ TIP!

Level 7 doesn't stay Level 7 very long.

224

Level 7 is really Level 6. It's only Level 7 in your head while you're at Level 7 thinking—while you *think* it's impossible. Once you shift to doing and implementing the change, it's not impossible anymore—you just did it, changing it into simply different. It has instantly moved down to Level 6.

WHAT'S NEXT TOOL #1:
Beyond Impossible

Don't wait! After you've done something big, something really different or impossible—and you have it working—it's not what it was. Now it's out there, subject to straightforward Level 5 copying and adapting by your competitors. And when you find yourself thinking about that, it's your inner signal to mindshift to beyond impossible. I'm not ready to call it Level 8 yet, but it is a change, and it means it's time to get off the curve you're on and jump on another.

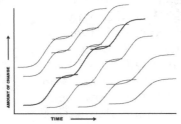

Don't ride your Level 7 idea all the way back down to Level 1, 2, or 3, where you can bog down in making it more effective or efficient or in trying to improve it. Look at where you are, look at the height you've reached, and consider the new perspective you now have with this Level 7 breakthrough idea of yours. Use that for leverage, draw on all the smaller Level 2, 3, 4, 5, and 6 thinking you did to position yourself to reach Level 7. Start looking for places where you can set up a new high camp, a new position from which you can break out and find a different route to new summits, to new and different areas to explore. And then do it again—and again, and again.

☑ **TIP!**
"KMF . . . Keep Moving Forward!"
—Chuck Gray, Exxon Chemicals

Change HOW You Think
- Think about the way you think
- Shift your perceptions
- Look at things differently
- Follow your intuition
- Force connections
- Be different   *... lateral thinking*

THINKING BEYOND IMPOSSIBLE

If all of this makes you exhausted, if you can't handle any more change, if the rate of change coming at you is overpowering, then move beyond impossible. *Change* change.

That concept hit me very hard a few years ago while I was talking with a U.S. Army brigadier general, the chief of staff at Fort Hood, Texas. He raised it as a challenge. "The army can't take any more change," he said.

> "We've gone through reengineering, downsizing, TQM, budget cuts, and a war [Iraq]. We've cut the fat, and we've given all the blood we can—and now it's down to bone and tissue. We've got to get hold of change. We've got to *change* change."

Bam! What a thought. *Change* change? How?

What if we viewed the 7 levels of change as having an underlying mathematical basis? What if we viewed change as a mathematical function, an expression of laws of physics and dynamics: I know from all the work we'd been doing with the 7 levels that the relationships between the changes—the delta or change between each of the changes themselves—is not a straight line progression or extrapolation.

When I graduated from college with a major in mathematics, I taught high school physics in California. Going back to those roots, you'll recall from Level 1 that the simplest form of change is a change of position: moving from point A to point B. The next is speed, the rate of change of position. That is followed by acceleration, change of change of position. With that in mind, I reflected on the thinking of some great minds (Level 5 copying) and hit on a hypothesis: The energy or effort, *e*, that's required to make a particular change is equal to the mindshift, *m*, required times the square of the level of change, *c*, that is being made.

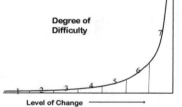

Degree of Difficulty

Level of Change

225

$$e = mc^2$$

The mindshift relates to the change in thinking that correlates to the particular level of change. How to *change* change?

226

What if we took the square root of change! That would flatten the upward-ramping curve of change into a flat line. It would convert the exponential aspects of change to a straight-line relationship.

$$\sqrt[2]{\overline{\text{Change}}} \cong \textbf{ootching}$$

WHAT'S NEXT TOOL #2:
Ootching

How to change change for nonmathematicians? Return to baseline. After each major change, touch back to the lower levels—Level 1—effectiveness; Level 2—efficiency; Level 3—improving. And on your way up, employ the highly technical tool of "ootching," which means shifting up increasingly steep slopes from level to level in *small increments*. I picked up the concept of ootching things while working a strategic redirection with David Messner, at the time the corporate strategic thinker for E-Systems, a high-tech defense firm in Dallas. David was a U.S. Air Force Academy graduate and Harvard M.B.A., and he is one of the sharpest and deepest thinkers I know. He used ootching to describe the way a lot of ideas and concepts were developed at E-Systems, and the word instantly connected for me. It says it all relative to change.

How fast can you make an ending, transition through the neutral zone—the vacuum the ending creates, and move on into a new beginning is all part of what makes each level what it is. It's easier for most people to make those lower level changes more quickly. The higher you get, the more ootching may be required. And thinking differently is ootching—the square root of change.

Dif*f*erent Thinking

Rethink yourself
- Get in the habit of changing your habits
- Redecide things regularly
- Shift perspectives and perceptions

ME, INC.®

The end? No . . . you're *never* finished with your mental incorporation. Now all you need is an action plan to ootch you toward your vision. There are a number of underpinnings that must be in place to support your future. These are critical success factors (CSFs)—things that either must or need to be in place for you to succeed. Try to limit yourself to no more than seven CSFs. None of them should contain the word "and," making them compound statements. Separate any compound thoughts into two CSFs. Each should contain the words "must" or "need." A must is necessary and means you cannot accomplish your goal without it. A need is important, and if you don't have it, your goal will be difficult to reach (Levels 3, 4, and 6 thinking). These CSFs form the baseline for determining your strategies.

Consider some broad strategies to follow as you carry out your mission, for accomplishing your goals, for leveraging your strengths, values, and principles to move you toward your vision (Levels 3, 4, 5, and 6 thinking).

Then move from strategic thinking to action thinking. Ask yourself, "What are the steps I need to take now to succeed?" And keep in mind that while you are creating your vision, you are moving up the 7 levels of change.

Now that you have put yourself through the entire Me, Inc.® process, look back at your work, edit, condense, and refine. KMF! Don't stop changing. Check your progress. Reevaluate regularly. Rethink. Reinvent your Me, Inc.®

227

LEVEL 7
Impossible

**Doing Things
That Can't Be
Done**

Getting Ready for Change
(Individuals)

My work with teams and organizations has led to some interesting insights into how people view change and deal with change. In February 2002, I was invited to give a presentation about the 7 levels of change at a Canadian conference focused on meeting the challenge of innovation in government. I heard some excellent talks and met some interesting colleagues with new ideas and insights, and of course wrote down some great ideas. This figure was developed by a Canadian group (An Idea Whose Time Has Come, Inc.) who were at the conference. Based on the eighty-twenty rule, their figure puts a big-picture perspective on how change may be viewed by an organization:

This is a great graphic because it resonates with something I've been saying in our School for Innovators and on Thinking Expeditions for the last twenty-five years: "They don't all want innovation. Go for the 5 percent who are excited, and worry about the rest later." I believe that if you are trying to make innovation happen in an organization, or are trying to roll out a *big change*, be selective. You need to find allies and you need them fast. They aren't going to be down in the 80 percent. Get the 5 percent working with you, and then team up with them to go after the next 5 percent and then the next after that.

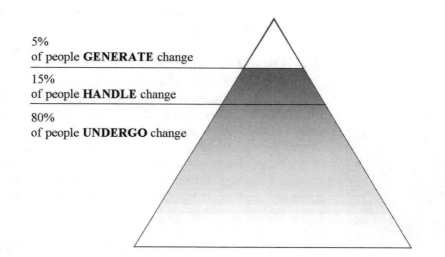

5%
of people **GENERATE** change

15%
of people **HANDLE** change

80%
of people **UNDERGO** change

230

Take a quick look back at the change "resistance-acceptance" chart.

How we see change clearly depends on where we sit in that pyramid—and the way I see it, where you sit in the pyramid isn't hierarchical, or related to the organizational structure. It's related to who you are in terms of your creative type and style, *and* who everybody else is in terms of their creative type and style. In your (or any) organization:

> ➤ What types and styles generate change?
> ➤ What types and styles handle change?
> ➤ What types and styles undergo change?

In the process of working with teams on Thinking Expeditions and with individuals in the School for Innovators, we've discovered some strong correlations between thinking style, problem solving style, learning style, personality type, and degree of comfort with the various levels of change.

Before joining a Thinking Expedition or attending the School for Innovators, everyone completes the Kirton Adaption-Innovation (KAI) Inventory and the Myers-Briggs Type Indicator (MBTI). These inventories are based on differing but broadly related theories of cognitive processes. The KAI defines differences in creative style (thinking), and the MBTI defines differences in personality type (behavior). I have been using the Kirton Adaption-Innovation (KAI) inventory in my work continuously since 1986 and the MBTI in combination with the KAI since 1992.

The combined use of the inventories gives us two different vectors of insight and creates leverage points around which we shape and customize the approach, design, content and flow of a Thinking Expedition.

CREATIVE STYLE

Creative style tells us quite a bit about how a person deals with their environment when solving problems, and I've found that it's also a strong indicator of how people are likely to deal with change.

Adaption-Innovation theory has roots that date back to 1961 and work done by Michael Kirton in observing organizational behavior, as well as to an early paper relating to an inventory developed by Kirton in 1976. Kirton's studies of organizations going through major change reflected, in many cases, substantial delays in the introduction of change and objections to new ideas, as well as the rejection of suggestions

IMPOSSIBLE!

by certain managers who were perceived to be "outside" of the establishment. Kirton believes that such resistance to change is independent of the abilities and intelligence of the individuals involved and much more related to the creative styles of the managers and differences in thinking.

The KAI inventory is extremely useful in compressing the time it takes for individuals or a teams to shift perspective. KAI theory helps us define and measure an individual's characteristic style of decision making and problem solving. According to the theory, everyone can be rated on a one-dimensional continuum of scores ranging from highly adaptive (those who solve problems within an existing system) to highly innovative (those who solve problems by challenging the norms of the system).

The KAI Inventory is a simple, one-page form of thirty-two questions with a five-point response range that yields a total KAI score which can range from thirty-two (extreme adapter) to 160 (extreme innovator). The scores are distributed normally over the general population with a mean of about ninety-five; men's scores are normally distributed around a mean of ninety-eight, and women's scores normally distributed around a mean of ninety-one.

Note that the KAI Inventory is not a measure of creative *ability*—it is a measure of *preferred creative style*. We do the feedback and debriefing in a group or team setting where the group is actively engaged in exploring and solving a problem, such as a Thinking Expedition, a strategic planning offsite, or a problem-solving workshop.

Generally speaking, the more strongly adaptive the score, the more the person prefers smaller, more incremental changes and in the extreme may be resistant to almost any significant change. The more strongly innovative the score, the more inclined the person is likely to seek out change, to prefer large-scale discontinuous change, and to function as a change agent, leading the way to change. In the extreme, the innovator is interested in change for the sake of change.

CREATIVE STYLE AND CHANGE: CORRELATION

I believe that there is a direct correlation between KAI scores and the 7 levels of change.

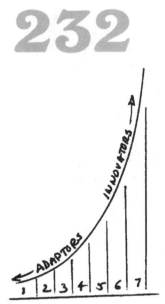

232

Strong adapters will tend to focus on Levels 1, 2, and 3 (effectiveness, efficiency and improving). Their operative change words are "better" and "improve."

Mid-range adapters will connect well with the concept of continuous improvement, moving into 2-sigma thinking at Level 4 (cutting) to eliminate waste. Typically, adapters will protect the *status quo* and try to work within the existing system, fine-tuning process and procedures, and clarifying rules and objectives. Time-management and redundant functions are favorite targets for their ideas. They tighten up the boundaries and borders of the system in which they work. In CPS sessions, adaptors tend to be more convergent in their thinking and approaches.

The mid-range innovator begins to start thinking about change at Level 4 (cutting) but with more of a focus on stopping doing things that don't make sense in order to make room to copy and adapt (Level 5) something interesting that they've seen someone else doing that will lead to effectiveness and efficiency. In particular they seem to want to get rid of rules and procedures that are "dumb" or restrictive or which are "simply common sense" and unnecessary.

When strong innovators think at Level 4 (cutting), they want to blow everything up and start from scratch. Their tendency is to use Level 5 change to copy something different in order to get a big change in place sooner and to more easily justify it for their more adaptive teammates ("Look, these guys at Kapow Corporation are doing it and it works great for them," they'll say). Their natural bias is towards 3-sigma thinking, the new and diffferent or Level 6 change. They continuously push their thinking into Level 7, generating lots of unusual, off-the-wall, extreme, and crazy ideas that occasionally turn into a really *big* change. In general, innovators will attack the *status quo* and try to bring in ideas from outside the system. They loosen up the boundaries and borders of the system in which they work, making it more "porous" by eliminating (or breaking) some rules and guidelines. During CPS sessions, innovators tend to be more divergent in their thinking and approaches. Charged with reengineering, they are likely to come up with two very different ideas:

Adaptor: "Cut fat and eliminate waste."

Innovator: "Fire all the managers!"

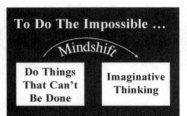

Similarly, adapters and innovators, looking at exactly the same change from their respective sides of the KAI fence, will often see the same thing as a very different level of change. The innovators will tend to *minimize* the implications of the scope and level of a change, while the adapters will *maximize* the implications of its scope and impact. Thus, an innovator may see some particular change as a simple improvement (Level 3 change), while the adapter might see it as radically different (Level 6), or in the extreme, as a change that is impossible to implement (Level 7).

I was reflecting on this during one of our early School for Innovators Expeditions in Colorado as there was a lull at the moment. Everyone had just changed seats again for the nth time, and I had regrouped them into table teams of four.

NOTE (AND TOOL #74):

We shift people around constantly during the School or on Thinking Expeditions in order to:

1. introduce "change" and "diff*f*erent" quickly at an experiential level;
2. disrupt everyone's normal behavior patterns (habits) of anchoring to one chair at one table for an entire course;
3. create a low level of continuous disequilibrium and uncertainty to reinforce the expedition metaphor;
4. ensure that everyone interact with and gets to know everyone well in a short period of time.

We know that the people with more innovative KAI scores enjoy the movement and change. Conversely, the people with more adaptive scores are uncomfortable with changing seats, often are stressed by it, and in some cases simply will not move when everyone else does—unless we tell them "that's one of The Rules on a Thinking Expedition." If it's The Rule, then it's okay. Generalizing,

adaptors avoid punishment,

while innovators seek reward.

KAI SUBSCORES

Which leads me into KAI subscores and "rules." The total KAI score can be broken down into three interrelated subscores:

234

> *Rule/Group Conformity (R)*, or style of relating to agreed structure and rules in a group or organization. The more adaptive tend to prefer rules and structure that provide them "good" guidelines within which to work or solve a problem ("It's the law"). The more innovative style tends to bend or break the rules as they see necessary ("That's dumb!").

> *Sufficiency of Originality (SO)*, or style of idea-generation, i.e., how much originality or novelty is preferred. The more adaptive style is satisfied with a sufficient number of good ideas that are well-focused to, and fit with, the problem—and have a likelihood of being accepted. The more innovative style will generate a large number of novels ideas, many of which will be seen as nonrelevant or useless.

> *Efficiency (E)* relates to how a person prefers to solve problems. The more adaptive uses the existing system or processes, and works within the system to make the system work for them more efficiently. They will make the end fit within their means. The more innovative style pays less attention to detail, and is less concerned with resources, time, and effort, and is often seen as inefficient by the general population. The will often use the ends to justify the means.

Each of the KAI subscores contributes a different "weight" to the total KAI score and are evidenced differently in behavior. They are also *not all normally distributed*, as shown below:

The O-Score ranges from 13 to 65 with a mean of 41

13 --------------------------41---------------------- 65

The R-Score ranges from 12 to 60 with a mean of 35

12 --------------------35------------------------ 60

The E-Score ranges from 7 to 35 with a mean of 19

7 ----------19-------------- 35

Imaginative Thinking

imaginative thinking (ĭ-măj′ə-nə-tĭv thĭng′kĭng)
n. 1. The formation of a mental image of something that is neither perceived as real nor present to the senses. 2. The ability to confront and deal with reality by using the creative power of the mind. 3. Mental resourcefulness.

Now let's go back to the four teams I was watching in the School for Innovators. We had arranged them by their rules subscores in preparation for the going outdoors and doing some rock-climbing. The teams were developing a list of important principles, obligations and rules for their own team of four.

How you view and deal with rules and guidelines is a strong reflection of your values. And people with similar values trust each other, particularly under dangerous conditions. They know they are operating on the same wavelength.

What I noticed was that the principles, values, and obligations within each team were very similar, and there was strong and excited agreement on their importance. They were about to go out and do something that had never been done before that was perceived as being risky and dangerous. They were going to climb some big boulders, tied together with the other three people at their table, and they were going to be depending on them for their own safety.

There is a big difference between perceived risk and actual risk. Rock climbing is a very safe activity because it is based on a few simple safety rules, simple special equipment, and simple communications protocols (all Level 2 stuff, remember?). Believing that, however is not so simple. Chris Argyris, a Harvard Business School professor, points out:

> *"When trust is high, precision can be low;*
> *but when trust is low, precision*
> *must be very high indeed."*

Unless trust has been established that your team knows the rules, and is going to follow these rules the same way you will, trust is gong to be pretty low—and there will be a lot of questioning about almost everything.

When the four teams went out to start climbing, they were in tight consensus about the values and obligations on which they had agreed. But the ranked the order of importance of the values of all four teams were quite different. On the rocks, their R-Score similarities and differences were very evident—we could see them in action. They all succeeded (differently) beyond their expectations, and they did some very different Level 6 stuff. Later, when we started breaking them up to regroup them again, there were violent protests. They wanted to stay together for the next five days!

235

R-Score is a derivative of your values and principles

We have used the R-Score, reinforced by MBTI types, in every School for Innovators since then and also, whenever it was appropriate, on operational Thinking Expeditions.

And we, the Thinking Expedition guides, work very, very hard to establish trust with the team as quickly and as early as possible.

Idea-Finding in Teams (O-Scores)

We form teams with their O-scores similarly, but for a different purpose—to highlight communication and understanding. We give them a task that relates to the group "mess" on which the whole Expedition is focused. Here we want to bring out the differences in the type of novelty, the degree of originality, the volume of ideas, and the manner in which common concepts (among the four teams) are presented. What comes out clearly here is that groups formed up with similar O-scores communicate very well—they more readily understand and accept each others' ideas than when in diverse teams, and there is less explaining of the ideas. We get a much more diverse set of results across the entire group—and the contrasts between each group really bring home the point.

Efficiency and Doing in Teams (E-Scores)

We have not yet been able to highlight E-score differences in teams as well as we have with the other subscores. I suspect this is because the "throw weight" of the O-score and the R-score overshadows the visible effect of the E-score in group behavior. What we have been able to do, however, is construct three-person teams with very widely separated E-scores (trying to hold all other factors constant), and those groups have regularly imploded over how they were "*not* getting the job done effectively." Great insights for everyone there!

If It Works, Keep Doing It

I'm pretty empirical. If something works, keep on doing it, and do more of it better. If it doesn't, stop doing it, and start doing something else. The KAI worked for me with teams right from the start. Do more of it better? We moved into the subscores. The example above goes back to 1992, and we've used the subscores to form and reform teams in the School for Innovators and on Thinking Expeditions since then. Again, it works.

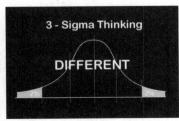

PERSONALITY TYPE

In 1993, we took team dynamics up another level and began integrating the Myers-Briggs Type Indicator (MBTI) into most of what we do with teams as well. It works, too.

Myers-Briggs theory and the use of the MBTI is complex and not something that is quickly understood and easily applied. The apparent simplicity of the various types, described in four-letter combinations, can be misleading. However, in the context of understanding human behavior around change and particularly with teams and teamwork, it is well worth studying. That said, I am not attempting to cover the MBTI in any depth but rather want to provide the reader enough information and background to have an appreciation for most of what I say about our use of the MBTI with teams on Thinking Expeditions and off sites.

The MBTI provides us with a second vector of perspective that complements the KAI very well in dealing with change and working with teams. The MBTI is a forced-choice inventory that operationalizes much of Carl Jung's theory of individual differences in human behavior or type. As with the KAI, we have found it to be far more effective to debrief the MBTI team engaged in working on a problem integrated into the flow of an ongoing Thinking Expedition. Getting feedback in the context of actual working situations is powerful.

Jung developed a comprehensive theory to explain human personality based on patterns in behavior. He referred to these patterns as "psychological types" and used them to classify the way people prefer to take in information (perceive things) and how they organize the information once they have taken it in (how they make judgments).

Jung classified all conscious mental activity into processes and functions—two perceiving functions and two judgment functions. The perception functions are sensing and intuition, and the judgment functions are thinking and feeling. His theory was that anything that comes into the conscious mind does so either through the senses or through intuition (how we become aware of things and gather information). For perceived things to stay in the conscious mind, they must be used, so the judgment processes—thinking and feeling—sort, compare, weigh, analyze, and evaluate them

237

style KAI ≠ Type MBTI

238

(how we come to conclusions and make decisions about the information we've gathered).

The MBTI gives people insights into their functions and attitudes, identifying 16 different combinations or patterns possible through the four pairs of preferences that follow Jung's theory.

The Perceiving Functions

These functions are the driver behind Jung's model of psychological type. Just like your hands, you use both on a daily basis, but one is more dominant and therefore "preferred" for your normal use. Sensing (S on the MBTI grid) is the term used for perceiving concrete things by using the senses—sight, touch, smell, taste, and hearing. Intuitive (N on the MBTI grid) is the term used for perceiving abstract things such as meanings, relationships, and possibilities through insight. The perceiving functions have the most influence on how a person sees and deals with or reacts to change.

Sensing (S): Individuals with a more dominant sensing function prefer to start with what is known and real—solid ground—relying on actual experience and proven results, not theory. They trust the conventional way of doing things and like simplicity. It is from this kind of mental baseline that they explore outwards, systematically, step-by-step, linking each new idea back into past experience and forward into relevant, practical applications. Their focus tends to be the current and the now, using sound, conventional wisdom. They approach change carefully, slowly, incrementally, and critically. Seventy-four percent of people tend to have a sensing preference, and sensing types are generally the most resistant to change.

Intuitive (N): Individuals with a more dominant intuitive function like complexity, theoretical relationships, and connections between things. They have the ability to see future possibilities, often unusual and abstract ones, using imagination and theory. They rely on inspiration rather than past experience and learn through an intuitive grasp of meanings and relationships, skipping steps and often making apparent leaps between new ideas. They have strong interests in the untried, the new, and the unknown, and are motivated by intellectual challenge. They approach change openly and optimistically, preferring larger-scale, fundamental jumps to incremental steps. Twenty-six percent of

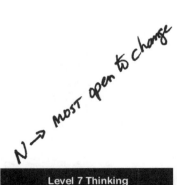

S → MOST Resistant to change

N → MOST open to change

Level 7 Thinking
Imagine and Visualize

MindShift your brain into high gear
- Imagine: Wouldn't it be great if ...
- Conjure up a miracle
- That's impossible
- Get a little crazy
- Make 90° turns
- Breakout!

... imaginitive thinking

people tend to have an intuitive preference and, in general, intuitive types are the most receptive to change.

The Judging Functions

Jung divided judging, the manner in which we reach conclusions and come to decisions, into thinking and feeling. Again, you use both on a daily basis, but one is more dominant and therefore "preferred" by you for normal use. Thinking (T on the MBTI grid) is the term used for the function of logical and impersonal decision making. Feeling (F on the MBTI grid) is the term used for arriving at conclusion through a process of appreciation employing a system of subjective personal values. Both are used when coming to a conclusion, evaluating, or making decisions. Both are subjective, based on a person's knowledge and environment.

Thinking (T) types apply logical analysis to allow them to weigh facts and examine consequences (cause and effect). They develop attitudes of impartiality, a sense of fairness and justice, and tough-minded objectivity.

Feeling (F) types develop personal values and standards, and knowledge of what matters most to themselves and other people. The attitudes they develop typically reflect a warm understanding of people, compassion, empathy, and a need for harmony.

The Attitudes

A third personality dimension that Jung identified deals with how a person gets personal energy and how they act in their environment (the physical direction or their mind's eye). Jung chose the terms *"extroversion"* and *"introversion"* to label these attitudes and defined the terms much more broadly than their normal, everyday usage. The extroverted attitude (E on the MBTI grid) focuses *outward from self,* and has a higher awareness of the environment it relies on for stimulation and direction.

Watch out! Because people confuse the terms with traits commonly associated with "extrovert" and "introvert," real effort is required to insure clear understanding of the words as *attitudes* and to stick with Jung's definitions.

Extroverted (E) focuses *outward from self* and has a higher awareness of the environment it relies on for stimulation and direction. Extroverted types are action-oriented and tend to

240

be impulsive ("when in doubt, act"). They communicate easily and literally think out loud, throwing out half-thought and incomplete ideas in an almost constant stream of psychological vomit. For them, things often don't make sense until after they say them. As a result, they are seen as more outgoing and sociable. Someone sitting next to an extroverted type on an airline flight will get off the plane knowing virtually everything there is to know about the person; anything they don't know is simply because they weren't listening.

Introverted attitude (I on the MBTI grid) focuses *inward into self* and the inner world of concepts, ideas and thoughts; as a result they are thoughtful, contemplative, reflective ("when in doubt, think about the issues more deeply"), and enjoy privacy and quiet time alone. Introverted types keep their half-baked ideas inside, examining them and working on them mentally, until they are fully done and ready to be exposed. Introverted types are typically seen as being uncommunicative and more reserved socially. The person sitting next to an introverted type on an airplane will have a quiet, undisturbed trip and at the end will know very little of a personal nature about the other passenger. Anything they don't know about the person will be a function of their not having specifically asked.

Innovation of Myers-Briggs to Jung's Theory: Attitude toward the Outer World

In the process of developing the MBTI, Isabel Myers and Katherine Briggs added a fourth dimension to Jung's model of psychological type—attitude toward the outer world in which people find themselves or the manner in which they run their lives. This attitude defines how people actually apply the perceiving functions (sensing/intuition) and the judging functions (thinking/feeling) to their lives. Myers and Briggs defined this attitude as judging (J) and perceiving (P).

The judging (J) type tends to be convergent, driving towards closure and results, and toward having a system or systems to work within. When a person favors a judging function (thinking or feeling), things are organized, scheduled, on time, settled, and managed by plans and priorities. As a result, the judging attitude is not particularly keen on change (i.e., having change impact their plans, priorities, and organization), and after sensing (S), judging is the next

Imagination

imagination (ĭ-măj′ə-nā′shən), *n.*
1. The formation of a mental image of something that is neither perceived as real nor present to the senses. 2. The ability to confront and deal with reality by using the creative power of the mind.

most resistive to change (56 percent of people). The percentage distribution makes this fairly "normal" behavior.

The perceiving (P) type tends to be divergent, open, flexible, and unconstrained. When a perception process (sensing or feeling) is used for life, the natural bias is to keep things open to new and more perceptions and possibilities as long as possible. The perceiving type doesn't want to miss experiencing anything. Their tendency is to minimize plans, organization, rules, and structure to adapt freely to changing circumstances. As might be expected, people with a perceiving preference enjoy and often seek out change. In fact, after the intuitive type, perceiving (P) is the next most receptive to change (44 percent of people).

☑ TIP!

The judging/perceiving aspect of a person's life is often the first element of their type that we notice as we get to know them to any degree. It is difficult even for a strong introvert not to disclose through behavior whether he or she is spontaneous or organized. This is useful information when forming or reforming small teams during a Thinking Expedition.

These eight characteristics in their corresponding four preference combinations define Myers-Briggs types. How those combinations are arrived at is shown with the corresponding pairs below:

Extroversion	E	⟷	I	Introversion
Sensing	S	⟷	N	Intuition
Thinking	T	⟷	F	Feeling
Judging	J	⟷	P	Perceiving

These preferences create sixteen possible combinations, traditionally arranged in a matrix:

242

ISTJ	ISFJ	INFJ	INTJ
ISTP	ISFP	INFP	INTP
ESTP	ESFP	ENFP	ENTP
ESTJ	ESFJ	ENFJ	ENTJ

The matrix can be divided into quadrants by common characteristics: IS, ES, IN and EN. Research on the distribution of types (MBTI Manual, 3rd Edition [1998] from Consulting Psychologists Press—CPP, p. 379) reveals that:

- 40% of people fall in the **IS** Quadrant and are referred to as "detail oriented"
- 34% of people fall in the **ES** Quadrant and are referred to as "pragmatists"

74%

- 11% of people fall in the **IN** Quadrant and are referred to as "academics"
- 15% of people fall in the **EN** Quadrant and are referred to as "innovators"

26%

Imagination

imagination (ĭ-măj′ə-na′shən), *n.*
1. The formation of a mental image of something that is neither perceived as real nor present to the senses. 2. The ability to confront and deal with reality by using the creative power of the mind.

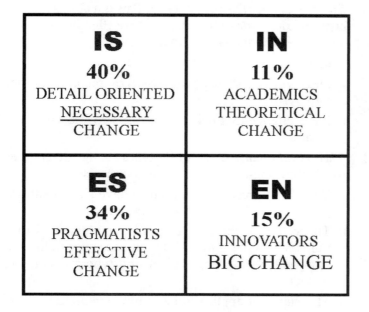

With what we have discovered on Thinking Expeditions about change and people, I have used this quadrant grid as a lens to classify change generally into four categories and to tie them back to the 7 levels of change for a baseline. From these classifications we can then look at how types of change and personality types mesh:

1. ***Necessary Change (Level 1, 2, 3, or 4).*** This is a change that is being made because of clear necessity. It is clear that the change will be implemented step-by-step at a steady pace, and the plan for the change has a significant amount of detail:

   ➢ why the change is necessary

   ➢ what, exactly, the change is going to do

   ➢ what the results are expected to be

   ➢ when the change will start and when it will end

   ➢ who is going to be in charge of the implementation, and whom it will effect

   ➢ the immediate impact of the change on what is presently being done is clearly evident

244

2. *Effective Change (Level 3, 4, or 5)*. This is a change that is being made to make something more effective, and it is a practical and realistic change:

   ➢ there will be specific, measurable results

   ➢ there will be a steady progression of implementation, step by step

   ➢ it is a change that people can relate to—it will effect what they do

3. *Theoretical Change (Level 6)*. This is a change that relates to new, cutting-edge theories and concepts.

   ➢ The change has the potential to have significant impact on existing concepts and thinking.

   ➢ Theoretically, the change can be implemented in a number of areas and at different paces depending on who will be working with it and where it is being introduced.

   ➢ The plans for application and implementation of the change can still be influenced or changed with additional new ideas or experimentation.

4. *Major Innovation (Level 6 or 7)*. This is a change that could impact and change the world.

   ➢ The change relates to current events or other large-scale changes at the global level (e.g., technological, scientific, national).

   ➢ At this stage the change is still developing and needs more input and definition.

   ➢ It is difficult to predict how the change will finally be implemented or what the results will be, but they will be big.

Using these general classifications of types of changes, we can look at the implications of tension between different types (across the quadrants) when they try to introduce change. Given the percentage distributions, resisting or accepting change is clearly not evenly split out, and the challenge of rolling out change can be even more appreciated with this in mind. Do you realize how much time and effort it may take to adjust to a big (perceived) change, or one of a particular type?

CRAZY!!

What's the
Craziest Idea
you can come up with?

...BLUE SLIP

A new manager taking charge, a transfer to a new job, forming up and launching a new project team all bring this out. There is a new task, a new leader, new associates, additional (but not "different") rules and procedures, new objectives—perhaps even new organizational structure and relationships. There are new team dynamics and personalities. However, most of the changes are "normal"; they fit within our experience base, and the degree and amount of unknowns is small.

Not so with a Thinking Expedition. Because an Expedition moves rapidly into the unknown—"unusual" (non-normal) change is a constant. As the Thinking Expedition unfolds, there is less and less clarity about anything. The kinds of changes that occur change, and change as an element of the Expedition shifts from a daily experience to hourly. This causes the basic needs and wants of the different types relative to change to surface very rapidly and to become more visible, more evident, and much more of a active dynamic.

TOOL #72 (GETTING READY FOR CHANGE):
Low Altitude Stress—LAS

On Thinking Expeditions we refer to this as "Low Altitude Stress" (LAS). It surfaces in the early stages of every expedition, generally on the long trek into the unknown. Why? Some types love this environment and others can't stand it, creating tension—LAS. The most visible tensions occur at the extremes, between the IS and EN types, and their differences usually surface first in a team (contrast the two in the comparisons that follow).

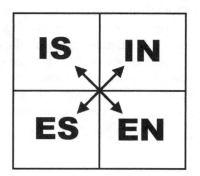

246

The following are some tips and insights for reducing stress for each of the four different personality types when introducing change:

The IS type needs specific details, facts, clarity, structure, rules, timelines, logic, and results. Organization and order. One thing at a time. Slowly. Control. Time to reflect. No nonsense. Conservative. *Necessary change* is acceptable.

The ES type wants well-defined problems, roles, boundaries, logical approaches, data, costs, practicality. They want visible results. *Effective change* is good.

The IN type wants new possibilities, meaningful impact, discovery, big picture, and time to reflect. They need harmony, freedom and autonomy, variety, and change. Change driven by *new theory* is great.

The EN type wants the big picture, flexibility and options, intuitive instructions, and new big stuff. Variety! More new and abstract stuff is better. They need involvement and lots of communication. Freedom and choices. Fast forward. Fun. Improvisation on the fly. *Big change and major innovation* is the way to the future.

So What? How Do You Use This?

First know yourself—your type. Then know each person, individually, on your team or in your organization—in terms of type and style. Know the types of changes that they prefer or that seem to fit with them. When you are going to work with them or talk about change, tailor what you do to fit *their* type, not yours. Statistically you can start by assuming that 74 percent of them (three out of four people) are going to do best with either necessary or effective change—Levels 1, 2, 3, 4, and maybe 5. If you can shape the changes or break them down some so that they start out at those levels, you're much more likely to be successful. Knowing the level of the change you are dealing with—from their perspective, not yours—is also important.

THE SPECTRUM OF CHANGE

When all the basic attributes and functions (behaviors) are combined into the sixteen types and overlaid across the 7 levels of change, some strong patterns relating to change emerge. When further combined with the percentage distribution data, we can make some powerful generalizations about relative strength of resistance and receptivity to change and at what levels of change:

247

#1 **Sensing (S)** is the most broadly resistive factor to change (74 percent of people – 3 out of 4). The percentage distribution then defines this as "normal" (1-Sigma) behavior.

> **74%**

> **Intuition (N)** is the most broadly receptive factor to (26 percent of people).

#2 **Judging (J)** is the next most resistive factor to change (56 percent of people). The percentage distribution again highlights this as "pretty normal" behavior (approximately one out of every two people).

> **56%**

> **Perceiving (P)** is the next most receptive factor (44 percent of people).

#3 **Feeling (F)** is the third strongest factor in resistance to change (61 percent of people)

> **61%**

> **Thinking (T)** is the third most receptive factor (39 percent of people).

#4 **Introversion (I)** is least in effect on resistance to change (51 percent of people)

> **51%**

> **Extroversion (E)** is least in effect on receptivity to change (49 percent of people).

248

Again—So What?

The next diagram, overlaid on the spectrum of the 7 levels of change, conceptually shows the relative strength by type of both resistance to change and receptivity to change—or said differently, preference for incremental change or fundamental change. The diagram and the relationships are based on the degree of acceptance-resistance and the percentage distribution of the factors in a normal distribution. The change "resistance-acceptance line of demarcation" which this highlights raises some interesting hypotheses and questions.

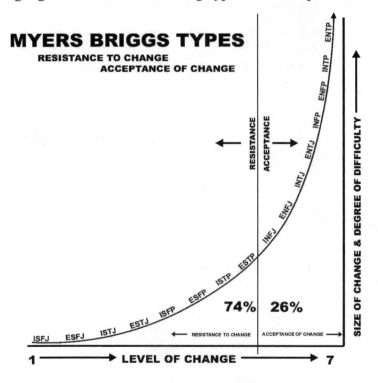

SOME OBSERVATIONS:

Undergo Change {

1. We can generalize from this and then hypothesize that "normal behavior" is to resist change or to prefer smaller, more incremental changes. Statistically, we can expect two out of three people to *broadly resist* change (74 percent of people are sensing in type).

2. Close to half of all people will *strongly resist* change (the 47 percent who are SJs).

3. Approximately one-fifth of all people will be *broadly receptive* to change (the remaining 18 percent who are NPs).
4. Only 6 percent of all people (the NTPs) will be *strongly receptive* to change and act as change agents (3-sigma "different" behavior).

It is evident once again that accepting or resisting change is very clearly not evenly split, and the challenge of rolling out change can be even more appreciated with this in mind. How can we leverage this?

"Typing" individuals or a team that is going to generate changes or lead a change, and typing the target group that is going to undergo the changes, makes a good case for using tools like the 7 levels of change, the MBTI and the KAI to help people better understand and deal with change in the context of who they are and how they are likely to react.

In this chapter, we presented some of the key aspects of individual preferences, characteristics, and differences. A team that is unaware of these important aspects of personality style will struggle or succeed without understanding why. A team that takes the time to understand its differences can leverage them to great advantage. Forewarned is forearmed, which takes us to the next chapter.

249

Generate and handle change

Getting Ready for Change
(Teams)

THE CHANGE FACTOR IN TEAMS AND ORGANIZATIONS

Much of my experience in working with organizations and change has been at the team level—executive leadership teams and offsite, strategic planning teams, military project management teams (PM) and project management offices (PMO), tiger teams, and wannabe teams (groups in trouble). These have largely been teams with a high-visibility task, or an unusually difficult problem, or the expectation of big, innovative results—all with an urgent timeframe.

Sometimes we're lucky enough to be in on the initial launch of the team—and we kick-start them. But often they are groups that have been working on something for a while and now find themselves "stuck." At a minimum they are looking for "out-of-the-box" and "different" (Level 6 results). In a number of cases, the team will also be responsible for rolling out and leading the changes they come up with.

We normally use the format of a Thinking Expedition (three to five days long) or a Strategic Thinking Adventure (two days maximum) with these kinds of groups, and we customize the design to fit both the psychometric profile of the team and the profile of their "mess."

These formats compress and accelerate timelines, highlighting individual and group type/style in the process.

The other groups we work with regularly are the ones who muster up for an eight-day School for Innovators Expedition. They are *all-volunteer* and are "invited" selectively. Most of these are very diverse, as people come from a wide range of very different organizations, companies, and backgrounds, and generally none of them have ever met each other before.

In either case, we have everyone do some prework, at a minimum the Myers Briggs Type Indicator (MBTI) and Kirton Adaption-Innovation (KAI) inventory. Depending on the problem, we may also ask them to do the Problem Solving Inventory (PSI) and the Grigorc Learning Style inventory.

The corporate Thinking Expedition teams are generally homogenous in type and style. Interestingly, so are the mixed bag of School for Innovators volunteers, but their profiles are homogeneously different from their corporate counterparts. It has been from this background and such empirical observations that I have become increasingly interested in the impact that the type, style, and character of a team has on the results they produce.

252

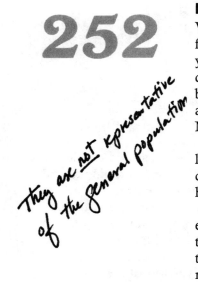

They are not representative of the general population

LOOKING AT RISK WITH TEAMS

Would you go on an expedition if you *knew* it was likely to fail? Or worse, if you knew that statistically some people on your team were very likely to die? The statistics for the expeditions that climb Mt. Everest have changed significantly, beginning in 1921 with the first recorded history of a summit attempt (George Mallory and Andrew Irvine, who died on Mt. Everest in 1924).

On 29 May 1953, Tenzing Norgay and Sir Edmund Hillary stood on the summit of Mt. Everest. Every other expedition prior to that had failed, and thirteen mountaineers had died.

Thirty years later, in 1983, for roughly every three climbers who made it to the summit, one member of the expedition team was likely to die. By 1983, 158 climbers had made it to the summit of Everest and sixty-five people had died on the mountain.

On 10 May 1993, forty climbers reached the summit, the largest number to reach the top on a single day. In 1993, 129 climbers summitted. Only eight people died that year.

On 10 May 1996, three years later, eleven climbers died near the summit, the largest number of people to die on Everest on a single day.

By 1998, the odds had improved significantly: for roughly every forty climbers to the top, the expeditions had only one death.

In 2001 alone, 182 climbers summitted—the most ever in a single year. There were five deaths. Everest had moved from Level 7 in 1953 to Level 6, and over the last ten years had become at best Level 5 in the purest sense. Climbers were "just copying" what many others had done.

So what? What does this have to do with business, or with your project teams?

Corporate teams have been climbing mountains of change every bit as big and tough and challenging as Everest. For most of them it's still 1952. On the mountain they're climbing, no Sir Edmund Hillary has broken the change barrier and shifted the unknown and the impossible down to simply different.

How can we improve the survivability odds for corporate teams the way they have improved for Everest expeditions?

TOOL #75 (GETTING READY FOR CHANGE):
Typing Teams

253

> Teams are well worth "typing," and a team's type is not a simple sum of its individual team members' types. By determining a team's dominant attitudes and spotting its "holes" in terms of both attitudes, functions, and style early, a number of potential difficulties and stress points can be anticipated and planned for, and we can shape the design of the processes we will use with the team appropriately. One size does not fit all. The end effect of pretyping is nearly always a compression in the time it takes the team to come together and bond, and correspondingly, the time the team needs to get into breakout thinking and high value results.
>
> Classifying teams by their most dominant behavior (MBTI "attitudes") and their creative style in approaching problems (KAI style) are the first steps in looking at their change factor—how they will function at the various levels of change and with the corresponding mindshifts in thinking at each level.

I will first follow this section with the profiles of two different teams: a two-company, two-team Thinking Expedition (Procter & Gamble and Honeywell), and a research team on Mt. Everest. Both show type and style in action. Then we'll move on into some case studies of operational Thinking Expeditions.

ORGANIZATIONAL CHARACTER

William Bridges, in his book *The Character of Organizations*, suggests that organizations differ in character and type in the same way that individuals do. He has developed an inventory which he calls the "Organizational Character Index" (OCI) that is similar to the MBTI but focused on organizational type, and he then uses the OCI to classify organizations. With the baseline of the MBTI, he explains why organizations act as they do, how each type of organization deals with change, and why they are so hard to change.

The following is a brief synopsis of each of the "orientations" that play into the make up of an organization's character. The synopsis builds on what I covered earlier in this

254

chapter on type, and again (as with the MBTI), this is *not* an in-depth coverage of Bridges' book nor the OCI; however, it should be enough so that you can follow how we use this in working with teams and organizations on innovation and change initiatives and the interplay of type and style with the 7 levels of change.

Following the descriptions is an example of a jointly-sponsored Procter & Gamble and Honeywell Thinking Expedition (two teams working together).

Sensing teams focus on the present and reality, making only step-by-step, incremental change. They are good at fixing, remodeling or enhancing how things are already being done and can always make something better, including the team itself. They do best with Level 1, 2, and 3 changes (effectiveness, efficiencies, and improvements). Level 4 changes (stopping doing things or cutting things out) can be a conceptual stretch for them. They do not look particularly far ahead and can become disoriented if there are no clear transition procedures. Sensing behavior as a type is the most dominant in resisting change. (The P&G team was a strong sensing team.)

Intuitive teams are excited by change and move the most quickly. They are much more likely to see the big changes (3 sigma) that lie ahead but not problems right in front of them. They believe that you need an overall design to integrate the whole project and in big, all-at-once changes in which the whole system is transformed. Their focus is on possibilities, and they are far more aware of new ideas, trends, shifts, and factors that sensing organizations will not recognize for months. They do well with visionary Level 6 and 7 changes (different and breakout) as well as more radical Level 4 changes (blowing things up!). Intuition is the behavior type most receptive to change.

Judging teams look at change as a disruptive interruption in what is otherwise a natural state of stability. They are uncomfortable with change and hunker down until the storm has passed and they are on solid, unchanging ground again. Once they have bought in on the need for the change, however, they are the most effective at implementing it. They risk moving too quickly in an effort to get change over with fast and once in execution are difficult to redirect. Because they favor order and stability, they do

Sensing Teams work on incremental change

Intuitive teams want to create BIG change

Judging Teams are interested in the effective implementation of change

best with Level 1, 2, and 3 changes (effectiveness, efficiency, and simple improvements) aimed at making things even more stable. Overall, judging behavior runs a close second to sensing in resisting change.

Perceiving teams are more likely to see change as the norm and stability as boring. They have little discomfort with change and respond easily to changing situations, going with the flow. Because they see an unchanging situation as unreal, they tend to seek out and initiate more dramatic levels of change—Levels 4, 6, and 7 (killing sacred cows, the really new and different, and the impossible)— or they are motivated to copy (Level 5) a mind-boggling systemic change (Level 6 or 7) which some other organization has implemented.

Feeling teams are wary of change because of the unavoidable impact and disruption change has on people. They are more likely to respond to the second-order distress and disruptions that a change causes—the changes behind the change—than the basic change itself and often become engaged in change efforts which have something to do with organizational values. For the feeling team, logic and numbers are not the issue; the right thing to do is the humane thing. So changes which improve people's lives or working conditions (Level 3, improving) and changes which get rid of burdensome bureaucratic requirements (Level 4, cutting) appeal to them. However, most big, systemic, organizational changes don't have those kind of effects on people; instead, they create stress and worry. Because of that, feeling teams are often strong resistors of change—they worry about impact change will have on people.

Thinking teams approach any change or unexpected situation by almost reflexively applying logical analysis and sequential planning. For the thinking team, the right thing to do is the logical, effective thing, and the team will focus on insuring that change leads to improved results. They look at a big change logically and simplistically, and are able to see it as Level 1 change—doing the right thing. Thinking teams frequently initiate Level 4 change (stopping and cutting), since they are unlikely to continue a course of action that is not working well and simply cut their losses—even though such a change may impact the people involved. When planning change, thinking teams tend to overlook or

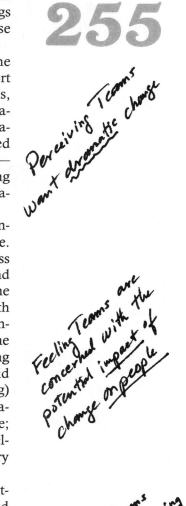

Perceiving Teams want dramatic change

Feeling Teams are concerned with the potential impact of change on people

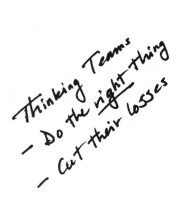

Thinking Teams
- Do the right thing
- Cut their losses

256

downplay the fact that it is people who will have to implement change and make change work. Thinking teams are able to mentally handle almost any level of change thrown at them. Logically, they think other people should be able to do that, too

[Observation: in my work with a large number of strategic planning and corporate change teams, I have found that they are consistently, at the 90 to 95 percent level, made up of thinking types. It has been extremely rare to find more than one or two feeling types on a strategic planning change team. If you are a senior leader who is likely to form such teams, this is a strategic *black hole* to be aware of.]

Introverted teams are slow to respond to change and sometimes actively resist responding to allow themselves some quiet time to figure things out and work out their responses completely. Because they are focused on and driven largely by their own internal processes and values, they tend not to stay particularly aware of external events. They are much more active in responding to internal change, especially shifts in thinking, belief structures, and value systems—things an extroverted team might not even notice.

Extroverted teams are in constant touch with what is happening around them, so when changes arise in their operating environment, they view them as normal events and are usually comfortable with them. They are relatively quick to respond to any external change, and reorient themselves with little difficulty to create new connections with what is going on. They need to talk a lot about change and have a continuous flow of communication relating to it. Extroversion as a team attitude runs a strong second to intuition in being receptive to change.

So what? How do we use all this?

JOINT THINKING EXPEDITION
Honeywell-Procter & Gamble

One of our most illustrative Thinking Expeditions in terms of creative style and psychological type was the Procter & Gamble and Honeywell Expedition. P&G was the customer and Honeywell was their long-time preferred IT supplier (Information Technology). There were some difficulties with requirements definition and deliverables, which had prompted the Thinking Expedition. The *initial* strategic focus and challenges they had mutually agreed on were: quicker, faster, better software deliveries and products.

The team of people was made up of two equal-sized groups, one from P&G and one from Honeywell.

The composite KAI score and distribution of the team followed a relatively normal distribution, basically ranging from mid-range adaptors to mid-range innovators, a good mix for creative problem solving. Because of this we started out using their MBTI scores more heavily than usual in making up subteams and in pairings.

However, on day two of the Thinking Expedition, we discovered that the *averages* of each company's individual half of the team were widely different: Honeywell's average was 122 and Procter & Gamble's was 93—a thirty-point spread or a 2-sigma difference! No wonder they had had some challenges! A difference of five points in *team averages* can cause communication difficulties, and a ten points can cause real working difficulties. Breaking this down further, the P&G range was 73 to 108, and the Honeywell range was 108 to 129.

The only common denominator was that each team had someone with a score of 108: there were two "bridgers." With no overlap area between the teams, they were *more*

than different.

The P&G team members were biased toward an adaptive tendency; the Honeywell team members had a strong tendency towards the innovative style.

In terms of MBTI type, the P&G team was solid STJ (sensing-thinking-judging) and the Honeywell team appeared to be heavily ENTP (extroverted-intuitive-thinking- perceiving). They were again essentially opposites (with the exception of their thinking behavior). When we broke out the individual types and charted them, P&G owned the four corners, the classic executive or supervisor and engineer types, and Honeywell sat solidly in the classic "innovator/inventor" spots. One side was going to be driving for details, practical results, and no bells and whistles; the other side was going to be talking big picture concepts, new technologies, and great possibilities. The P&G engineers were going to approach change and new systems slowly, carefully, and incrementally, and the Honeywell folks were going to be pushing the conceptual and technological change envelope.

We "randomly" paired everyone up to work on a *big idea*—so that the highest KAI scores from each company were paired together and they were as opposite as we could make them in type (ISJ+ENP). However, because of the very unusual distribution in KAI style, this amounted to pairing a high innovator Honeywell person with a normal P&Ger, and on down the line to the final, strong adapter P&Ger pairing with the "normal" Honeywell person.

While people from both Procter & Gamble and Honeywell were frustrated with one another, the Thinking Expedition format got them all to the same place fast— diff*f*erent. By learning more about one another through KAI and Myers-Briggs, both organizations were collaborating on ideas in a better way fast—diff*f*erent. By learning more about one another through KAI and Myers-Briggs, both organizations began collaborating differently on ideas in a better way—faster—developing creative solutions that would benefit both organizations. P&G would get global hardware and service at affordable prices and rates, and Honeywell would get higher volume and continuing business.

A year later, both organizations—using many of the tools learned on the Thinking Expedition—were developing common business objectives that would meet each organization's unique business needs as they both expand globally. Keep in mind that the P&G team went into the Thinking Expedition focused on better, quicker, faster, better software deliveries and products, and the Honeywell team went in to solve the problem creatively and give P&G some great support (ideas!).

Authors' note:
Thea Goldin Smith, my oldest daughter, and her husband, Grant Goldin, each participated on separate expeditions on Mt. Everest in May and October, 1999. Thea is a 1996 graduate of the School for Innovators (Expedition XX) and Grant is a 1997 graduate (Expedition XXII). Both are experienced Thinking Expedition guides. Thea is our expert on type, style, stress behavior, and characteristics/profiles of teams. She compiled the following "case study" on the interplay of type, style, and stress in a team on a big mountain under extreme conditions. Additional information and data can be found on the following Web sites:

www.meditac.com/e399/Default.htm
www.explorers.org/

BACKGROUND AND HYPOTHESIS

We have found that the large majority of people who volunteer to go on expeditions tend to have definite type and style characteristics in their profiles. Consider the dictionary definition:

> **Ex·pe·dí·tion** An excursion, journey or voyage made for some express purpose, as for exploration, to investigate unknown regions to gain insight or knowledge of something previously unseen or unknown.

This is Level 6 and 7 stuff. The majority of people who go on expeditions tend to be open to change and new possibilities and ready to go with the flow of whatever might happen (NP in type). Similarly, they also tend to be more on the innovative side of the KAI scale, and on the higher end of the 7 levels of change graph. Their nature is to loosen up the boundaries and borders of the environment surrounding a problem by breaking new ground. As the nature of any expedition is to explore the boundaries of the unknown (thereby changing the realm of what is known), we would expect to find a higher percentage of more innovative individuals (as opposed to the normal population) on most expeditions.

In the process of working with teams on Thinking Expeditions and with individuals in the School for Innovators, we've discovered exactly that. There are some strong correlations between thinking style, problem solving style,

260

learning style, personality type, and degree of comfort with the various levels of change. This has led us to hypothesize that there is a significant bias in the personality type and creative style of those who *choose to go "on expedition."*

PRACTICAL APPLICATION OF TYPE AND STYLE ON THE EVEREST EXTREME EXPEDITION (E3)—MAY 1999

In May of 1999 a team of fifteen expeditioners on Mt. Everest spent fourteen days at base camp (17,500 feet). The entire expedition took six weeks (three weeks trekking in, two weeks at base camp and higher, one week trekking out). The Everest Extreme Expedition (E3) of 1999 was sponsored by NASA, Yale University, and the International Explorers Club. E3 was a research expedition organized to investigate medical on treatment, procedures, and advanced technology under extreme conditions (e.g., high altitude effects, vital signs monitors, telemedicine). Team members were predominantly medical doctors, volunteer research assistants, and professional mountaineering guides. They were supported by ninety-nine Sherpas and twenty yaks

Grant Goldin, an experienced Thinking Expedition guide, joined the Everest Extreme Expedition team with the intention of conducting research on change and stress caused by an expedition, as well as the effect of extreme environments on individual and team creative-problem-solving styles.

The Everest Extreme Expedition offered additional opportunities to investigate behavior connected with transitioning through the 7 levels of change under extreme conditions: mindshifts, fears, stresses, and resistance-acceptance of change. We could also further validate "typical" events that take place over the end-to-end process of an operational expedition (i.e., as depicted on the process flow map of "How expeditions happen") Further, there were upwards of fourteen other expedition teams operating on Mt. Everest.

TYPE AND STYLE PSYCHOMETRICS

The psychometric instruments and the data-collection processes Grant used on the Everest Extreme Expedition were much the same as those developed for Thinking Expeditions and in the School for Innovators.

Before joining a Thinking Expedition or attending the School for Innovators, everyone completes the Kirton Adaption-Innovation (KAI) Inventory and the Myers-Briggs Type Indicator (MBTI). Depending on the purpose and focus of the Expedition, we also use the Grigorc and the Problem Solving Inventory (PSI). All of these inventories are based on differing but broadly related theories of cognitive processes. (The KAI and MBTI have already been covered in some detail in the preceding "Getting Ready for Change" chapter.)

The KAI defines differences in creative style (thinking) and the manner in which a person deals with their environment in solving a problem; we also use it as an indicator of how the strongly the person is likely to resist or accept different levels of change.

The MBTI highlights differences in personality type (behavior)—how people prefer to take in information (perceive things), how they organize the information once they have taken it in, how they make decisions, and how they move through life.

The Grigorc gives us insights into a person's learning style—the manner in which we perceive and order the world around us (concrete, abstract, random, sequential).

The PSI assesses an individual's awareness and evaluation of his or her problem-solving abilities or style. Problem-solving confidence (self-assurance), approach-avoidance style, and personal control while solving problems.

E3 DATA COLLECTION

The data from the psychometric inventories indeed supports the hypothesis that there is a significant bias in the personality type and creative style of those who *choose to go "on expedition."*

KAI NORMAL DISTRIBUTION VS. EVEREST EXTREME EXPEDITION TEAM

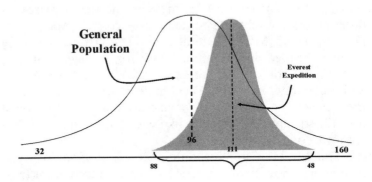

The chart above shows the normal KAI distribution (32 to 160, with a mean of ninety-six), and the E3 Team's distribution (83 to 148, with a mean of 111). Visually the differences are profound, and the team is a full standard deviation away from the norm in the direction of innovative style. This distribution and average score correlates strongly with the urge to explore different (Level 6 change) and the previously unexplored (Level 7 change). Not surprising, as expeditions by definition represent a Level 6 or 7 change "going into the unknown."

Consistent with the theory of "resistance-acceptance to change" (diagram on page 248), we would expect teams going on expedition to be predominantly NP, highly accepting of change and the unpredictable results and events on Expeditions.

In psychological type, the make up of the team was as follows.

MBTI DISTRIBUTION
Everest Extreme Expedition 1999

ISTJ	ISFJ	INFJ	INTJ 1
ISTP	ISFP	INFP 4	INTP 2
ESTP 1	ESFP	ENFP	ENTP 4
ESTJ 2	ESFJ	ENFJ 1	ENTJ

If we contrast the Everest Extreme Team with the general population, the differences (Δ) are glaring:

MBTI DISTRIBUTION COMPARISON

	Norm	**E3 Team**	**Δ**
I Introverted	51%	47%	-4%
E Extroverted	**49%**	**53%**	**+4%**
S Sensing	74%	20%	-54%
N Intuitive	**26%**	**80%**	**+54%**
J Judging	56%	27%	29%
P Perceiving	**44%**	**73%**	**+29%**
T Thinking	**39%**	**67%**	**+28%**
F Feeling	61%	33%	28%

Strongly biased towards NTP, this is not a "normal" team at all!

Where the general population is 74 percent sensing, the Everest Extreme Expedition team was only 20 percent sensing. Conversely, the Everest Extreme Expedition team was

264

80 percent intuiting where the norm is 26 percent—*more than 3 times the norm.*

Furthermore, where the normal population is made up of approximately 56 percent judging types, The Everest Expedition team was only 26 percent judging. In contrast again, the Everest Extreme Expedition team was 74 percent perceiving versus a norm of 44 percent, or *nearly double.*

Finally, where the norm is split roughly 40:60 between thinking and feeling, the Everest Extreme team was 67 percent thinking and 33 percent feeling in style, a *difference of nearly 30 percentage points.*

The differences in introversion and extroversion are negligible on the team, although it is slightly biased towards the extroverted style.

The Everest Extreme team is more than a full standard deviation from the normal population in terms of preferred type—coming out very strongly with the profile of an NTP team.

LEVEL 6 THINKING AND DOING (DIFFERENT)
The E3 Team Profile

While the type distribution and profiles for the Everest Extreme Expedition team is anything but normal, it is very similar to the profile of many of the groups participating in School for Innovators Expeditions (which are specifically designed to be unusual, different, and unfamiliar—and are all-volunteer). These findings are what we had hoped we would discover and will continue to explore more closely in the future.

Going back now and using William Bridges's descriptions to construct a picture of the characteristics of the E3 team:

Intuitive teams are excited by and receptive to change, and they move quickly into action. They believe that you need an overall design to integrate the whole project. Their focus is on the possibilities that are under the surface of many situations, and the long-term. They are much more likely to see the big changes (3-sigma) that lie ahead but they don't see problems right in front of them. They are far more aware of new ideas, trends, shifts, technologies, and factors that sensing teams will not recognize for months. They do well with Level 6 and 7 changes (different and breakout) as well as more radical Level 4 changes (not just cutting but blowing things up!).

Thinking teams approach any change or unexpected situation by almost reflexively applying logical analysis and sequential planning. For the thinking team, the right thing to do is the logical, effective thing, and the team will focus on insuring that change leads to improved results. They look at a big change logically and simplistically, and are able to see it as really only a Level 1 change—doing the right thing. Thinking teams frequently initiate Level 4 change (stopping and cutting), since they are unlikely to continue a course of action that is not working well and simply cut their losses. They will do that even though such a change may impact the people involved. When planning change, thinking teams tend to overlook or downplay the fact that it is people who will have to implement change and make change work. With their logical perspective on change, thinking teams are able to mentally handle almost any level of change thrown at them. Logically, they think other people should be able to do that, too

Perceiving teams are more likely to see change as the norm and stability as boring. Because they see an unchanging situation as unreal and inherently unstable, they tend to seek out and initiate more dramatic levels of change—Levels 4, 6, and 7 (the really new and different, and the impossible)— or they are motivated to copy (Level 5) a mind-boggling systemic change (Level 6 or 7) which some other organization has implemented. They have little discomfort with change and respond easily to changing situations, going with the flow.

LEVELS OF CHANGE = STRESS

MBTI and KAI research has established that a person is comfortable with certain tasks based on their particular personality type and style. Because of the nature of Expeditions, and our hypothesis, we would *not* expect a typical expedition team to be composed of a wide variety of types and styles. Therefore individuals on an expedition team are often required to perform tasks in opposition to their preferred style. This is especially true on very small, fast moving expedition teams.

Many individuals initially have no trouble "flexing" their behavior and coping with the tasks they are assigned.

266

Over time however, the "cost" to the individual of coping and altering their preferred behavior becomes higher. The likelihood of stress and declining performance can increase, depending on the length of the expedition. Not only can this create tension amongst the members of the expedition team, but the declining performance could possibly put the mission and safety of the expedition at risk.

Over the eight-week course of the Everest Extreme Expedition there were several instances of behavior which could be anecdotally associated with the long-term mismatching of task to type and style, as well as adapting to a level of change incompatible to the type and style of that individual.

LEVEL 1 & 2 THINKING AND DOING
(Effectiveness & Efficiency)

The person responsible for the movement of the Expedition Team, fifteen research physicians and explorers, ninety-nine Sherpas and twenty yaks, as well as the accountability of hundreds of pieces of equipment typed as an INFP with KAI of 104.

This personality type is likely to become highly stressed by long periods of detailed work (Level 1 and 2—doing the right things and then doing them right—every day, all day) combined with the rigid schedules required to keep an Expedition Team of this size operating and on the move. It was inevitable that as the Expedition progressed, this individual would begin to lose the ability to "flex" and begin to stress. This has also been our experience on a number of Thinking Expeditions, when several of our own vTx guides (who all typed as NFPs and who were more innovative in relation to the general population, i.e. range 109–145) have been tasked with running and organizing our base camp.

CONCLUSIONS AND OBSERVATIONS
Level 3 Change (Improving)

It is useful to know and understand the personality type and style of the expedition members as well as relating that to the tasks that they will be required to perform. Just as on a Thinking Expedition "stretchers" are brought in to fill in potential "weak spots" in the team in order to get better results, the same kind of preplanning could be used on other types of Expeditions. In future expeditions, this can facilitate the selection of additional team members whose style can be associated more closely with the tasks.

Alternatively, this knowledge would provide an understanding by the team members of the potential weakness in the structure and allow them to take the necessary steps to reinforce that position if the information can be disseminated ahead of time. The Expedition leader of the Everest Extreme Expedition recognized what was happening when members of the team began to become stressed and was able to deflect potentially damaging situations. His KAI score turned out to be exactly the same as the group average, making him an ideal bridger between the different KAI scores on the team, and a major contributor to the team's ultimate success.

While the data and observations collected on this Expedition correlate with our hypothesis and previous findings of the predominance of certain types who tend to "go on Expedition," the presence of other types and styles of individuals on expeditions whether out of necessity or interest must also be considered. The usefulness of heterogeneous teams made up of individuals with not only different skills and talents, but also of different personality types and styles and therefore different problem-solving styles cannot be denied. Having a strong understanding of team dynamics and a working knowledge of the interaction between different types and styles can prove extremely useful in the future of exploration. Developing education and training programs for Expedition Leaders and team members regardless of their type and style profiles, can help them prepare for, minimize, and anticipate the expected changes in a person's behavior and thinking that inevitably will occur when teams are isolated and operating in stressful conditions for long periods of time, such as the International Space Station, underwater exploration, polar exploration, or military underground command posts.

The benefit to the Expedition Leader (or the project management leader) and team members of understanding which personality type and styles are best suited to which tasks cannot be emphasized enough. Further, what kinds of probable uncontrollable expeditionary events are most likely to cause stress for specific members of the team can

268

also prove invaluable. This knowledge will enable team members to create better cohesiveness and thus give the expedition or project team a greater chance of success.

NOTE: Since our discoveries on the 1999 Everest Expeditions, we continue to see a strong NTJ bias in corporate Thinking Expedition teams. Further we have noticed an even stronger and consistent bias towards NFP/NTP and high Innovator KAI scores in the volunteers who join our School for Innovators Expeditions in Colorado.

Much of the information and observations on the heels of Stress and Fear behind the 7 levels of Change has emerged through this work. We are continuing to study team dynamics, Type and style under pressure and extreme conditions.

— Rolf Smith
10 May 2002

Appendix A
The Thinking Expedition—Five Case Studies

Some things just happen. However, the concept of the Thinking Expedition evolved deliberately. For more than ten years, since 1991, the School for Innovators has increasingly integrated mountaineering, rock-climbing, expedition metaphors, and experiential learning into the basic curriculum of thinking diff*erent* and Creative Problem Solving (CPS). The results have significantly stretched and changed our graduates. They do not return to normal, and our postgraduate feedback has been overwhelmingly powerful.

Why? Because we run the School for Innovators on Expedition lines.

What's an Expedition? It's a journey or a voyage made for an express purpose—focus. It's an exploration of discovery into unknown regions to gain insight or knowledge of something previously unseen or unknown. An Expedition is about different. You come back different.

Expeditions transform people.

How do Expeditions happen, and how do you move through the 7 levels of change on expedition? In very predictable stages—take a look:

We have tied the map closely to mountaineering and climbing expeditions because these correspond most closely with the 7 levels of change model and because our own validating expedition experiences have been on mountains and rocks. The map moves through a series of very distinct stages and transitions:

- ➤ The idea
- ➤ Funding: Backers and sponsors
- ➤ Organizing and forming up the team
- ➤ Staging: The long trek in and the approach
- ➤ Base camp
- ➤ Acclimating and assessing the mess
- ➤ Reconnoitering and route-finding
- ➤ The 7 levels of change: Climbing and higher camps
- ➤ Discoveries and results
- ➤ The summit

> Descent and return
> Celebration
> Follow-on

Any group on expedition can quickly and easily identify their position on the map at any point in time by having each individual on the team mark the position they see themselves at relative to the stages immediately behind them and in front of them.

LEVEL 1: EFFECTIVENESS
Doing the Right Things (The What)
The idea. The urge to explore. What an expedition really is, the basics of everything. Expectations. Sponsors and backers. Funding. The guide. Staging. Volunteers wanted! Forming up the team: Who's who? Where to focus and *what* to do. Watch-outs and dangers. Planning and problem-finding.

LEVEL 2: EFFICIENCY
Doing Things Right (The How)
Rules, roles and S.O.P.s. Safety. Learning *how* to do things: New tools, techniques; how to survive. How to discover and explore, how to find ideas. Communications protocols. Developing basic expertise. The mission. Setting priorities, charting a route. Time. Crossing the frontier. The long trek into the unknown. Noticing. Realizing . . .

LEVEL 3: IMPROVING
Doing Things Better
The search for ideas. New and better ways to be more efficient and effective. Acclimating to changes: environment, altitude, attitude, people, weather. Lost??? Regrouping, rethinking. Base camp. Acclimatizing: building strengths, skills, becoming flexible. Mess-finding and data-finding.

LEVEL 4: CUTTING
Doing Away with Things
Letting go of old habits, beliefs, perceptions. Developing 80/20 focus, shedding unnecessary weight. *Mindshifting*, negative-positive tension. Moving to higher ground, camp 1. Leaving the comfortable behind.

LEVEL 5: COPYING
Doing Things Others Are Doing
Transitioning to *out-of-the-box* thinking and doing. Knowing what you don't know. Observing and noticing more. Copying and adapting what others know and do.

Clipping in: pairs, triads, quads, small rope teams. Listening diff*erent* to yourself, others. Route-finding—the long, slow climb to higher camps. Moving as small rope teams.

LEVEL 6: DIFF*f*ERENT
Doing Things No One Else Is Doing

Thinking diff*erently*—experimenting, trying things. Reflecting, *thinking up* ideas. Creating new things out of old things, new ways of doing things. Path-finding. Exploring new ground. Risking diff*erently*. Becoming a guide: leading the team. Discovering diff*erent*. Thinking about thinking. Levels of fear. High camp.

LEVEL 7: BREAKOUT!
Doing Things that Can't Be Done

Accelerating the rate of change, changing changes that have already occurred. Mindshifting the team beyond present rules, roles, and operations. Leveraging adversity, the unexpected. Higher-level obstacles, barriers, unknown routes. Breakout and the impossible. The summit! Insights. Results. The long trek back. Return and celebration.

∼

What follows next are seven very different case studies, stories really, of Thinking Expeditions that I've led or that have been led by graduates of the School for Innovators . . . or by someone who simply read this book and used the 7 levels as a template for change. Each one is different and told in a different way.

———————————— CASE STUDY ————————————

TEXACO
Knowledge Thinking Expedition
Houston, Texas, October 1998

In the fall of 1998, Betty Zimmerman came up with the idea of a Thinking Expedition to explore knowledge in Texaco. Betty was a recent graduate of the School for Innovators (Expedition XXVI, September 1998) and had previously been a team leader on several major Thinking Expeditions we had designed for the Electronic Messaging Association (EMA).

Texaco, a multinational petroleum company with technologists scattered across the world, needed to collect and consolidate its knowledge to bring effectiveness, efficiency, and improvement (Level 1, 2, and 3 change) to its exploration and production operations. Petroleum is a maturing industry where success depends on finding oil faster and delivering gasoline and other products to consumers at less cost. How could the company create a knowledge management system that would enable it to work smarter than the competition? To answer this question, Betty and several Texaco executives asked us to design a Thinking Expedition for experts from across all business organizations in the company and several of its partner companies.

Ron Robinson, Vice President of Technology and the backer of the Thinking Expedition, had set the strategic focus: Explore Knowledge and Knowledge Management (KM). The desired results: A long-range, ten-year "Outlook for Knowledge Management at Texaco."

Betty Zimmerman and John Old, the Expedition sponsors, worked with us on recruiting the team. We adapted (Level 5 thinking) Sir Ernest Shackleton's advertisement in the London Times for his ill-fated 1914 Expedition to Antarctica, and Betty sent out the ad and note to candidates:

"This promises to be an experience like no other meeting you have ever been part of. Space and time are limited. Not everyone will be able to go. To submit your application for consideration and to obtain more information, click on the Web page address."

Volunteers Wanted
For Hazardous Journey

Small wages. Little sleep. Paltry rations.
Long periods of intense thinking. Much Unknown.
Increasingly difficult levels of change. Constant danger.
Route unclear. Continual frustration.
Normal return doubtful.

If Interested, Apply:
www.Thinking-Expedition.com

Everyone whom Betty and John had nominated signed up to go! "As soon as word spread through Texaco's human network that we were planning the Expedition, we had people 'knocking down the door' to participate," Betty said.

TOOL #74 (LEVEL 3):
The eVISA Questions

To set the stage for the Knowledge Expedition, all nominees for the team completed an "Expedition VISA Application"—Level 1 pre-work that was framed around questions such as these:

1. Unusual skills, knowledge and experience I bring to the team:
2. Some new skills I would like to develop on Expedition:
3. Knowledge I have about knowledge management initiatives in other companies:
4. Some critical issues & challenges we face in knowledge management:
5. Some things I *don t* know about knowledge management:
6. Other unknowns I would like to explore on expedition are:
7. Some things I hope we discover about knowledge management on expedition are:

8. Results! Some specific results I hope the expedition returns with:

Initial Level 2 & 3 Doing and Thinking: The eVISAs were sent to our virtual base camp where we integrated, synthesized, and summarized them. Note that these uncoordinated individual viewpoints approach gave us the widest possible perspective of the initial "mess" we were going to explore. In addition, everyone completed the KAI and MBTI inventories, so we also had an excellent type and style profile of the team. Using all this information as a baseline, we designed the flow of the first two days of the Thinking Expedition in detail, customized to leverage the group's thinking profile.

EXPECTATIONS—RESULTS AND DELIVERABLES

Working with Betty and John, we sketched out what the results of the expedition might look like—our vision for the Knowledge Expedition. From that we then developed an outline and table of contents for the deliverables: a long-range "Outlook for Knowledge Management." Deciding on a three-ring "living document" approach, we preloaded the "Outlook" with tabs in the "for sure" sections (e.g., the summarized Issues, Challenges and Unknowns from the eVISAs; a bibliography; background) and included a number of blank tabs for other "to be discovered" sections.

Expect the Unexpected

A team of twenty-eight expeditioners gathered at Del Lago, Texas, a remote location away from offices. The guide team issued everyone Thinking Expedition vests, Idea Passports and Expedition Journals, and we began forming up the team—accelerating the rate at which everyone got to know everyone else, who's who. With these Level 1 changes, we worked through what an expedition really is and began shifting expectations fast as the guides explained roles, procedures and rules, and what to do. The skeleton (empty) three-ring "Knowledge Outlooks" binders were passed out to everyone, and we walked the team through the projected contents to set the focus of the expedition. Finally, we highlighted the need (and expectation) of producing a Texaco Knowledge Outlook (TKO) go-forward action plan by the end of the Expedition.

WHY A THINKING EXPEDITION?

We'd worked ahead of time with Ron Robinson, the Knowledge Expedition's senior backer. He made several short video clips that fitted into the flow of the Thinking Expedition at appropriate key spots.

And on day one, shortly after launching the expedition, we popped in one of Ron's video clips:

> I believe the task you are facing over the next few days is an unusually tough one—one that requires doing things much differently than we do them today. We need this team to break with past experiences and the current paradigms and find the best path. We need you to think differently so we can work differently in the future, to provide the maximum benefit to Texaco.

He continued:

> We've asked you to tackle a particularly critical challenge, namely, what do we want the Texaco knowledge worker's environment to be like in ten years? We want you to learn from each other and identify what is *best* for Texaco as a whole.

Then Ron got to the bottom line, the payoff:

> Now, what results do we want? As you're aware, we expect you to return with more than a handful of great ideas . . . we want to know how to make them a reality within Texaco. The last day of this expedition is intended to define an outlook for the Company to implement. What we are going to come back with is a long-range outlook for Knowledge Management at Texaco.

TEXACO'S KNOWLEDGE MANAGEMENT OUTLOOK

Ron's video instantly energized the team. Especially when he stood up in the back of the room and said: "I walked in just now while that was playing. I couldn't have said it better myself!" Then he rolled up his sleeves and joined the Expedition.

Level 1 Thinking—Focus, Awareness and Exploring the "What." We moved the team immediately into examining "knowledge" and began basic idea-finding:

1. What is a **Thinking Expedition**?

2. What is **Knowledge**?

3. What do I **Know**?

4. What **Knowledge** do I have?

> *NOTE:* Wherever I have included the actual Knowledge- exploring Questions from the Expedition, I have capitalized and highlighted the **KEY WORDS** to emphasize the focus.

The team paired-and-shared on these and then formed into small rope teams to converge on working definitions of knowledge. Those were rapidly processed in the base camp and passed back to the team, clipped into the "Outlook"—and *voilà*, we were moving forward at high speed. From this baseline then mentally began exploring all aspects of a knowledge management "system." Looking back in history, Betty highlighted that one of Leonardo da Vinci's desires was to ". . . collect *all* knowledge." Already an impossible goal in his lifetime, Betty pointed out how far bigger a challenge that is today with the ever-expanding knowledge that surrounds us. Even within only a single company, it is simply not possible to collect all the corporate knowledge. "Corporate" knowledge lies in the minds of people, and corporations need to draw on *what* their employees know.

Moving from there on into Level 2 doing, the expeditioners rapidly learned *how* to use their new creative thinking tools, techniques, and processes to explore, and how to discover and find ideas—*how* to be efficient and effective on expedition. They developed expedition protocols and ways to communicate effectively and efficiently, began setting priorities and charting a route. As they developed expertise and a sense of mission, they began to look simultaneously at the "how" of knowledge.

> *"There are two types of knowledge. One is knowing a thing. The other is knowing where to find it."*
>
> —Samuel Johnson

Level 2: Efficient Thinking—Discovering the "How"

> ➤ How do I get knowledge?
>
> ➤ What is a great example of leveraging know-how in your organization today?

The team "crossed the frontier" and began the long trek into the unknown—acclimating to changes slowly as they moved forward: environment, altitude, weather, and people. Building strengths and skills, becoming flexible, gathering data were all signs that they were already connecting with Level 3 change—coming up with new and better ways to be more efficient and effective in their approach to knowledge.

Level 3: Thinking Better, Increasing Knowledge

> ➤ What do I need to know?
>
> ➤ How do I learn?
>
> ➤ How do I share knowledge?
>
> ➤ What are the critical issues and challenges facing us with knowledge management?

The team regrouped into new rope teams and, using all the blue slips and idea summaries that they had come up with thus far, sketched out "the Knowledge Mountain Range" that was beginning to clarify ahead of us. New questions (Level 3 doing) were developed to explore knowledge further, and as the Texaco expeditioners looked under every mental rock and behind every forgotten leaf, the unexpected happened. These knowledge experts realized that "KM" was not about creating and managing a "system" for collecting and publishing knowledge, it was about knowledge workers and ultimately, it was simply about knowledge.

With that conclusion, the team shifted momentarily into Level 4: Cutting and *doing away with things*—shedding unnecessary weight. "KM" disappeared and was left behind for the rest of the expedition.

Level 4: Rethinking

> ➤ How do I unlearn things that are no longer true?
>
> ➤ How do we let go of old habits, perceptions, and preconceptions?

Mapping and sketching the Knowledge Mountains Range, both clarified and opened up understanding across the team (mess-finding). Now we were able to determine where we were relative to the major peaks (goals), the big mountain immediately ahead in front of us, and had some glimpses of possible summits.

WHERE *ARE* WE?

We paused, spent more time getting our bearings, and determined where we were. As it turned out, the team was spread out all over the map—literally. It took us some real effort to reorient and regroup, pull everyone back to the same reference point—and from there we were able to establish base camp. "The long trek in" was behind us. We caught our breath, tried to acclimate (some Level 3 work), and spent time thinking up ideas for the base camp that the team now realized they would also need to support them back in Texaco when they returned.

That led us into another eighty-twenty refocus, and to also thinking about what we no longer needed (mentally) and could leave behind at base camp. We hit on the idea of "If it's dumb, it's not our policy," and dug into that with some deeper Level 4 rethinking:

> ➤ What are we doing that's dumb?
>
> ➤ What could we stop doing?
>
> ➤ What could we riiiippp out?

SITUATION ASSESSMENT:

The mess with which we had started the expedition now looked significantly different from the vantage point of base camp, particularly with the various teams' perspectives of the Knowledge Mountain Range.

With what we had discovered on the long trek into the unknown and in getting to base camp as our baseline, we ran a five-minute meeting focused on knowledge and what we knew about knowledge in Texaco up to this point:

> ➤ What interesting new ideas have surfaced thus far?
>
> ➤ Based on where we are, what are the three most critical issues facing us?
>
> ➤ What are three most pressing challenges for you personally?
>
> ➤ What are some opportunities you see for us?
>
> ➤ What actions might we take *now*?

Reforming the whole group into pairs, everyone discussed these new blue slips with someone else. We then shifted into new rope teams of six based on creative style and background, and each team was tasked to "build the mountain" out of all the available blue slips they had, including any left over from their Level 4 work. After some heavy-duty work, we had six quite different mountains coming together. These were first-cut models of knowledge and what our Texaco Knowledge Outlook might look like.

All but one team member were rotated out of their team and sent off to scout another team's mountain. This was the first stage of transition to *out-of-the-box* thinking (leaving your work and compiled knowledge) and into copying and adapting, doing things others are doing, and to more clearly knowing what we don't know.

Level 5: Learning What Others Are Thinking

The scouts made observations, noticed differences, looked for reinforcing similarities, took notes, and asked questions of the team member who had remained on each mountain. They then returned to their own mountains and used their new insights to refine and reshape the structure of their model.

At this point we began to put more and more emphasis on the mountaineering metaphor. The first stage of route-finding began as the team on each mountain attempted to work up through the baseline issues and challenges to find a location for "Camp 1"—the first subcamp in the long, slow climb to higher ground. Negative-positive tension was more discernible now in the teams as they began leaving base camp and the comfortable behind. Additional new questions were developed to probe the possible routes:

> ➤ What informal networks are you part of?
>
> ➤ How do you share knowledge?
>
> ➤ How do you discover what is no longer true?
>
> ➤ What are the great problems facing us?

Camp 1

The concept of "KaK" was one of the big discoveries at Camp 1. To quote the discoverer:

> Sometimes knowledge about knowledge (KaK) is more important than knowledge. Getting people to be receptive to answering questions of others can often be more valuable that having the person write down what they know—it may not match what is needed.

From Camp 1 on each of the mountains, the teams began the hard work of path-finding through the mass of blue slips they had spread out (covering the six-foot-wide round tables). These were being continually rearranged as they explored new ground, risking diff*erently* in the search for potential points to locate "higher camps." This was done by working down backwards from the summit blue slip(s) with "if-then" thinking: "If we could get to here, then we could do this . . . And if we could get to here, then we could do this . . ."

For me the most fun on the Expedition was watching the small rope teams building the mountains out of their blue slips. Their intra-team and inter-team dynamics were amazing displays of personality type and creative-problem-solving style in action! Their high-speed connection with the expedition and mountaineering metaphor leapfrogged us right over many aspects of "more typical" Expeditions where we have to work very hard to get people comfortable with this kind of different.

Doing Things No One Else Is Doing

We were definitely at Level 6 now—experimenting, trying things. Camp 2. Creating new things out of old things, new ways of doing things—Camp 3—discovering diff́erent. Soon all the rope teams were moving towards High Camp—The point from which we would have a high likelihood of summiting, getting some breakthroughs.

Level 6—Creating

We pushed further into what we knew, what we needed to know, what we didn't know:

> ➤ How do I create knowledge?
> ➤ What do I know I don't know?

Reflecting deeper, *thinking up* really different stuff—the *big ideas* coming out of Level 6 were big indeed. At High Camp everything and everyone started accelerating. The teams now were mindshifting themselves beyond present rules, roles and operations, and unexpected conditions, sprinting upwards—"moving like greyhounds unleashed" as Canadian mountaineer Laurie Skrislet once described his summit climb on Everest.

Level 7—Imaginative Thinking

Unknown and unexpected routes were discovered through some very sticky thinking:

> ➤ What do I know I don't know that no one knows?
> ➤ What don't I know that I don't know I don't know? (Don't know x 3)
> ➤ What won't work?
> ➤ What can't be done?
> ➤ What is impossible today, but if it were possible it would fundamentally change the way we do business?

Level 7—Breakout!

Doing Things That Can't Be Done. Sparked by these questions, the participants shared their unique perspectives with other members of the group in order to produce new knowledge by the convergence of existing, albeit untapped, knowledge. These questions and the work the teams then did moving from their High Camps to the summit, late on the night of day four, completed both the content and the framework for the Knowledge Outlook. Their answers and thinking over the course of the expedition produced more than twenty-eight thousand ideas in the sixty hours.

THE LONG TREK BACK AND RETURN

Betty Zimmerman later commented that all of the answers to the questions contributed key perspectives on knowledge and knowledge sharing in Texaco. "Upon completion of the expedition, a group of us (John Old and his team; Dave Wisch, a Texaco Fellow; Tom Lionetti, one of the Expeditioners; and Rolf and his team), began synthesizing the results into Texaco's Knowledge Outlook (TKO), which is being published internally; that was on the Friday that the Expedition ended. We also created the Strategic Knowledge and interactive innovation Process, or "SKiiP"—and a two-hour briefing that drove it.

Upon return from the Expedition, we immediately began conducting a two-hour session to engage Texaco people who were not able to participate in the Expedition itself. During theses SKiiPs, we solicit additional information for the TKO and identify potential pilot projects. As we solicit information during the SKiiP, we help individuals develop their own personal knowledge outlook and identify a new knowledge habit that they will incorporate in their daily work.

At a Petroleum Industry Knowledge Management Conference some months later, Betty stated that "the expedition was such a success that Texaco has continued to refine the process and consider it to have produced a strategic advantage for their organization."

From my point of view, this was our most immediately successful Thinking Expedition ever. Because of the proprietary and strategic nature of the material, all I can show here is a summary outline of the TKO and the SKiiProcess process.

THE TEN-YEAR TEXACO KNOWLEDGE OUTLOOK (TKO)

A 182-page mini-plan that included:

- ➤ Seven Great Problems (problems that go beyond Texaco and require unusual knowledge and thinking)
- ➤ Twelve Strategic Thrusts
- ➤ Summary of Major Issues & Challenges
- ➤ Important Trends on the Horizon to Leverage
- ➤ Six Areas to Explore Further:
    1. Texaco Business Areas
    2. The Value of Knowledge
    3. Return on Knowledge (ROK)
    4. Cultural Issues & Challenges
    5. Technical Culture
    6. Organization & Infrastructure
- ➤ A manageable collection of Big Ideas to move forward
- ➤ A detailed 7-Point Near-Term Action Plan (SKiiP)

THE SEVEN-POINT ACTION PLAN
Texaco's Strategic Knowledge and interactive innovation Process (SKiiP)

- ➤ Identify the intellectual capital of Texaco (current state)
- ➤ Communicate a new/different "value of Texaco"
- ➤ Build the Knowledge Culture—GUS: Get it. Use it. Share it.

- Grow Knowledge & Harvest Knowledge
- SKiiP—Strategic Knowledge and interactive innovation Process. Texaco Knowledge Network
- What Don't We Know?
- Take Knowledge to the Marketplace (the SKiiP)
- Run Texaco Run: Use it

―――――――――――― CASE STUDY ――――――――――――

U.S. NAVY SMART SHIP PROJECT
USS Yorktown (CG-48)

The Smart Ship Project was launched by Admiral Mike Boorda, Chief of Naval Operations, in November 1995. Admiral Boorda laid out his vision clearly in a message to the fleet. Commissioning the Smart Ship Project, he said that the navy was faced with challenging fiscal choices. "It is imperative that we keep fleet performance high while striving to operate our ships more efficiently," Admiral Boorda said. "Personnel expenses combine to utilize over one-half of the navy budget, and I am initiating a project called 'Smart Ship' which will help us focus on ways to achieve the benefits of reduced ship crew size."

Admiral Boorda set the focus clearly: "Today, we can explore improvements through the application of proven, currently available technology, changes in ship-board equipment, embedded training, and a new look at ship-board personnel requirements." To emphasize the importance of making something happen fast, Admiral Boorda designated the USS Yorktown, a large guided missile cruiser with a crew of 370, as the operational platform on which to test ideas.

The Level 7 mindshifter, however, and the words that really opened things up were: "*. . . we must be willing to selectively break with culture and tradition* and employ technology as a work saver—not as backup."

And with that, the Smart Ship Team got under way. Captain Tom Zysk was named the project team leader. At the kickoff meeting on 15 November 1995, the team started by describing the Smart Ship Program as "a rare opportunity to revolutionize. Technology is not a roadblock—manning can be reduced substantially using only demonstrated technology. The roadblocks are to be found 'in culture and tradition'."

The navy's approach centered on setting up a single operational ship to serve as a model using innovative technology aimed at reducing manning requirements and lifecycle costs. The Smart Ship Project goal was to install and to maintain (through the demonstration period) innovative projects onboard a U.S. Navy commissioned surface ship and to demonstrate the resulting reductions in manpower and benefits associated with life-cycle costs.

Committed to working outside the box, the navy was willing to accept any and all ideas for evaluation in all areas that might be a candidate for reducing manpower requirements onboard surface ships as long as they would not have an adverse impact on readiness or create additional manpower demands on other requirements (e.g., operations, training, maintainability, and reliability).

TEAM I—FIRST PHASE, DECEMBER 1995

Captain Tom Zysk called me shortly after the team was formed and asked if we could put together a short course on out-of-the-box thinking and innovation tools for the team of twenty naval officers and civilian engineers. We agreed on a two-stage "lite" Thinking Expedition, which would heavily emphasize applying creative thinking on first-cut idea finding. Chief Petty Officer David Purkiss, a recent graduate of our School for Innovators (July 1994), assisted me as an Expedition Guide.

Smart Ship Team Profile—Type and Style

On short notice, the team completed the KAI and MBTI. I had made an operating/planning assumption that the group's profile would be that of traditional military officers: TJ, conservative, and biased toward the adaptive side of the KAI scale. Further, I thought that they would generally have an engineering mind-set/background. I was wrong. They were delightfully different, diverse, unnormal, fun to work with, and full of new thinking.

Their average KAI score was 2-sigma off the norm! The typical ENTJ team intuitively grasps change, takes command, and acts decisively. They are focused outward and respond quickly to external shifts, developments, and opportunities. Looking for possibilities, they have no difficulty coming up with big and visionary changes as well as strategies for implementing them. They plan well and handle any and all of the 7 levels of change easily.

Often an ENTJ team will have a tendency to approach things with an "engineering" mind—an impersonal point of view of the issues and factors connected with the problem—and because of that, they are not particularly well suited for major changes centered around people. The team had almost no feeling types at all, a huge hole in understanding people. This flagged a concern for me since the whole thrust of the Smart Ship Project was built on sailors, and sailors would have to implement the changes in the end.

ENTJ teams can grow quite large and still remain focused and effective. They hate inefficiency and don't tolerate incompetence. They like things spelled out and definite. They focus on closure, and they aim for clear results (go back to the "Getting Ready for Change" chapter for more insights into Team type and style).

With a KAI average score strongly biased towards the innovative side, they were well suited for their out-of-the-box thinking mission. A team with scores such as they had can easily be perceived as fitting with the normal organization, can slip in innovations under that appearance, and is usually good at manipulating adaptive structures, Their high originality score would ensure out-of-the-box concepts, and there was a high probability that their innovative ideas would have practical applications and could be implemented easily. They would be intuitive in their approaches and very comfortable determining their own agenda.

STAGE I: LAUNCH OF THE SMART SHIP TEAM

With their type and style in mind, we initially ran a pretty focused "lite" expedition. We worked primarily at setting the stage for thinking different—Think 101 basics—and for recognizing that this was in fact a Thinking Expedition into the unknown. We concentrated on arming the team with creative thinking tools and skills for changing at Levels 1 through 6

> *Level 1 Change:* How to have an idea with blue slips: "Write it down!"

> *Level 2 Change:* What to do with their ideas, how to process their thinking.

> *Level 3 Change*: How to leverage each other, particularly the diversity of thinking styles within the team; the power of two pairing-and-sharing ideas and concepts.

> *Level 4 Change:* PIN—How to suspend judgment as long as possible, focusing on positive thinking and perspectives first, before moving into negative or critical thinking.

> *Level 4 Change:* How to change the nature of meetings and briefings into creative, innovative idea-finding sessions.

> *Level 5 Change*: Looking outside the box: noticing, clipping, and copying ideas, shifts, and trends in magazines, newspapers, journals, movies, and TV.

> *Level 5 Change*: The basic creative-problem-solving (CPS) model and how to apply each stage of the model depending on the challenge. I also explained the rules/roles (Level 2 change) of brainstorming and modeled how to apply those within CPS. Then I coached Captain Ross Barker, one of the senior team members, through stand-up use of the CPS process (thirty-minute version) with the team on a real Smart Ship focus-area. With Ross, we had imprinted Level 6 different—a U.S. Navy captain leading a CPS session!

> *Level 6 Change:* We had the team work on several different things grouped by their KAI/MBTI scores (as usual, without their knowing it). Afterward, I explained KAI and MBTI theory, gave the team individual and group feedback on their scores, and pointed out where differences were clearly operating among them. We worked through understanding how each member of the team individually approached problem solving and idea finding, and action finding. I worked with the team on understanding the differences in creative

style within the group—and how to flex and cope with those differences to leverage their diversity as much as possible.

➤ *Level 4, 5, 6, and 7 Changes*: We generated a number of *big ideas* focused on out-of-the-box operational concepts and departed with the team ready to make things happen.

MORE! ON EXPEDITION!

Captain Tom Zysk called me again almost as soon as I got back to Houston. He was excited about the results we'd gotten with the mini-expedition and the noticeable shifts in thinking and energy in the team. Tom wanted to know if we could come back for a second stage the next week to accelerate the momentum we had created. We turned around and went back the week before Christmas, and the team rapidly moved to higher levels of thinking with more tools and techniques. They were more than ready for change.

Looking back, this was one of the most exciting and rewarding things I've ever been involved with—a great project, absolutely superb, innovative, motivated people, and a lot of them officers in the US Navy! For me, it was a real Level 7 mindshift—it couldn't be happening (as an air force colonel with twenty-five years on active duty, I knew what I knew about the navy!)

The project was started without program funding, with the intention of seeking funding for all projects found to be advantageous to the navy.

In addition to traditional contracting methods, all types of acquisition and nonacquisition methods were to be utilized, including cooperative agreements and other collaborative efforts between the government and industry.

Any kind of transaction was to be used when other forms of procurement weren't feasible.

Level 7 Change: Instead of issuing a formal Request for Proposal (PFP), the normal approach under the dreaded Federal Acquisition Regulations (FAR), the team issued a Broad Agency Announcement (BAA). The BAA allowed the team to express its intention and to solicit ideas without implying that anything further would happen with them. Further, the BAA had no telephone numbers in it—rather, it directed interested parties to access an Internet server on the World Wide Web to submit proposals or to ask questions. Some five-hundred-plus proposals were received in the first five months, and the contracting office only had to mail out five information packages. A project of this scope normally would have generated requests for thousands of information packages. Instead, proposals were submitted by E-mail with attachments (Level 6 change) and were limited to ten pages in length.

Level 4 Change: This process change to the FAR created space to get some work done instead of answering the phone and reading proposals for the first six months. It generated an E-mail explosion. Any callers who did manage to get through were told, "Go read the Web page." There was some resistance to taking this approach (Level 7 change) with the Broad Agency Announcement . . . critics shrieked that it couldn't be done, that the Q&A section could not be built into the Web page. In the end it worked great. Everyone submitting a proposal had access to the same information and answers. More than eight hundred concepts and proposals were ultimately received.

Levels 2 & 3 Implementations: The team got pretty focused. They wrote up the ideas as one-page Smart Ship Implementation Proposals (SSIPs) and then implemented and bolted as many as they could onto the ship. This phase was primarily idea finding, idea processing, and relatively small-scale implementations. Any ideas requiring large-scale physical changes and major engineering work were queued into the future.

TEAM II—SECOND PHASE, JUNE 1996

Captain Tom Zysk called me again and asked me to do some planning on how to transition in a new team to replace most of the old one. He would be retiring in June, and most of the team members would go back to their primary commands since they had only been on loan to the Smart Ship Project. With replacements coming in, Captain Grey Glover had been named to lead the project into the next phase of implementation and measurement. Tom felt team II would need to go through everything the first team had and thought that a one-shot (instead of two-stage) Thinking Expedition would be the way to go.

Commander Bill Olsen, a real out-of-the-box innovator on the first team, began the planning with me, and CPO David Purkiss and I went back to Carderock.

Our mission and objectives were team building and training in innovation tools. However, just before we left, we learned that Vice Admiral D. J. Katz, the executive director for the Smart Ship Project, was going to show up in the middle of things for a briefing on the project. Several other unexpected events began to make this look more and more like an operational expedition, so we changed our plans.

Level 1 Change: Because 85 percent of the original Smart Ship Project team had rotated in June, we designed a fast-forward, two-day-plus (forty-two hours!) Thinking Expedition focused on bringing the new team up to speed on innovation tools, techniques, and thinking different. We also developed some ideas for assessment of implemented ideas on the Smart Ship, and in the process build the new team.

Level -2! Chief Purkiss and I discovered that we were going to be ninety minutes late for our kickoff with the new team. Our plan had been to come in at 3:00 PM, but *their plan* had been to start with us at 1300 hours. This was not a great way to start doing the right things.

Level 2 Change: Having given up on our arrival, the new team had moved into developing an update briefing for Vice Admiral Katz—focusing on the right things and doing the right things right.

Level 3 Change: Coming in late, we walked into the middle of the discussion on the briefing design. Chief Purkiss immediately stepped into the breach and kick-started the group with a five-minute meeting—a simple Level 3 change for us. For the team, however, it was pure Level 6 different! The energy level of the room went right through the roof. David had them pair-and-share the ideas they had just written down (a Level 2 change).

> NOTE: This was the only time we had demonstrated and *taught* the how-to's of a five-minute meeting. Keep your eye on LCDR Ed Kenyon as this expedition unfolds. Ed is a strong KAI adaptor with an amazing innovative streak and a "take charge" attitude.

Level 1 Change: When the team settled back down, we started at Level 1 and did the right thing. We moved into a quick overview of what a Thinking Expedition is, how we were going to operate and lead it (rules and roles), and how an expedition works. This was not our normal, no-agenda-up-front approach. However, we've learned over time that for a team with a strong STJ bias, up-front clarity and details are pretty important. We had sent the new team KAI and MBTI inventories to complete prior to our arrival and already knew what to expect. This team was different in type and style for the first Smart Ship Team.

Level 6 Change: Captain Jim Baskerville, commander of the Carderock R&D Center and co-chairman of the steering group for the team, decided to join the Thinking Expedition. My own air force mental filters had put navy captains at the far end of conservative. Here I was with three of them! Jim gave me a fast mindshift. He proved to be a real innovator, open to anything, and ready to make just about anything happen.

Level 2 Change: Straight off, we introduced the team to the process of capturing ideas by writing them down on blue slips and Just-in-Time (JIT) Journaling. Only four people remained from the original team, so this was essentially all new stuff for the team. They'd been hearing about blue slips and idea-capturing, seen others using them, but weren't quite sure about them yet.

Level 4 Change: Chief Purkiss got the team to write their expectations for the Expedition on blue slips. Then he had them wad them up and throw them away, a straightforward Level 4 change (cutting out blocks to new thinking). We moved from that on into negative self-talk and both team and external Not Invented Here (NIH).

Then Vice Admiral Katz's perturbation began to register on the expedition. He was going to be coming in the next day, and Captain Grey Glover and the newbies on the team were starting to defocus. Level 3 and 4 fear kicked in. Grey was open, though, and the new team decided to use the briefing as a mission objective for the Thinking Expedition. We used the tools and techniques the team was learning to explore and get ready for the briefing. From here we mindshifted into higher levels of thinking fast.

Level 6 Changes and more: We taught the team mindmapping and a lateral thinking crayon technique we call Picasso. Forming them into small rope teams by KAI scores, each team had to imagine (Level 7) that they were the only ones who were going to brief the admiral and that they had to use their mindmaps to do it. Further, that it had to be Level 6 different because by this time, they realized that was what the Smart Ship was about.

Level 7: Grey Glover stood up on his chair exactly like Robin Williams in *The Dead Poets Society* and told the team that he was going to start off the briefing with Admiral Katz that way. He would give a very minimal outline of what was going to be covered, no timeline for when it would be over, and let the team run with it. A lot of mouths dropped open in the room—this was a real mindshift. Nobody believed him but . . . crayons and mindmaps started flying, and it was difficult to shut things down at 10:30 PM that night (22:30 in Navyspeak).

Level 6 and 7 Changes: The next morning we pressed on, now reorganizing the teams into their actual working areas relative to the project. Using the previous night's crazy ideas and diverse mindmaps, they focused in and created five major mindmaps to cover every aspect of the status in each functional area. The energy level on the expedition had gone through the roof again. We then loaded up and drove from the offsite location back to Carderock and the Smart Ship Team base camp to set up for Vice Admiral Katz.

Level 7 Change: The Summit. Grey Glover was unreal. When he said "Admiral . . ." and climbed up on his chair, the team was galvanized. He did exactly what he said he'd do! He stood on the table. The mindmaps seemed like second nature, and Admiral Katz played right into them as each team walked him through them. At the end, as Grey was about to close the briefing, Lieutenant Commander Ed Kenyon stood up and said, "Just a minute, Captain. Admiral Katz, we're going to run a hot washup five-minute meeting. If I could ask you and everyone else to take some of these blue slips"—and quiet Ed, with the strongest adaptive KAI score on the team, ran a perfectly executed five-minute meeting. He then paired up Admiral Katz and Grey Glover to share their blue slip ideas, along with the whole team. The place was electrified! It was magic.

THE PAYOFF?

From my vantage point—$500 million to $1 billion in long-term savings. Where'd that figure come from? The Yorktown was commissioned July 4, 1984. She's eighteen years old and has an expected ship life of thirty-five years, leaving twenty-two years of remaining ship life. Using a cost figure of $34,000 per year per manpower slot times the ship life, with a projected reduction of fifty billets or military positions, Yorktown could save the navy $37 million. One hundred billets, the high-end estimate, would yield $75 million in savings. Carrying this out into the fleet in Yorktown's class of ship only, with forty-seven ships in the class, overall long-term savings would be $500 million to $1 billion.

THE RESULTS

A few of the many changes implemented on the Smart Ship in the first six months:

Level 1 Changes: Doing the Right Things

➤ Shifted all hands to coveralls, making laundry simpler and faster.

➤ Reduced fire watch requirements. Smart Ship Team hit upon a change to the traditional way of manning fire watches, which had been an exhaustive workload on the crew. This change was immediately passed on to the fleet. This was a leap of faith in the face of policy and has potential to reduce occasional fire watch requirements both at sea and in port by 50 percent.

Level 2 Change: Doing Things Right

➤ New Automated Tag Out System (ATOS) called Taglink replaced a cumbersome, manual safety program. Taglink is a proven Dbase III Windows-based software program that performs the ATOS functions with significantly reduced workload and a substantial increase in audit, accuracy. Will realize a 50 to 60 percent reduction in all work centers using Taglink and will not eliminate billets but reduce collateral duties for four to five billets.

➤ EZ Pup fire hose nozzle handling device. The process of breaking out, handling, maneuvering, and drilling/fighting fires with the navy standard firefighting hose nozzles is tiring work. For that reason the navy trains and mans hose teams with sufficient numbers of people to rotate the number-one nozzleman. The EZ Pup fire-hose nozzle-handling device can be readily backfitted onto any fire hose and significantly reduce effort, fatigue, and manpower associated with handling hoses. It allows the crew member on the front of the hose to run the hose for forty-five to sixty minutes without getting tired. Present equipment tires the front crew member in five minutes and requires continuous rotation of positions. The cost of the new nozzle is $300.

Level 5 Changes—Copying and Adapting

➤ Switched paintbrushes to Paint Sticks, a home use product from Home Products Corporation. Commander Bill Olsen, visiting the smart ship, saw a Bosun's Mate painting a big bulkhead with a two-inch brush, dripping paint all over and getting paint on his uniform. Bill went home, got a Paint Stick, came back in uniform, and demonstrated how it worked without spilling a drop.

➤ The change to Reliability Centered Maintenance (RCM) was a very dramatic change seen as quite risky, but private airlines have been doing it for quite some time. Much of the current preventative maintenance requirements are on a time-directed basis. PCM methodology emphasizes condition-based maintenance, enabling direct workload savings by repairing only what needs to be repaired. It has an estimated bottom-line reduction of 30 percent of total maintenance man-hours shipwide.

> Pilot house manning—take people off the bridge. The plan was to go from twelve people to a minimum manning of five, as it is done in the Merchant Marine. Successful implementation resulted in a net reduction of twenty-one watch standers, 168 man-hours per day, and required no funding, but does require watch standers to have more training.

Level 6 Changes—Things No One Else Is Doing

> Shifting to cashless services reduced operations for shipboard office, ship's store, vending machines, and morale-and-welfare expenses. The idea is tied to the use of a SmartCard as an enabling technology (doesn't reduce workload, improves quality of life). Saves one to three billets and reduces collateral duties for six to ten senior personnel.

> Instituted the use of the Smart ID Card called "MARC" for Multi-technology Automated Reader Card. MARC makes the process of properly and accurately identifying shipboard personnel significantly more efficient and accurate, reducing independently-done and unintegrated administrative effort. Magnetic swipers/readers would be installed at all muster points and key watch locations, allowing accurate muster to be taken in minutes.

Level 7 Changes—Things That Can t Be Done

> The Broad Agency Announcement (BAA) process itself was an impossible idea that met incredible initial resistance. The attitude was "can't be done" because of the existing Federal Acquisition Regulations (FAR). The BAA allowed the Smart Ship Team to express its intentions and interests only and to solicit any and all ideas without implying that anything further would happen with the ideas. Using the Web page saved time on both ends.

THE HAMMER SURPRISE

On August 29, 1996, the Honorable John Dalton, secretary of the navy, on behalf of Vice President Al Gore, presented the Smart Ship Team with The Hammer Award for reinventing government processes in support of the President's National Performance Review Principles. The citation accompanying the award read:

> The Navy's Smart Ship is the antithesis of "bureaucratic red tape." The project brings together a very diverse group of energetic and talented civilian and military individuals representing a variety of organizations who have succeeded in breaking with past practices by challenging policy, culture, and tradition of procuring and operating Navy ships. The Smart Ship Team has been charged with rapidly changing policies and identifying new technologies which will reduce the workload for a Navy ship's crew, improve sailors' quality of life, and enhance the ship's mission readiness.

THE AFTERMATH

Smart Ship Team members Commander Bill Olsen and Arnie Ostroff both attended the August 1996 School for Innovators in Estes Park, Colorado. Bill returned to find he'd been extended on the Smart Ship Team, Stage 11, and Arnie found himself on the new Smart Base Team.

The Smart Ship spun off two more Thinking Expeditions shortly afterwards—Smart Base and Smart Staff—and three Thinking Expeditions were run for US Army Materiel Command (AMC) to kick-start Project Management Offices (PMOs) teams.

Once you've hit the summit, Level 7 doesn't stay Level 7 for very long!

CASE STUDY

INTERNATIONAL PROJECT MANAGEMENT
Mindshifting from Chaos to Leadership
by K. Kent Malone
Halliburton Company

OK, admit it. You always questioned when you would ever have a real-world use for all that theory you learned in Macro and Micro Economics or your required college calculus class. And, you were right—you have never once used a function or derivative since that door smacked your fanny on the way out. The 7 levels of change, however, is real-world stuff—concepts and ideas you can apply to your everyday work, your long-term career and your longer-term life.

Me, I'm one of the lucky ones. I got to attend a life-changing training experience in expedition mode with Rolf and his crew of different guides back in August of 2000 (School for Innovators—Expedition XXXIII). The training was intense but extremely effective in getting this very conservative manager to not only live, work and think differently, but to indeed embrace and encourage change.

One of the best examples I can give is to show a real-world application of the concepts described in this book. About nine months after going on the Vanguard School for Innovators Expedition, I visited one of our large international projects and was simply astounded by what I saw. The project requirements, the location, and the accumulation of participants from all over the globe had given chaos a free hand in ruling the project. If you've ever disturbed an ant mound, you will immediately recognize chaos—hundreds of people running around in dozens of different directions.

To combat the chaos, management had implemented reams and reams of processes and procedures. Management had gotten their arms around the chaos and was starting to do the right things. They didn't even have to read Rolf's book to know that doing the right things was effective management. It was common sense to move right into Level 1.

So now that management was in control, and chaos was mostly overwhelmed, hundreds of people were focused into dozens of pockets of activity, with everyone doing the right things. There is nothing like a few rules and requirements to stifle initiative, however. With all these rules, how can anyone get anything done? Overall progress on the project had ground to a halt. Management brought the pockets of activity into touch with each other. As they talked, they began to realize how their work impacted the next pocket of work. They began to shift into doing the right things right (Level 2 change) to help their downstream flow and, lo and behold, efficiency broke out. Again, no prompting was necessary to move into this common sense second level of change.

I showed up after several months of this effective efficiency, about the time the project team realized they were getting farther and farther behind in the schedule. One of the critical aspects of this project was that if they didn't do something quickly, they would be facing some tremendous liquidated damages for late completion at the end of the project. The 7 levels of change was the perfect tool for me to use to explain the predicament they were in and the steps necessary to move toward a successful outcome on the project.

As shown in the diagram below, the first thing I did was lay the management-to-leadership continuum over the 7 levels of change and add the concept of chaos to round it out. It was then easy to show them how they were very effectively controlling the chaos by managing things and ensuring the compliance of their personnel to processes and procedures.

The 7 Levels of Change

In fact, they had such good control of the project at this point that it was now painfully apparent there was no way they could avoid incurring significant liquidated damages at the end of the project without tremendous increases in their productivity. In other words, they needed to quickly quit managing things and start leading toward the desired results—and higher levels of change.

The quickest way to do that would be to implement an atmosphere of change into the project, and it had to start at the top. The next two levels of change, improving and cutting (Levels 3 and 4), would be very helpful in getting the project back on schedule. Improving is still in the less innovative, more management side of the continuum, but it definitely helped to improve the processes that were broken and make other minor changes that were obvious to improve efficiency.

Level 4 is the first change level where leadership qualities are required for implementation. That requires a hard look at the organization and a conscientious decision to make a significant change. We're talking about cutting here and that just doesn't come easy to managers. We've become accustomed to those steps, processes, tools, whatever's that we use everyday, and the idea of *not* doing it is heresy. Here is where the mindshift model must come into play. What are we doing that is too good, too perfect and must therefore be totally done away with so we can move on to really doing the things that will get us diff*f*erent results? It wasn't easy, but once we committed to cutting, significant progress was realized on the project.

Copying was an easier sell to project management. Top level personnel were brought in to implement innovative concepts that had proven successful on other projects and, as with Level 4, Level 5 again brought significant improvements in progress, but there was still a lot of ground to make up.

The heart of the matter was that we were going to have to quickly get to Level 6 to overcome the time we had wasted during the period of chaos and the subsequent autocratic-management period focused on Levels 1 and 2. This was a very hard sell to project management. "We've done dozens of projects just like this—why do anything different?" they were heard to say, along with many other head-in-the sand comments. The reality was we had never done anything like this project—it had the same names and was similar in many ways to previous projects, but the unique circumstances surrounding this project made it, indeed very different. It required a diff*f*erent approach, and Level 6 was where we would find the answers.

Fortunately, Level 7 wasn't required for this project. "The impossible" is a specialty of the company I work for and has set us apart—diff*f*erentiated us—from our competitors time and time again over the years. Do not be afraid to set your company—and your life—on a diff*f*erent path to achieve impossible results!

NOTE: Kent Malone is senior manager of sub-contracts in Kellogg Brown & Root, the engineering and construction division of Halliburton Company, Houston, Texas, and has just been promoted again—for the second time since graduating form the School for Innovators eighteen months ago.

CASE STUDY

A CHANGE PLAN FOR DENTISTRY
Ronald Konig, D.D.S.
Houston, Texas
www.konigdds.com

I was visiting my dentist, leaning back in the chair with my mouth wide open, and Bam!—an idea hit me. I reached up quickly, pulled a blue slip out of my shirt pocket, and started writing it down. Dr. Konig immediately stopped: "What are you doing?" he asked. I took off the headphones he'd given me and said: "I just got a great idea. I always get some new ideas or insights while I'm here and I don't want to lose them." That got me explaining blue slips and what I do.

Ron Konig isn't really a dentist—he's a change agent and innovator. He knows that people don't just want cavities filled; they want their teeth to look good, feel good and last a long time. They want a beautiful smile. Ron and his staff know what it takes to create smiles that look and feel good. And technically, he's recognized as being in the top 1 percent of the dentists in aesthetic skills in the United States.

I gave Ron a copy of the 7 levels of change, and each time I'd visit his office, he'd update me on how he was using the book. Here's how Ron Konig has taken his practice, his office, and his staff of professionals through the 7 levels of change. It's a blueprint for dental excellence and a strategy for change.

LEVEL 1 CHANGE: *Effective*—Doing the Basics
> Getting started. Two-minute exam by dentist.
> Quickie cleaning, in-and-out mindset.
> Patient needs filling work, has large silver-mercury fillings.

LEVEL 2 CHANGE: *Efficiency*—Tightening Up. More basics, but explaining things to patients.
> Taking a little more time to educate patient.
> Still doing "drill bill fill" dentistry.
> Staff is still just "there" with little direct involvement.
> Call and remind patients the day before scheduled appointments—keep their time in mind too.
> *No* wait time for appointments.

LEVEL 3 CHANGE: *Improving Everything Constantly.* Starting to understand and listen to the patient better. Begins to discuss and involve patient in diagnosis and treatment planning. Providing better care and better treatment.

➤ Treat more comprehensively. Begins to include periodontal (gum) evaluation during exam.

   I.   Begins training staff to a different level—they understand the care and treatment needed as well as the patient.

   II.   Constantly upgrading the "total office look" visually. Patients immediately see what can be done when they walk in the door

      A.   "Smile Gallery" of framed *portrait* photos of patients—with their endorsements.

      B.   Large book of before-and-after photos in waiting room—not of teeth, but of smiles!

   III.   Continuous education for everyone—Dentist, assistants, technicians, reception and administration. Holds offsite staff retreats with entire office to build a real team.

   IV.   Variable office hours: very early on some days, late on others—to accommodate patients' busy work and life schedules.

LEVEL 4 CHANGE: *Getting Clarity*—Starting to see the whole picture. Eighty-twenty shift into longer-term relationships with the patients, families.

   I.   Beginning to see payoff of educating and raising awareness in patients, and patients are also seeing benefits!

      A.   Focus shifts to the 20 percent that is most vital for the long-term. Exam includes whole patient: jaws, bite (occlusion), gums (periodontal) health, cancer screening.

      B.   Understanding what is happening, understanding the patient, learning to really listen to what the patient desires and temperaments are.

      C.   Time is based on patients' needs. Taking time to properly diagnose patients' needs, implementing new technology.

      D.   Intraoral cameras, taking diagnostic models of teeth, proper x-rays.

   II.   Staff has dropped "just there" to becoming friendly *people* who know and like you; they ask about family members and remember details and conversations from last visit.

      A.   Everything is absolutely trustworthy in terms of quality. *I know* I am getting excellent care and advice.

      B.   Staff understands and participates in caring for patient. Dentist leaves discussion of costs to staff, thus making money a neutral issue.

LEVEL 5 CHANGE: *Copying and Adapting from the Best of the Best—Comprehensiveness*

Comprehensive approach, major behavioral and lifestyle changes in dentist, staff and patients.

> New dentistry: adopting new techniques, cutting-edge technology, and elective care such as bleaching and basic cosmetic care.

> Staff and doctors are now learning excellent new communication skills as well as advanced treatment skills. Patients' depth of understanding in all areas increases significantly.

> Dentist and staff survey patients' likes and dislikes about their appearance, looks and teeth.

> Offering patient the best care doctor knows of, learning to complete care in timely manner with no pain and maximum efficiency. Referrals to specialists when needed.

LEVEL 6 CHANGE: *Different. Doing things no one else is doing.* Developing long-term patient-dentist relationships.

    I.   Patients have an "educated" understanding of everything that is being done and their dental health history. Questions and answers go deeper from both sides.

        A. Delivering what is promised and expected; patient expectations are now extremely high.

        B. Doctor and staff understand the homage "five-star care and service"— not just lip service.

        C. Deliver only the best—no exceptions.

        D. If it isn't right, fix it.

    II. *Changing lives daily with every visit!!!*

        A. Reshaping bite, teeth, and jaw alignment, implant treatment.

        B. Major aesthetics/cosmetic dentistry that looks natural and beautiful (no "Chiclets" or black lines).

        C. Patients leave the office not just feeling different, but *looking and being* different.

LEVEL 7 CHANGE: IMPOSSIBLE—*Doing things that can't be done.* Beyond comprehensive in approach. Creating a new smile, a new look, a new life with every patient.

> Taking the "Five-star care and service" to new levels.

> Doctor and staff both continue taking classes to stay on the leading edge of care and service—this becomes a much more challenging objective.

> Practice now gets frequent referrals from other doctors and patients with complex problems as well as from those who demand the best.

> Level of professionalism, communication, and treatment extends to levels unforeseen in the medical world. *This never stops—Level 8 is in sight!*

—————————————— CASE STUDY ——————————————

CAMPBELL JUNIOR HIGH SCHOOL
Cypress-Fairbanks ISD, Texas

How do you energize junior high school teachers and students? Gwen Keith, the principal of Campbell Junior High School in the Cypress-Fairbanks Independent School District of Houston, Texas, did it by running her school like a Thinking Expedition on a day-to-day basis. She had attended the School for Innovators (Expedition XIV-April 1995) on a scholarship and had been immediately taken with the power of the expedition concept and the tools and techniques used to teach creative thinking. At the time, she was principal of Frazier Elementary School, but shortly after she returned, and before she could try out many of the new ideas she had, Gwen was promoted laterally to become the principal of a junior high school.

New to junior high and moving into a new leadership position, Gwen found her different (Level 6) ideas met with some resistance. To further complicate her ideas, she wanted her new school to be run by teams. Initially, in August 1995, her teachers and staff voted it down. But Gwen didn't quit. One year later, only five eighth-grade teachers were not on teams. How? By ootching in change.

Levels 1 and 2 (Efficiency & Effectiveness): On the first day of her Thinking Expedition, Gwen introduced the idea of blue slips and asked plenty of tough questions. The next morning she began her work on team building. At 2:00 PM, she taught the entire staff how to tie a water knot, a basic mountaineering tool for securing webbing and ropes. She had learned how to tie the knot during the School for Innovators while rock climbing. She then formed them all up into small rope teams.

Level 1 (Effectiveness): Her first goal was to form the A Team (Administration) into a working team. The A Team consists of a principal, director of instruction, assistant principals, counselors, and diagnostician. We conducted a half-day KAI and MBTI workshop for the A Team, which then led to their supporting using another staff development day with us to orient the entire school of 125 professionals and para-professionals on thinking type and style (KAI and MBTI, a Level 5 change and a good example of ootching).

To emphasize the expedition theme, Gwen says she used the theme of risk-taking and teamwork throughout all of her staff-development activities. While most of the actual changes she initially implemented at Campbell were lower-level changes, the idea of running the school like a Thinking Expedition was beyond Level 7 (impossible) for many of the teachers and administrators. But in August, at the start of the 1996 school year, I went out and, with Gwen helping as a guide, launched a volunteer team of fourteen sixth-, seventh-, and eighth-grade teachers as a Thinking Expedition at Campbell. They would in turn be leading 360 of the eleven hundred students on a special Expedition Track for the next ten months.

Gwen's still going. Her school is always on expedition, looking for ways to keep Campbell on the innovation track. Following are some excerpts from Gwen's Thinking Expedition journal notes outlining some of the changes realized.

Level 1 (Effectiveness): We worked on team building with the A Team. Established new ways of doing business with them. Approached the mountain very slowly. Decided what I would ignore and what I would change regarding past practices of how the A Team meetings worked. Did a lot of talk regarding expeditions and risk taking.

Level 2 (Efficiency): Sent Laurence Binder, director of instruction, to the School for Innovators in September 1995 (Expedition XV), so we could speak the same language and hook into the mission together. Later sent Assistant Principal Bonnie Pnegra to a School for Innovators sponsored by Exxon Chemicals (Expedition XVII) just for educators. Built from the expertise of other members of the A Team.

Level 5 (Copying): We had a half-day workshop on MBTI and KAI. Began to get results and buy into the Thinking Expedition idea and teaming. The A Team decided that the entire staff should do MBTI and KAI!

Levels 3, 4, and 6 (Improving, Cutting, and Different): Converted a storeroom into Base Camp. Used the expedition theme for decorations. Have mountain-climbing artwork on walls. Large table to work together (Level 3). Began to hold A Team meetings here for problem solving, setting goals. There was a sense of change in the air as we worked in the room together very differently than we had elsewhere before (Level 6). No phone in the Base Camp conference room (Level 4). We are on expedition, therefore no interruptions from outside.

Levels 5 and 6 (Copying and Different): We copied ourselves! I used the A Team and what it had learned to change the format of the faculty meetings (Level 6). They had been done the same way since 1978 right down to people sitting in the same chairs. We used blue slips (Level 1, but for this group Level 6!). We modeled teaming by using the A Team as an example (Level 5). We walked our talk. We conducted the meeting as a team. Got people up out of their chairs and moving around. A Team members became facilitators for meetings and taught tools like brainwriting and blue slips.

The Results (Level 5): Gwen's ideas and example are spilling over (Level 5) into other schools in Cypress-Fairbanks Independent School District, and CyFair ISD now has a large cadre of educators who are graduates of the School for Innovators. Special assessment and measurement processes are being developed to monitor (Level 2) the long-term effects and changes of the Expedition track on student learning. Whatever they are, excitement and enthusiasm is high for students and teachers alike!

UPDATE—MARCH 2002

Five Years Later . . .

Gwen's initial challenge was getting the staff behind her, using expedition thinking and levels of change as a roadmap and guide to leverage herself with various groups. Her goal was to become a change agent in the school, focusing on changing staff attitudes regarding staff development, TAAS (state mandated) test, working in teams, and technology.

She formed the first expedition regarding technology by creating a small rope team to do different. At the beginning only 22 percent of the staff was making use of school computers for themselves or their students. The computer technology course requirement was dropped; the objects and skills were integrated into the seventh grade. The computer technology teachers became guides and helped content teachers to plan lessons that would use their subject matter and integrate the objects and skills taught in the computer literacy course together. This allowed students to take an extra semester elective—a bonus for them. The guides taught alongside the teachers in the labs as the curriculum from other courses would be meshed together. Eventually the classroom teachers were using more and more technology on their own.

Level 7 Results: All students were able to pass the end of the computer literacy test and received credit for the course.

Level 6 Results: Subsequent years have expanded to all grade levels and subject matter. There is now a full time technology coach who serves as the guide for the use of technology. Labs are constantly full and they are now piloting some cutting-edge software in the school for selected academically at-risk students, ESL students, and special education students.

Level 3 (Big) Results: Students are still passing the end-of-the-year test and doing well, and 100 per cent of the staff has teacher tools in their classrooms. The staff has whole heartedly agreed that these students can be pulled out of regular elective classes for six weeks; the staff also agreed to spend over eight thousand dollars on the project. Talk about a change in attitude regarding the use of technology in this school!!!!!!!!!

Level 5 & 6 Results: On the staff-development front, in the beginning the staff demonstrated a less-than-positive attitude regarding staff development. Expeditions were formed for them with the first staff development offsite held at a new location—Galveston. It was a suburban expedition where the staff was sent into the community for a day. There were ten rope teams in ten rented vans. They were equipped with maps, cameras, supplies, and a field-guide notebook. They were to visit churches, home builders, businesses, retailers, and real estate offices to find out as much as they could about each team's section of our attendance zone. They created field guides for each zone. By going on expedition, each team was able to help the entire staff gain a much better understanding of the Campbell attendance mountain and ended up with a much better understanding of our school community. They all saw how important it is for educators to get outside their classrooms.

Level 3 Results: They revisited the Myers-Briggs and updated the type and style profiles of the various teams that exist in the school. They also were able to bring new staff members up-to-date on the use of MBTI to create teams and understand differences.

Level 3 Results: One rope team was formed for training in Capturing Kids' Hearts; it has become active in staff development. Another rope team was sent for training in Understanding Children from Poverty and have conducted staff development in the area of at-risk student population. Participation in rope teams helps everyone learn, who in turn can serve as guides for others.

Level 6 Results: For the past several years the staff has ranked the staff development at Campbell above 90-percent satisfaction on the job-satisfaction survey conducted by the district and the staff development liaison.

Level 7 Results: The TAAS Test. When Gwen first arrived, the staff regarded the mandated TAAS test (Texas Assessment of Academic Skills) as though it belonged to the counselors—not anyone else. An office of academic achievement was established, and a guide was found to help them pilot the use of data and statistical information to predict scores. Building funds were used to hire the guide (consultant), and now the district uses this consultant in every school! A rope team helped lead the rest of the staff, and scores have gone up dramatically. Seventy-five percent of the staff actively mentors between one and three students who are statistically most likely not to pass the TAAS test, giving up planning periods to help students. They have created intervention programs which require them to eat lunch (and sometimes breakfast) with students to tutor their students in TAAS objectives. Over 90 percent of our population is passing the TAAS test, and every teacher is involved in a TAAS studies class that is conducted twice a week. All electives teachers are involved in teaching TAAS. This includes coaches, band, art, orchestra, choir—*everyone* is involved.

Appendix B
The School for Innovators (SfI)

EXPEDITION XXXVII
Joshua Tree, California
6–13 December 2001

Planning for Expedition XXXVII began early in 2001 with 27 April as the start date. To accomodate everyone's schedules, the date slipped three times, from April to July 17 and then to September 21. On September 11, everything went on hold. By November we had decided that it was important to move ahead. We shifted the venue from Estes Park, Colorado, to California and warmer weather.

Eight stalwarts clipped in for Expedition XXXVII:

➢ Barbara Zelon—NASA/Johnson Space Center

➢ Gregg Shuman—Kellogg Brown & Root

➢ Jimmy Cook—Kellogg Brown & Root

➢ Kathryn Clark—NASA HQ

➢ Keith Ackley—Kellogg Brown & Root

➢ Kimberly Fernandez—Kellogg Brown & Root

➢ Marlo Del Rosario—Evans & Wood

➢ Susan Haunschild—Kimberly-Clark

During every School for Innovators Expedition, we pause regularly and take time to reflect on history that we all are making. We use those pause points to write brief "history snapshots" of the most significant events that come to mind.

The following is a composite history of School for Innovators Expedition XXXVII, extracted from the daily flashbacks of the eight participants and synthesized into the flow of events.

HISTORY SNAPSHOTS—DAY-BY-DAY
How Expeditions Happen: the Idea

One morning Bill handed me *The 7 Levels of Change*, saying "You *must* read this." Over the next couple of weeks we talked about the book as I read it. I started a journal, beginning with Me, Inc.® Fascinating process. About the time I was finishing, I got an E-mail from Rolf saying Bill had recommended me for the course. This had become an ongoing saga. First try was in summer, July I think. The timing of that was bad for most, so the school was moved to September. Then, 11 September, and few were able to fly. But Bill persisted, saying "This will be good for you, this will be good for NASA." So, I moved my entire schedule again for October.

From the first time I thought about this until "I'm going!" was a skeptical period. Surprise was my first thought as this was unexpected, certainly unplanned. Followed by skepticism and denial . . . not enough time . . . too much time . . . not a good time of year! Fairly quickly I moved into acceptance and planning, on looking forward. I talked with School for Innovators alumni and heard their takes on the School—very positive and upbeat. I started to get excited myself! "Life changing!" is what I was told. 11 September. My company banned travel; I cancelled again and thought "I'll never get out there!" On again, off again, on again . . .

Then we received a series of E-mails setting a new schedule for December in a different, warmer location, because Denver would have been too cold for an Expedition with outdoors work. Finally, we learned about Joshua Tree, California.

It's A Go! Rapid Preparations

First decisions were what to bring, what I have, and what I need to buy; then figuring out if my wife has any needs or conflicts this week. Was I going to miss anything with the kids? Yes! Christmas programs! I spent Monday and Tuesday making sure things got closed out at work. Didn't sleep well the night before in anticipation of the week.

Wow! What great excitement! After hearing others talk about their previous expectations, the thought of my own made me smile from ear to ear with excitement.What was it going to be like with me gone for ten days?

I was ready to do something unique and was a little sad about missing some "normal" activity around the holiday. I thought "Good, I can refocus on my thoughts and recharge." I think I was tired from expending so much energy on people and felt a break could be good for me, my family, and my relationships. Emotion high, thoughts of "is it really, really going to happen this time . . . where are we going—the venues all changed, what about timing—too many details to address around the house. Feel like a giddy child bolting out of the car on a promised trip to the zoo . . . what will it be like? who will I see there? . . . what's the weather?—what to pack, where's my flashlight?—no, I won't take long johns—I'll probably regret that . . . oh, oh yeah, this stuff has to get done at the office too, I'll shoot for four hours of sleep—well three, would be okay, two is better than none, one will have to do. I can sleep on the plane . . . ."

Day One—Arrival

Everyone gathered together at the Yucca Valley Inn at 5:00 PM, met one another, got neat stuff . . . one of which was our passports. Other useful tools we worked on were blue slips, noticing twenty different things, "realizing" and a hot washup.

The room is set as a mixture of the southwest, Christmas and Expedition with pan-pipe music (Incan?) in the background. Trunks are opened—vests and eVISAs passed out, and the Expedition begins in earnest. Travelers learn of each other's little known secrets as we all quietly begin the journey. Blue slips—the first fun tool of thinking different are introduced. Then the avalanche begins—at first slow but eventually taking on momentum.

There are some teddy bears that do some talking too, but are relatively quiet. "So what's next?"—we are all learning from the experience we are having. Even dinner becomes an adventure, and we tend more toward beer than grape, and all enjoy the conversation.

But there is more to come after dinner, and we all head back with heady thoughts about those bears. Some bears came from foreign countries; some were American. They didn't talk much and hung out in a group. Dressed strangely too, some were naked . . . no modesty at all. Me? I was fondest of the large, dark one. He was quick, agile, and stoic. I'm sure he has a sense of humor. I like his big paws, too. I'm glad they're here.

Many questions come into our minds as day one comes to a close. Will it be any colder? How much sleep will we really get? Will we truly be able to gather all this info coherently enough to use it once we get back to our old routines and environments? When does the rock climbing start? Do they have to play that mind-numbing synthesizer music?

Day Two: the Real Beginning

We started the morning with *"Namaste"*—the Nepalese greeting that means *"I see the spirit in you,"* took our "mental temperatures" and also began journaling. All three become daily rituals.

We worked through the concept of "different," the benefits of pair-and-share, and the dangers of expectations. Definitions of innovation, change, the normal distribution of ideas were first presented. As pairing-and-sharing continued, we started to connect with each other and also with each other's "messes."

The role of "base camp manager" was discussed, and duties, requirements, responsibilities were defined with respect to both a problem-solving situation and on a mountaineering expedition.

Me, Inc.®—Through Others' Eyes

The evening of day two was our first Me, Inc.® board meeting. To prepare for that, we were introduced to Me, Inc.® and wrote down our strengths, skills, abilities, needs, objectives. What is our dream job? What was our worst job? Why? What is something I want to change? What don't I know but wish I did? We took a walk on the golf course, sharing with one person a little-known fact or an aspiration. Later we held Me, Inc.® board meetings and got intensive feedback on our strengths/dreams and our messes. We also got ideas on things to do with our mess; primarily this was about each individual for the first time sharing some pretty deep feelings and seeing ourselves through the eyes of others.

Day Three—What Mountain Are We Climbing?

Day three began with some reflecting and journaling on the clubhouse patio! The rest of the morning and early afternoon were composed of viewing the experience of real-life Expeditions to Mt. Everest and inner Africa. We each defined our own mountains, summits, and "cages," and made preparations for scaling some real mountains. We also explored the concept of innovation as an active "doing" process (innovation is not innovation until it is implemented). Despite this busy morning's activities, there was an air of tense anticipation of the afternoon's climb . . .

Fear, Noticing and Shopping!

Midday three we worked on the 7 levels of fear, which correspond to the 7 levels of change. When we went through the fear discussion before the actual climb. Will see how it impacts our perceptions of the upcoming climb. We also learned how to notice and how to notice what we weren't noticing. We took a field trip to a shop and started noticing. We also noticed things that we wanted to buy!

How on Earth Are We Going to Get Down?

The beginning of the climb involved getting my footing. I learned to twist my feet and try not to use my hands too much. I concentrated on every step; before I realized it, we were actually pretty high. We stopped for a brief rest, and someone mentioned to looking out over the valley. Wow! I was pretty impressed, and not very scared; a couple of loose rocks—not a big deal. As we climbed higher, we started to run into more obstacles. We would look at all the options and choose what seemed easiest. We were very good at reassessing our positions. Awesome. The next obstacle was a bit more of a challenge. We chose a path that requires a bit of maneuvering. All I could think was "how are we going to get back down," but trusted Rolf's judgment and kept going. We summitted shortly after and stopped for a picture. It was a great feeling, but quite overshadowed by my fear of going back down. But all I can say is "Thank God for my team!"

Perspective Is Everything

Of course, the group had to choose the most difficult of the options before us—larger hill, unknown terrain—a little later in the day. It is odd being tied to the rest of the folks. The rope is too loose, the rope is too tight. Now it is my turn to lead—the mental work should not have been different; I had been calculating moves all along, but it felt different, like I was somehow more responsible. It is starting to grow dark. We have reached our summit—it is breathtaking, both the view and the feeling. Maybe I really can lead, at best when I have such a strong team.

Think It, Try It, Did It

Did not think I would make it here (the summit), not scary but major. Can't quite catch my breath. At least I didn't let the team down. Sunset on a chapter, got to go . . . trip down was short, sweet and easy. I like the end of the rope—more my pace; I can set my pace a bit better. Accomplishment for me was major. We'll see what the future brings. Me, Myself, and I are willing to try.

The parallels to "work" are numerous—false summit, losing clear direction, forgetting to preplan and look for alternative solutions. Team was *way* above my expectations. So much for expectations—there is a learning there also. Coming down was interesting. You could feel the tension increase as the darkness fell. Natural, I suppose. Letdown after success.

I liked the way the dynamic worked of leading, following, and learning to work interdependently. We had to come down in the dark, and it added one more level of excitement and challenge. However, it is sometimes hard to see the big picture when you are concentrating so much on what's directly in front of you. It's easy to lose your overall sense of direction.

Buzz, Buzz, Buzzzzzzz

One team already down; the other navigating slowly down in full darkness. There is a palpable buzz in the group. Excitement about the climb summiting and the novelty of the trek back. Exhaustion has not set in. Some blue slips and a bit of journaling before we relocate to the warm comfort of the hotel lobby for discussion of personal values. Each team member talked own values and remaining team shared their observations—powerful communication and connection; first tears shed.

Now the discussions! Excitement, camaraderie high, high, high. Good food, good friends. Then the buzz became zzzzzz's. Our sleep was infiltrated by dreams of our day. It must have been the adrenaline from the day's climb. All of the journaling, writing, and sharing our summit cards and then walking over to the hotel lobby to find another group was having a party at our base camp! Discussion of our values with our group. Powerful words and thoughts. Suddenly the alarm went off . . . day four already.

Day Five—What a Mess!

We had a very hard time getting everyone to remember what we had been doing since day two, not to mention focus . . . a very difficult thing for us. We started using "tell me more" and "do you mean" to add clarity, and it began leading us towards results.

The Canadian mountaineer gave us some tips on bouldering: Planning moves ahead of time; accuracy, balance, precision, and commitment. Don't go into areas you can't get out of. Talent vs. attitude. Be aware of changing conditions. Then we grabbed our gear to go climb!

THE BIG CLIMB

The Guides Who "Just" Climb Mountains

Everyone was happy and excited. The guides were laid back, patient, but revealed an incredible amount of insight into human behavior, fear analysis, and skill strength.

➢ Don: Capable of climbing a mountain in a single "bounce." Great sense of humor that he uses to disarm or focus the issue at hand. Lead mentor, innocent. Reminds me somewhat of the bass player (or guitar) from the Muppets band.

➢ Steve: great teacher, very patient. Takes the time to not just explain things, but to show you also. Very laid back, makes you feel comfortable in what you are doing, and his humor was very relaxing. Great at problem solving and making you feel invested in the outcome, made climbing look like he was "just" walking up the mountain.

We're psyched and ready to go.

I Know I Can, I Know I Can

The sheer emotions are bubbling through as I remind myself, yes I can! I have faith and magic shoes and gloves! It's possible! Just hang on! The first pitch was tricky, but it helped to be the first. The key was to just take it slow and assess each step one at a time.

Felt Absolutely Sure We Would Summit Today

It's beautiful up here. You can see for miles. This is an adventure I'll always remember. Fear was not the issue. Summiting was not the issue. Working it out was everything. Sun was warm—warm to the bones, like heaven. Lots of exhilaration getting the hang of the climbing routine—and willing to go again.

Getting ready—how do we decide order? How do we tie in? As a team, we are searching for the mountain in the mess, for the route in the mountain. I am in competition-preparation mode—focused on the devil I'm about to attack, and it's not the mountain. I watch the others. I took the route uncharted, and it has made all the difference.

SUMMIT THOUGHTS

Ok, at the top. This is it? Huge letdown! Don't want to stop.

The summit is great because I loved some of the maneuvers necessary to get there. My main feeling was one of ready-to-climb at least one more time. I feel slightly unfinished. Is that why climbers continue to climb?

A high—at least an eleven the whole day. I was and still am on the top of the world, and the vantage was renewal; I haven't felt so "unburdened" in years, I bet at least twenty. Feel like I have a clean slate to work with, a fresh toolbox, and a renewed purpose.

The similarities between the mountains of Joshua Tree and our metaphorical mountains and especially how we attack them are becoming more and more clear.

The rush was more than I had imagined. The view, more breathtaking, the sensation more empowering. I have made a major step in my life and have started committing to myself! I will carry this feeling with me for when I begin to think "I can't."

We've summitted, and everyone is psyched. I wish we could all be together as a group to celebrate together.

Who would have ever guessed I'd climb 160 feet to summit a mountain?! Not me. I guess that's what Level 7 change is all about . . .

It feels great to reach the top. It's absolutely beautiful up here. You can see for miles. Great to see for miles. Great to see how much can be accomplished if you "just" put your mind into it and commit. This is an adventure I'll always remember; I will carry this memory into life.

AFTERMATH

The Descent after the Descent

Once we returned from cold but exciting climb, we paired up and read our climbing observations to each other, discussed how our observations related to our personalities and how the climb related to the CPS model.

The ride back to base camp provided time for storytelling and for catching our breath.

Over dinner Kim started a blue-slip activity, but no one had brought blue slips to the table. Kim saved us, had us tear up our placemats ("place matting" instead of blue slipping), write on those about the facility, the people, the food. What would we do different?

After dinner there was a CPS facilitation demonstration lead by Rolf and Durwin. We gained specific insights and tips, rules, and techniques for facilitating our own CPS sessions. Then it was our turn and we practiced facilitating meetings.

So, Where Are We? Where Are You?

Rolf set the stage for the "Where are we?" process, and we located both the team and ourselves on the map (where we felt we were now)—and we were "all over the map."

> We discussed the most opposite views of personal interpretation. This revealed how differently we were interpreting the map, and our perceptions and thinking, but we didn't notice.

> We paired up to clarify and locate on the map where we thought the group was, and all hell broke loose! The two groups became two "camps," one trying to convince and persuade the other.

> As a result of all this two-camp, lack of listening, few facts with many opinions, and huge emotions . . . a "meeting" broke out. We broke every creative thinking rule we had learned so far, but it became the ultimate learning tool. Chaos! Rolf was sitting back trying not to step in and tell us what to do.

Before the beginning of great brilliance, there must be chaos.
Before a brilliant person begins something great,
he/ she must look foolish in front of a crowd.
—I Ching

THE FORCED MARCH TO BASE CAMP

After what seemed like hours of strong opinions about approaches, routes, and even which summit to ascend, and even if we were on the same planet, we backed down from the chaos and reassessed. The discussion was robust and passionate, and finally we did define the location of base camp. We consecrated base camp with a Nepalese Puja ceremony led by Durwin that was pretty amazing. Once camp was set up, we began acclimatizing by taking inventory of our tools and looking toward the summit.

And on that note we went to bed.

ANTICIPATION AND ANXIETY: THE LAST DAY?

My outlook was one of excitement towards "graduation" and sadness at leaving the new friends I had made that week. The day was packed with more learning, and doing, and experiencing along the way—new methods and techniques for creative problem solving, and we even had "client planning meetings."

The day sped by; anticipation and anxiety were palpable. We pushed on late into the night; practice, practice, practice—I am rusty, but it felt good. Then suddenly we were there—the end—our summit?!? The diplomas handed out, the images of our "shared" experience flashing up on the wall. The rope ceremony—moving. Final good-byes are incomplete, KC must dash and head for the airport now; others are exhausted, too much emotion to say good-bye. "Sleep 'til you get up" is the order. One last look at that amazingly clear night sky with stars that go on forever.

CLOSING DOWN AND BITTERSWEET BEGINNINGS

The week reinforced for me how well you can get to know someone when you put in the energy and time. Sleep deprivation and pent-up energy had mixed and was creating interesting dreams (or was I awake?) and perpetual thinking. I found out I could stay confined in a place sitting for longer than four days, and that I could live without aerobic exercise. Brainwriting was particularly energizing—the ultimate in piggybacking and idea jumping.

There was the anticipation of going home to see our families and loved ones, but also the hesitation of leaving Joshua Tree for the "real" world. We delved deeper into different techniques for CPS facilitations and collectively provided input for the rest of the group's individual summits. "Brainwriting" generated some particularly creative ideas . . . After a steak dinner with champagne toasts, we prepared for our final ascent to the summit. The evening/early morning ended with the presentation of diplomas, and an emotional closing rope ceremony. We said our good-byes and began mental preparations for our most challenging climbs awaiting us back home.

WHAT A WEEK!

It's hard to believe that this is the last day. We spent the majority of the day on the various CPS models and learning new tools that we can use in CPS, thus completing our toolbox. We stretched our minds and fed off the creativity of others and worked towards our own and group summits. *Namaste.*

RETURN AND DESCENT—DEPARTURE AND RETURN

Around 4:00 AM, we all found our ways back to our rooms and got ready for our return to the real world. I quickly packed and met the others of our "KBR-Evans & Wood" group at 4:30 AM, and we headed back to L.A.

Despite the lack of sleep, rest was hard to find on the flight back to Houston. The bonds that were formed, the memories and experiences that were shared, all raced through my mind as we flew back over the Rockies. The realization that our very real mountains were looming closer and closer on the horizon became more prevalent as we approached Houston.

Had a welcome, although brief, Expedition flashback as I bumped into Barb as she tried to track down a missing bag at the baggage claim area. However, driving home from Intercontinental Airport in Houston through afternoon rush hour served to further jolt me back into reality.

As I pulled into my garage, my mind was on unpacking, catching up on voice and E-mail, what bills need to be paid right away, how far behind I am at the office, has all the Christmas shopping been taken care of, what sort of name is "Durwin" anyway? Couldn't Michael try and be a little more laid back . . .? As I lugged my baggage into the house, my mind was quickly put back on alert as I was immediately ambushed by four small commandos. It was then that my mission, beliefs, values, and principles combined to hit me square in the pit of my stomach.

The clouds are parting to reveal the summit; it appears that a break in the weather is approaching. Assault on my mountain begins ASAP.

My husband picked me up from the airport; I extroverted all over him, and there was a tear! My thoughts were working on my camps back here at NASA, hugging kids and dogs, and enjoying the thoughts of all our differences and collective experience.

PACKING UP THE SCHOOL FOR INNOVATORS

Day Nine Postponement

In bed by 4 AM, everyone else has left, but up by 9:00 AM and out the door like some child in anticipation of Christmas. Can't sleep—even though I *need* it. It's sunny but very windy, and there is a distinct bite to the air. Climbing would be cold, oh so cold today. Shoot off rest of the roll of film so it can be processed (how may pictures of Joshua Trees does one need to survive in this world?) Off to the processing place, drop the film off, some shopping and then back to the Blue Skies Country Club—our erstwhile base camp for eight days. I am in total denial that the Expedition is over!

Day Ten: Going Home.

Truly want to be back on Expedition. Feeling very alien—"Stranger in a Strange Land." Resolve to call Rolf as soon as I get to and through the airport! Sleep deprivation is taking its toll—missed the exchange and have to backtrack—good thing I have plenty of time. Drop off car and stand in line at check-in. Starting to feel really lonely. Security check—take the vest off, with all its metal parts—and tuck it in the backpack—feel naked without it. Left message for Rolf—energy starting to come back up—sort pictures for "storytelling" when I get home. Need the journal, dig frantically through backpack—it must be in luggage. Sinking feeling settles in . . . journal has got to be in suitcase.

Grave potential for being an Expedition junky.

Appendix C
USAF Electronic Security Command (ESC) Innovation Strategy Paper

DEFINITION: Innovation is the effort to create purposeful, focused change in an enterprise's economic or social potential.

STRATEGY: Build a climate in ESC to foster and support innovative thinking and make the ESC the most innovative, forward-thinking command in the Air Force.

RELATED MASTER PLAN MISSIONS: Innovation applies to all mission and mission support areas with potential for infusion into every aspect of the command.

REFERENCES

- CSAF Innovation Task Force, 1984
- USAF Long-Range Planning Conference, Sep 1985
- CSAF Action Memorandum, 18 Nov 1985

BASIC CONCEPTS

- Innovation is aimed first and foremost at change.
- Institutionalizing innovation is a long-term initiative, won't take hold overnight: time is required for any noticeable change.
- To make innovation work, there must be deliberate corporate commitment and emphasis.
- There cannot be top management isolation, little contact with operations, trenches, customers.
- Executive-level vision is required: People at the top have to manage their organizations' atmosphere to support innovation.
- Innovation and Long-Range Planning are inextricably related.

GOALS AND OBJECTIVES

- Create purposeful, focused change in ESC. Institute a conscious, purposeful search for innovative opportunities throughout ESC.
- Target ESC leadership at every level. Focus that leadership on creating and supporting an environment that encourages innovation.

➤ Generate the active participation of ESC people at all levels throughout the command.

➤ Sustain the active participation of our people in the ESC innovation program.

➤ Actually be more innovative.

ISSUES

➤ Perception is that innovation is all "Hype"—just another buzzword.

➤ The Long-Range Innovation Team (LRIT) concept sounds good, but there is a perception that it is not working as presented.

➤ There is a perception that you can't "legislate" innovation, that it's not possible to organize, focus, create a structure for innovation.

➤ Ideas need to be able to flow to assure a fair hearing, it must not be blockable.

➤ Flexible management practices are required to make innovation a success, accommodate and allow change.

➤ Perception that middle management stifles innovation, creativity, and action.

➤ ESC now experiences excessive bureaucracy, causing delays, blockage at every turn.

➤ Leading technology companies, when faced with a new product or method, time after time, inevitably try to press harder with their old product or way of doing business.

➤ The command culture now fosters the attitude: "But we've always done it that way . . ."

➤ Perceived traditions, rules, policies "prohibit" new ideas and changes.

➤ There is a need to keep innovation program goals fuzzy, broad initially to avoid creating undue opposition to a new idea.

➤ Be willing to fail in non-critical initiatives.

➤ Day-to-day mode of work is the staff and the "in basket" syndrome really impact on people's ability to think creatively and to be innovative.

➤ To foster an environment where the staff can be more innovative, they must be taken out of the day-to-day operations mode. Decentralization of daily operations to the divisions and units will help.

➤ ESC's Form 0 concept and the USAF Suggestion Program (Form 1000) appear similar.

➤ Make the ESC Innovation Program active, responsive. The initiator of ideas should never have to seek a status update.

➤ Idea + Evaluation + Implementation = Innovation. Until an idea has been implemented it is not an innovation.

ESC INNOVATION STRATEGY PAPER ACTION PLAN	OPR	Timing
1. OBJECTIVE: Establish clear Command Section and top leadership commitment		
a. Make comments in briefings, meetings, unit visits, speeches to groups, JJOC, NCO Academy, 8035 Classes, etc.	CC/CV	*Immediate & Continual*
b. Hold informal CC/CV discussion sessions with HQ, unit staffers/operators, e.g., brown bag luncheons	CC/CV	Periodic
c. Develop CC/CV 2–3 slide briefing on innovation in ESC for unit visits.	XP	*Jan. 86*
d. Personal letters/calls from CC/CV on really good innovations. Advertise them.	CC/CV PA	Continual
e. Infuse innovation philosophy into ESC Master Plan: Foreword, Guidance section, Corporate Objectives on Innovation, DCS Objectives.	CC/XP	Oct. 85 Continual
f. Develop Corporate Strategy Paper on Innovation	LRIT	Apr. 86
2. OBJECTIVE: Establish a special HQ Staff function (LRIT: Long Range Innovation Team) directly interfacing with CC/CV to serve as ombudsman, honest broker for ideas, innovations in ESC.		
a. Spin-off HQ LRIT from XPX: Handpicked small group (5–10 people) for one year in that capacity. Innovative leader with no axe to grind. Rotate cross-staff people through the LRIT. Include some new people (non-ESCers)	CC/CV XP	Jul. 86
b. Set up unit-level LRITs to work with unit/CCs, permit field personnel to get ideas up to the top (unit or HQ) for a fair shake. Chain-of-command can make comments, but must forward or implement.	LRIT	May 86
c. Schedule monthly LRIT 1-on-1 direct interchange sessions with CV: status, Forms 0, new ideas, top-level emphasis.	CV	May 86
d. Use "Trends" briefing, Trends Group concept to spark innovation, get ideas moving	XPX	*Oct. 85 Ccontinual*

ESC INNOVATION STRATEGY PAPER ACTION PLAN	OPR	Timing
3. OBJECTIVE: Develop a simple, one-page Innovation form. No justification of idea is needed to implement ideas.		
a. Develop an ESC "Form 0" to solve bureaucratic problems of AF Form 1000/Suggestion Program; move ideas, get them approved/implemented fast . . . and also try to improve AF Form 1000 Processing	LRIT	Sep. 85
b. Make LRIT and Form 0 a "Win-Win" operation with a "no risk, you can't lose" approach.	All	Continual
c. Set up systems to turn around Forms 0 and innovations/implementations fast; rapid feedback to the innovator.	LRIT	May 86
4. OBJECTIVE: Get ESC closer to our customers: the flying, fighting Air Force.		
a. Understand the MAJCOM CINC's and Commander's concepts, needs better, as well as our own. Send non-ESC and EC staffers out to field units for some hands-on operational orientation; send ESCers out on assignments with operational USAF HQs/bases/units	All/DP	Aug. 86
b. Make more interface visits to USAFE, PACAF, SAC, TAC, et. al., to learn their business; develop innovative ways to work solutions to their needs, concepts, ideas.	All	Sep. 86
5. OBJECTIVE: Set up an ESC "Innovation Center" where people can go to brainstorm, get new ideas, listen to lecture cassettes and videos, hold LRIT sessions.		
a. Obtain office space, storyboards and try on a test basis for six months. Put innovative Lt. Col. in charge, focused on specific issue facing ESC.	XPX	Apr. 86
b. Develop ESCers' reading list on innovation, creativity. Work with library to buy, stock Innovation Center	LRIT	Apr. 86
c. Bring in outside thinking on innovation, ways to improve ESC. Learn from industry, other commands, academia, trends.	XPX	
(1) Invite MG Perry Smith (NWC) to visit ESC, share his ideas, concepts	CC/CV	Jul. 86

ESC INNOVATION STRATEGY PAPER ACTION PLAN	OPR	Timing
(2) Invite Prof. John Demidovich (AFIT) to lecture ESC Staff or a symposium.	LRIT	Jun. 86
d. Participate actively in advanced technology symposiums, conferences to collect ideas, learn of others' innovations.	All	Continual
e. Set up an LRIT "short course" on the "how-tos" of innovation (3–5 days): Running an LRIT, Innovation center; Form Os: creating climate for innovation; breaking down barriers/stagnation	LRIT	Jun. 86
6. OBJECTIVE: Structure and organize ESC to be more innovative, carry-out the corporate strategies and emphasize areas.		
a. Make ESC into an operational command: Reinvent the intermediate levels and the headquarters and centers.	CC/XP	Jun. 86
b. Evolve ESC toward small, flat organizations, less management structure/bureaucracy. Use Tiger Team concept to focus, innovate with the critical emphasis areas. Build some "skunkworks" with sunset clauses.	CC/XP	May 86
c. Set up creative relationships: consortiums, universities, other command "piggy-backs."	All	Jul. 86
d. Get into a "rapid-prototyping" mindset: test solutions/products in users' hands early, learn from interaction, adapt/evolve designs	All	Continual
7. OBJECTIVE: Set up PR campaign to highlight ESC as the most innovative command in the Air Force		
a. Publish articles on LRIT concepts in periodicals, newspapers, AU review; work with intra- and extra-ESC publicity	LRIT/PA	Continual
b. Brief "Innovation" and Innovation Center concept constantly to all VIP visitors to ESC. Modify Command Briefing to permanently reflect underlying innovation theme.	All	Apr. 86 Continual
c. Publicize ideas adopted and not adopted, and why in both cases.	LRIT/PA	Continual

Elvira Stestikova's Chart of the 7 Levels of Change

Tools to use	Habits and Characters	Thinking about Thinking	Mind Shift	Pros and Cons	Levels of Fear
LEVEL 1: EFFECTIVENESS—Doing the Right Things					
Blue slips Thinking Journals	Strong rule followers. Black-and-white thinkers. Like to gather the facts. Passionate about details. Complete their tasks to perfection. Highly focused. Accepts rather than challenges. Risk averse. More adaptive in style	Awareness. Focus. One thing at a time. Thinking that produces the intended result. 1-sigma thinking well inside the "normal" range. Convergent thinking.	Focus on the right things. Notice a new definition of what's right. Move from thinking to doing with a new perspective of what's right.	You are focused. The results are immediate. The results are right. . . . . Too focused on the existing process. It closes you off from new ideas.	Paralysis. Fear of doing the wrong things. Doing nothing. Waiting.
LEVEL 2: EFFICIENCY—Doing the Right Things Right					
To Do Lists. Day-Timer/Planner. Blue slips. Voice mail. Phone Logs. E-mail.	Great at finding ways to conserve time, energy, and resources. Task oriented. Structured, orderly. Serious-minded. Tries to fit things into current situation. Seen as "company person." Adaptive in style.	Focused thinking. JIT (Just In Time) Thinking, producing ideas with a minimum of waste, expense, efforts. Logical, analytical.	How to do the right things right? Have to focus on the right things, which also keeps you from doing the wrong things right.	Positive change. Results show up quickly in energy, money, and time. . . . . Can lead to stagnation of ideas. Because of high competency, strong bias against change could exist.	Inefficiency. Fear of wasting time. Fear of doing the right things wrong. Asking constantly for directions.

Tools to use	Habits and Characters	Thinking about Thinking	Mind Shift	Pros and Cons	Levels of Fear
LEVEL 3: IMPROVING—Doing Things Better					
Thinker's Toolbox. Good questions. "Do you mean . . ?" The 5 Whys. 5-Minute Meetings. Pair-and-Share. Power of 25-Minute Meeting. Rules for Creative Meetings. Brainwriting. BIG Idea. NIH. List 101 Goals. PIN—NIP. CPS Model	Focused and task oriented. Not as rule oriented as Level 1 and Level 2. Neat and organized. Looks for ways to improve things. More efficient. Maximizes available resources. Reliable, stable. More consistent.	Better thinking. Positive thinking that moves things toward progress. Thinking to understand. Thinking beyond your own and other people's thinking. Highest level of "normal" or 1-sigma thinking.	In what way might I think better? Focus on better from a positive angle—What's right and how it could be made better, as opposed to "What's wrong?"	Easy measurable changes in time or money savings, more sales or better products. . . . . Overlooked (neglected) interrelatedness of higher level changes associated with those of Level 3.	Catastrophizing. Seeing only the worst case. Fear of bad weather. Fear of things getting worse. Fear of making things worse. Worrying . . .
LEVEL 4: CUTTING—Doing Away With Things					
60 Words for lowering costs.10% less. Re-Red Tagging. Riiippp! Use E-Mail proactively. DUMB Stuff. Pareto Post-its. Convergence-Nominal Voting. Look back down the trail. No more "No." Stop bad Self-Talk.	Preoccupied with saving money, not time. Tends to emphasize utility over novelty. Less rule oriented. Translators. Integrated, versatile, highly employable. Flexible. Can see both sides of an argument. Seen as indecisive.	Stop distorted thinking of blaming, personalizing . . . Rethink, Reframe, Redecide, Revisit, rediscover . . . RE-everything	To stop doing things, refocus your thinking and ask questions "Why?" and "Why NOT?" Level 4 thinking moves you into 2-sigma or interesting thinking.	Effects are immediate and bigger. . . . . Have to give up things that were enjoyable or comfortable. Have to learn something new, which is a negative to some people.	Holding On. Fear of letting go. Focusing on the 80% that only brings 20% of the value. Fear that stopping doing something will be a mistake. Wanting to keep on doing it the old way. Just-in-case thinking: "We may need that—take everything just to be safe."

Tools to use	Habits and Characters	Thinking about Thinking	Mind Shift	Pros and Cons	Levels of Fear
LEVEL 5: COPYING—Doing Things Other People Are Doing					
Dilbert on Management. Benchmarking. Read it for 'em. Write in Books. Let TV be your guide. Copy Great Thinkers. Start listening differently. Trends spotting. Trends Network. Trends Briefing. Tear out new ideas. Visual connections. Visual controls system.	Curious, outwardly focused. Love new. Have more piles and less files in their office. Dress more casually than Level 1 and 2. Bridge people at Level 6 and 7 to those at Level 1, 2, 3, and 4. Can manipulate adaptive structure. Calculated risk taker	Visual thinking— produces image in the mind. Think about what's different and what's missing. The highest level of 2-sigma or interesting thinking.	To copy things other people are doing, you have to see and notice things. Begin noticing things that are different and unusual when compared to the things you normally notice.	Requires to focus outward (Levels 1–4 are inwardly focused). Changes can be easy and can jump-start innovation. • • • • • • • • Over-focusing, isolating an idea that might not work the way it works anywhere else. Stall efforts at originality. Not terribly creative to copy.	Self-Doubt. Fear of not being physically able. Fear of not copying the right thing. Fear of copying the right things wrong. Fear of being laughed at. Fear of criticism. Fear of self.
LEVEL 6: DIFFERENT—Doing Things No One Else Is Doing					
Turn your life into adventure. Feng Shui (promote change and harmony). Change = Move. Different focus. Different perspective. Humor, Jokes & Laughter. Categorically Different. Create New Words. Divergent Convergence. Mountain Building. Mindmaps. Strategic Visioning. The School for Innovators. A Strategy for Innovation. Makes new rules.	Habitual rule breakers. Lots of ideas from 3-sigma thinking. Many different hobbies and interests. Desks, shelves, cabinets covered with piles of information. Redefines limits. Starts many projects. Impatient.	Intentional thinking. Lateral thinking. This thinking reverses basic assumptions and accepted logic or reasoning. Distinct and separate in style and process. 3-sigma thinking. Pushes the envelope.	Thinking is moving away from, disconnecting and moving off to the side, to see from a completely different angle. To do things no one else is doing, you have to think different. This requires lateral thinking.	Huge impacts in dollars saved. New markets. New directions. Necessary for BIG changes. • • • • • • • • Too many ideas. More difficult to sell ideas because so different. Idea generators, not implementers. Seen as a flake, weirdo.	Normalcy. Fear of being different. Fear of being noticed. Fear of being laughed at. Fear of rejection. Fear of tradition. Fear of trying different things that might not work. Fear of falling off trying. Fear of the unexpected. Fear of getting hurt. Fear of exposure.

Tools to use	Habits and Characters	Thinking about Thinking	Mind Shift	Pros and Cons	Levels of Fear
LEVEL 7: IMPOSSIBLE—Doing Things That Can't Be Done					
Can't make a wish. Have a Crazy idea. Impossible technologies. Break the rules. Make your own rules. Beyond Impossible. Ootching.	Dreamers, envisionaries. Challenges rather than accepts. Makes unusual connections. Creates own environment Adventurous. Sense of humor, sarcasm, punsters. Laughs at self. Welcomes problems. Hates details. Hates structure, red tape, and bureaucracy. Breaks the rules. Risk taker. Tends to be disorderly and messy. Very impatient.	Breakout and forceful thinking— pushes through restrictive mental conditions. Highly intuitive. Childlike thinking—naïve and forever questioning. Pushes everyone's envelopes.	To do things that can't be done, you have to break out normal patterns of thinking. To do that, you have to think imaginatively. When you suspend judgment, anything possible!	Fame, wealth, incredible success come with incredible change. . . . . Lots of risk to Level 7 ideas. Impact could be unmanageable.Too many weird ideas. Seen as crazy, out of control. Irritates others.	Disbelief. Fear of the unknown. Fear of not having a basis of comparison. Fear of problem size. Fear of believing. Fear that I can't do that. Lack of self-confidence. Fear of a fault, a weakness in the safety system below you. Fear of total failure. Fear of the point of no return. Fear of death—not coming back alive. Fear of others dying. The sum of all fears.

Index of Tools and Techniques

NOTES:

NOTES:

NOTES:

NOTES:

NOTES:

NOTES:

NOTES:

NOTES: